THE TAKEN

A book in the Latin American and Caribbean
Arts and Culture initiative.

Latin American and Caribbean Arts and Culture is
supported by the Andrew W. Mellon Foundation.

The Taken

TRUE STORIES OF THE SINALOA DRUG WAR

By JAVIER VALDEZ CÁRDENAS

Translated and with an introduction by Everard Meade

University of Oklahoma Press : Norman

Library of Congress Cataloging-in-Publication Data

Names: Valdez, Javier, 1967– author. | Meade, Everard, translator.
Title: The taken : true stories of the Sinaloa drug war / Javier Valdez Cárdenas ;
    translated by Everard Meade.
Description: Norman, OK : University of Oklahoma Press, 2017. | Includes
    index.
Identifiers: LCCN 2016029481 | ISBN 978-0-8061-5576-0 (paperback)
Subjects: LCSH: Drug traffic—Mexico—Sinaloa (State) | Organized crime—
    Mexico—Sinaloa (State) | Kidnapping—Mexico—Sinaloa (State) |
    Kidnapping victims—Mexico—Sinaloa (State) | BISAC: HISTORY / Latin
    America / Mexico. | HISTORY / Modern / 20th Century. | HISTORY /
    Modern / 21st Century. | SOCIAL SCIENCE / Violence in Society. |
    HISTORY / World.
Classification: LCC HV5840.M4 V357 2017 | DDC 363.450972/32—dc23
LC record available at https://lccn.loc.gov/2016029481

LATIN AMERICAN
AND CARIBBEAN
ARTS AND CULTURE

The paper in this book meets the guidelines for permanence and durability of
the Committee on Production Guidelines for Book Longevity of the Council on
Library Resources, Inc. ∞

1 2 3 4 5 6 7 8 9 10

Contents

THE TAKEN

Introduction

EVERARD MEADE

For two years, Sandra Luz Hernández skirted an abyss of violence and impunity that threatened to swallow her up at every turn. But she refused to back down. "I'm going to be a rock in his shoe," she declared of the prosecutor in charge of investigating the forced disappearance of her son, Édgar. On February 12, 2012, a group of armed, masked men stormed into his house in Culiacán, Sinaloa, and carried him away. He was never seen again.

It was a typical *levantón*—literally a "taking," where unknown men forcibly carry someone off, usually to a safe house or some remote location, sometimes for torture and interrogation, sometimes for ransom, sometimes for execution, and often for some combination of these and other torments. The perpetrators include organized crime, the police, and the military, often cooperating with one another. The victims are sometimes set free and sometimes killed, sometimes celebrated and sometimes denied, sometimes dumped in public places and sometimes forcibly disappeared. The constant is an armed commando taking and holding a person or group of people against their will, exercising near-complete power over their bodies for a period of time, and then leaving them and their family and friends with very little means of explaining what happened, why, or who is responsible. Terrified survivors often avoid public space, civic engagement, or encounters with the authorities. Solitude and self-doubt strike even the most courageous and outspoken, but not because they think some big brother, panoptic state is watching them or because they've internalized its propaganda. Taken by an amorphous combination of armed men—a thundering but spectral force almost impossible to identify or thwart—they fear that *no one* is watching, that no one else is capable of bearing witness to their suffering, of giving it meaning or common cause.

The *levantón* has become an everyday modus operandi of the current drug war in Mexico. Its particular brand of intimate yet anonymous, patterned yet unpredictable violence is the ultimate expression of the nature of power in a place where the dismantling of the one-party state spurred a democratic efflorescence but also a power vacuum filled by gangsters and pistoleros; where free trade has opened up new markets and created massive wealth but done little to address crushing poverty and inequality; and where globalization has created new networks of solidarity and resistance in the face of mass violence but also provided nineteenth-century-style warlords with access to twenty-first century weapons, communications, and supply chains. Like the forms of power it represents, the word *levantón* is relatively new—it was rarely used before 2003 or so, and it is not included in the classic dictionaries of Mexican criminal slang.[1]

Mexico is living through a decade-long drug war that has produced casualties and atrocities on par with the dirty-war dictatorships of the late 1970s in Chile and Argentina and the civil wars of the 1980s in Central America. Since the intensification of the present drug war in 2006, more than 100,000 people have been killed, 30,000 have been forcibly disappeared, and at least 250,000 have been forced from their homes.[2] The use of rape, torture, and mutilation as weapons of war is widespread and well publicized. Mexico ranks in the bottom 11 percent of the Global Peace Index, next to Lebanon and just above Yemen and Libya.[3]

At the same time, Mexico is a prosperous and cosmopolitan place that attracts more than twenty million foreign tourists and nearly $20 billion in foreign investment each year and recently displaced Spain as the largest economy in the Hispanic world. Mexico is a vibrant center of art, culture, and intellectual life, and on the whole suffers less violent crime than most of the rest of Latin America and many large North American cities. Its GDP has grown by 25 percent since 2009; women hold more than 35 percent of elected positions nationally; and civil society is booming like never before, despite media monopolies and the persistence of political corruption.[4]

Compared to other societies wracked by chronic violence, Mexico's relative prosperity and functionality are stunning. Things just seem to work in Mexico in a way that they don't in Honduras, Egypt, or Venezuela. And it's not just for foreign tourists or traveling businesspeople. Mexico City—Mexico's financial, artistic, intellectual, demographic, and administrative capital—has been relatively unscathed, even as the states that surround it have descended into garish violence and gangsterism. There's also the general vibe of renaissance that one finds at a TEDx event in Tijuana; the booming wineries of the Valle de Guadalupe; a national cinema that went from producing fewer than twenty-five to more than one hundred films per year and claiming nearly every international prize over the last decade; and the explosion of vibrant online magazines and blogs.

Considerable signs of progress and peace can make it exceedingly difficult for the victims of violence to stand out, to represent a larger phenomenon worthy of solidarity or demanding of collective action. In the best-case scenario, they come off as tragic but idiosyncratic victims of pathological individuals or groups. In the worst-case scenario, they are assumed to be complicit in their own victimization—they must have done something to have deserved or at least provoked it. This is the environment in which *levantones* thrive.

Nowhere is this reality more important than in Culiacán, Sinaloa, the birthplace of modern drug trafficking in Mexico and the epicenter of the current drug war. In this book, veteran local journalist Javier Valdez Cárdenas presents thirty-three firsthand accounts of *levantones* from a wide variety of perspectives. Following a rich tradition of testimonial literature from Latin America, these stories provide a vivid human perspective on what it is like to live in a situation of chronic violence, how this experience fits into a broader and incomplete democratic transition, and what lasting legacies it will leave behind.

Rather than gangsters with private jets, generals with piles of cash and hidden torture chambers, or exotic "murder cities" along the border, these stories offer the perspective of migrant workers, schoolteachers, single moms, small businessmen, bored teenagers, petty criminals, aspiring assassins, municipal officials, and local journalists. These are the kinds of stories that are often missing from press coverage of the drug war, particularly in the United States. The extreme danger for journalists, the contraction of newsrooms and foreign bureaus, and the myopic focus on border security and drug enforcement in the policy community have made it increasingly difficult for even the most diligent of journalists to invest the time and energy necessary to cultivate these kinds of deeply personal, local stories. This is precisely where we need to hear from seasoned local reporters like Valdez Cárdenas, writing about the place where he lives and where he's built a network of trusted sources over the past twenty years.

In addition to the methodology of the *levantón* and the spectrum of suffering it inflicts, the common thread in these stories is the nebulous and volatile nature of power that the *levantón* represents. The use of terror and intimidation tactics by a broad mix of government and criminal actors, the uncertainty about who wields the power to carry out these acts and to what ends, and the failure of the formal apparatus of the state to protect people from the harm they cause (or even to acknowledge it) threaten more than just the bodily integrity of ordinary citizens. Their feeling of moral agency and the coherence of their communities are at stake. *Levantones* make people question whether their lives really matter, and to whom. The repression that Sandra Luz Hernández faced while she searched for her disappeared son relied as much on systemic doubt and uncertainty as it did on government goons or assassins' bullets. Hers is the most infamous of recent efforts to uncover the truth about a *levantón* in Culiacán. It shows just how deeply this particular method of violence is interwoven into a broader web of crime, politics, and business, and just how high the stakes of exposing these connections can be.

Édgar García Hernández, twenty-five, worked as a messenger for the public prosecutor's office in Culiacán, and he was assigned to District Attorney Marco Antonio Higuera López. The connection was not lost on his mother. From the moment Édgar disappeared, Sandra Luz demanded that Higuera investigate the case and staked out his office. When the authorities dragged their feet, she cultivated her own sources, visited gravesites and other places where people were rumored to have disappeared, and led bloodhounds scouring the hillsides in rural areas across the state. Sandra Luz quickly became a leading voice for the family members of the other fifteen hundred disappeared in Sinaloa, particularly the mothers. Forceful, but never shrill, the former saleswoman of cosmetics and cell phone plans pressured the authorities to find her son and injected the cause of the disappeared with newfound hope and energy. Governor Mario López Valdez promised to get involved in the case, and the State Human Rights Commission opened its own investigation. From her insistent, methodical tone to her neat, short haircut, hip purple eyeglasses, and carefully selected accessories, Sandra Luz cut a modern professional figure—not a wealthy or entitled *fresa* (bourgeois) from the power-lunch set, but one of those strong, matter-of-fact, urban, middle-class women who head households all over Mexico. Most important, she never lost her composure in front of the camera or the microphone, despite the obvious pain in her voice. She was just plain compelling.

On May 12, 2014, immediately after a morning meeting with Higuera and other officials, Sandra Luz received a call on her cell phone from someone promising information about the whereabouts of her son. The caller made an appointment to meet with her later that afternoon in Colonia Benito Juárez, about twelve blocks from the prosecutor's office in the historic center of Culiacán. On her way to the meeting, while she was walking across 30 de Septiembre Street, a man jumped out of a car, aimed an automatic pistol at her head, and shot her fifteen times. Motionless on the gray concrete, with yellow evidence tags radiating out from her head like a surrealist crown splashed by a narrow stream of red blood, surrounded by lab coats and photographers, Sandra Luz appeared in the national and international media. Here was another activist killed for speaking truth to power in Mexico, another assassination victim among tens of thousands in the "drug war," and another martyr for the missing in a country where 30,000 have disappeared over the past decade.

In the aftermath of the murder, Higuera revealed a new theory of the case: Édgar had been taken because he was part of a criminal gang responsible for the kidnapping, robbery, and murder of Manuel Alonso Ruiz Haro on January 29, 2012 (two weeks before he was taken). In a national radio interview, Higuera claimed that this alleged connection, which he had never mentioned before, was the key to Sandra Luz's murder. One of the other members of the supposed gang, Antonio Benítez, had turned up dead the previous April, shortly after Sandra Luz had gone to him and another of Édgar's friends, seeking information about his whereabouts. Three weeks after Sandra Luz's murder, the police arrested the other "friend," Jesús Valenzuela, as the triggerman. Sandra Luz had repeatedly accused his brothers, Joel and Gabriel Valenzuela, in the disappearance of her son. All three brothers shared a house in the town of Paredones, in the hills just north of Culiacán. While the authorities publicly denied that they were suspects, sources within the prosecutor's office told a different story to local journalists. Facing fifty years in prison for feminicide, Jesús Valenzuela confessed that he had killed Sandra Luz when he saw her coming down the street, because he feared that she would kill him first. He claimed that Édgar had been taken so that he wouldn't betray the other members of the gang, and his mother was taking revenge, man by man. Valenzuela denied setting a trap—he'd gone out for tacos and run into Sandra Luz by chance. To most observers, the theory that the unarmed activist and mother of five could order assassinations or strike fear in the heart of a seasoned criminal like Valenzuela was plainly absurd, as was the "random" killing of a prominent activist by alleged criminals whom she had named to the police.[5]

Adding insult to injury, ten months later Valenzuela was released from jail without charge, for a lack of evidence. Apparently, about a month after his arrest, he had ditched the public defender assigned to his case, taken on a "miracle-worker" private attorney, and retracted his confession. A criminal court judge had granted a motion to dismiss the case on the grounds that the confession was coerced and the government had presented very little evidence implicating Valenzuela in the murder. Governor López and prosecutor Higuera accused the judiciary of favoritism; Valenzuela's lawyer is the son-in-law of a powerful superior court judge, and he has a reputation for making charges against his more infamous clients disappear. The prosecutor and the governor condemned the court's decision and claimed that they would continue to fight to bring Valenzuela to justice.[6] A year later, at this writing, nothing has changed.

Whether or not there's any truth to this theory of the case, it's difficult not to view the outcome as the ultimate smear. Higuera was able to blame the original victim and his champion for their fates, or at least to plant needling doubts about them that they were not alive to contest. By condemning the legal outcome and blaming judicial favoritism, he and the governor were able to acknowledge a base level of corruption in the case—just enough to make it believable in a place wracked by corruption—while deflecting attention from their own agencies and even claiming to stand for truth and justice. To those most suspicious of their motives, the message was more sinister: whatever really happened, the government could effectively manipulate the truth to suit its own ends. Valdez Cárdenas calls it "the three deaths of Sandra Luz"—her son, herself, and the truth for which she fought.[7]

The manipulation of rumor, doubt, and plausible deniability, magnified through carefully controlled media outlets, is a standard tactic of dictatorship. And even the most grandiose dictatorships have used paramilitary forces, vigilantes, or plainclothes agents to carry out their dirty work under an aura of mystery or outright denial. But there is something different about *levantones* in this regard. While they clearly overlap with the authority of the state, they are also independent of its formal apparatus and hierarchy to a much greater degree than secret police or death squads working for a military dictatorship. And their purposes are far more diverse and idiosyncratic.

Witness the forced disappearance of forty-three teachers-in-training from rural Ayotzinapa, Guerrero, on September 26, 2014. The indigenous scholarship students were on their way to Mexico City via bus to protest education reforms initiated by President Enrique Peña Nieto. Ayotzinapa students have a reputation for aggressive but peaceful tactics, including the erection of roadblocks and the commandeering of busses. Acting on orders from Mayor José Luis Abarca, municipal police officers in Iguala, Guerrero, attacked five busses that the students had commandeered, captured the forty-three, and handed them over to members of the Guerreros Unidos drug cartel, who more than likely tortured and murdered them. That specific orders to attack the busses had gone out is substantiated by eyewitness testimony and the fact that the police mistakenly shot up a charter bus carrying a youth soccer team earlier that evening, killing the driver and a fifteen-year-old boy. According to the official federal investigation, Abarca was worried that the disappeared students' participation in local protests would interrupt a campaign event for his wife, María de los Ángeles Pineda, who was running to succeed him as mayor and whose family is deeply intertwined with the Guerreros Unidos and Beltrán Leyva drug cartels.[8]

The federal government's response was flat-footed and tone deaf. President Enrique Peña Nieto failed to cancel or curtail an Asian tour when news of the massacre broke, and he offered the stalest of platitudes to the parents of the missing. The governor of Guerrero, Ángel Aguirre allowed the mayor and his wife to escape, and they were on the lam for weeks. Aguirre later resigned in disgrace, and the mayor and his wife were arrested hiding out in Mexico City. Over the next few months, each new theory of the crime that federal law enforcement officials floated not only was debunked but also revealed evidence of further crimes— such as the discovery of multiple mass graves, first in Guerrero and then elsewhere. Captured members of Guerreros Unidos confessed a bit too readily, and each time one of them parroted the government's rendering of events, it magnified official embarrassment when that version was disproved. After a Swiss laboratory confirmed a DNA match for one of the missing students from a bone fragment found in a river where some of the captured Guerreros Unidos members claimed they had dumped bags of their charred remains (after killing them and burning the bodies), the government declared the case closed on January 27, 2015. However, a panel of independent experts convened by the Inter-American Commission on Human Rights (with the consent of the Mexican government) declared the official explanation of the case "scientifically impossible." Questions about the participation of the Federal Police and the army in the *levantón* continue to arise, along with mounting evidence of all sorts of other unsavory connections and conspiracies.[9]

Obvious government malfeasance, coupled with the obvious innocence of the victims, provoked widespread outrage. The utter banality of the apparent motives behind the massacre crossed a moral and cultural Rubicon that previous acts of violence had not, or at least not so publicly. There were marches and mass demonstrations across the country and around the world. Creative displays commemorating "the 43" appeared on T-shirts, signs, banners, public art, punked-out haircuts, social media posts, and even carved into a wheat field in Norway.

More than previous waves of protest, Ayotzinapa generated solidarity that crossed entrenched sociological and cultural barriers within Mexico. Middle-class urbanites who hadn't lifted a finger when two activists from the same school were killed by federal police a year earlier rallied to their cause this time. It's not that people didn't care before. They had simply run out of ways of telling themselves that it couldn't happen to *them* after a decade of escalating violence. One of the memes that caught fire after Ayotzinapa—*Ya me cansé* ("I'm tired [of it]" or "Enough already")—referred to being tired of constant fear, but also of making excuses for it.[10] "The victims must be *narcos*, criminals [or prostitutes, drug users, illegal immigrants, rebellious Indians, rabble-rousers, et cetera]"—these old refrains rang increasingly hollow. They had been disproved by incidents small and large, and here was a big, bold, brazen case where those responsible showed neither recognition of the humanity of the victims, nor of the capacity of the broader public to figure out, care about, or rectify the situation. Ayotzinapa became a watershed precisely because people knew that "the 43" were not isolated victims, that they represented uncounted thousands of others who have been "taken," and the prospect that it could happen to anyone.

The clarion call "It was the state!" echoes through the global protest movement. But who or what is "the state" in this scenario? Are drug cartels really a part of the state apparatus? Have they supplanted the Mexican government? Do they aspire to govern or dominate a territory indefinitely?

The slogan implicates the Mexican government in the killing and places it alongside a history of state terror in modern Latin America, right there with the Tlatelolco (Mexico, 1968), El Mozote (El Salvador, 1981), and Accomarca (Peru, 1993) massacres. The apparent motives and involvement of government officials and police certainly justify the label, and so does the cover-up. But the relationships between Ayotzinapa, drug trafficking, and the broader wave of violence in contemporary Mexico also challenge conventional definitions of state violence.

Rather than the actions of an entity holding a monopoly on the use of violence in a given territory—the classic social scientific definition of a state, Ayotzinapa seems to have happened (and happened the way it did) precisely because no entity had a monopoly on the use of force in Guerrero at that moment. Most other massacres carried out by drug cartels and the worst explosions of violence during the present drug war have taken place in the absence of a dominant faction, or in the rush to fill the power vacuum after a previously dominant faction has been destroyed or weakened.

Rather than an entity recognized by other sovereign entities—the classic international relations definition of the state—the murky combinations of forces responsible for Ayotzinapa and other *levantones* are not precisely defined, much less recognized as sovereign authorities in a given territory, even as a belligerents or pretenders. They are not like the Revolutionary Armed Forces of Colombia (FARC), whom the Colombian government has a mandate to exterminate but with whom they also negotiate, as a belligerent, with de facto sovereignty over its territory. Nor are they like the Taliban or the Tamil Tigers (both of which, like the FARC, traffic drugs to fund their movements).

Thinking of those responsible for massacres like Ayotzinapa as simply a representation of the Mexican ruling class and its interests—the classic materialist definition of a state—doesn't work either. Those responsible for Ayotzinapa might have represented the interests of the local ruling elite in Iguala or even the vanguard of brutal new form of capitalism. But those interests do not align with those of a coherent national political, commercial, and financial elite. There are strands of such interests that one can trace across partisan, industrial, and geographic boundaries in Mexico and beyond, and organized crime has infiltrated organizations across a broad ideological and institutional spectrum. But there are massive conflicts of interest along the same axes and among the same groups. Simply put, agents of the Mexican state and supposedly legitimate businesspeople have acted like gangsters, gangsters have acted like agents of the state and legitimate businesspeople, and they have collaborated in many acts of violence. But the underlying institutions remain quite distinct, and there is no singular determinant or "state behind the state" responsible for the wave of violence now washing over Mexico.

Most of the analysts who have claimed that Mexico is somehow a "failed state," whose territory has been usurped by a "*narco* insurgency," are interlopers with a vested interest in Mexican chaos—a motley crew of security contractors, risk consultants, and attention grabbers with pre-packaged solutions or splashy headlines to sell.[11] Careful and committed observers, like sociologist Luis Astorga, point to deeper social determinants and patterns in the use of power by the Mexican state that have persisted below the surface of various crises of authority.[12]

Take, for example, the meteoric rise of "self-defense forces" in Michoacán beginning in 2012—the catalyst for a new round of "failed-state" hyperbole. In less than a year, these vigilante groups occupied a significant portion of the state with overwhelming public support. Their leader Dr. José Manuel Mireles became a national figure, and they successfully drove drug traffickers out of many towns and rebuffed repeated disarmament efforts by the Mexican army and federal law enforcement. A year later, however, most of the self-defense groups had joined the new federal rural police force, much of their leadership had been co-opted into government positions, and Mireles, who opposed incorporation, was in federal prison on weapons charges. Public support had eroded, and the former self-defense forces were accused of operating their own drug cartels and kidnapping rings.[13] It became a perfect example of the corporatist nature of the Mexican state going back more than a century: infiltrate, co-opt, and water down a social movement, while persecuting those who get in the way. This kind of co-optation allows the government to project an image of power, despite the fact that it cannot control the underlying phenomena—in this case drug traffickers and armed groups holding local communities hostage. The lack of a master villain or master conspiracy may be unsatisfying, but the uncertain reality beneath the displays of power projected by the government and the drug cartels is where most people live and how they have experienced the past decade in Mexico.

It's no secret that organized crime is a driving force behind this muddled reality, creating hundreds of thousands of jobs and injecting billions into the economy but also hijacking nominally representative institutions. Less clear is the simple association between the violence carried out by organized crime and the protection of the international market for illicit drugs. For one thing, drug cartels have diversified into identity theft and protection rackets, and they traffic dollars, weapons, sex workers, international migrants, and forced laborers as well as drugs. Perhaps more important, it has become increasingly difficult to link particular acts of violence carried out by organized crime to contract enforcement or even the forcible seizure of retail space or transit routes in a black market. Rather than punishing witnesses, whistle-blowers, or confederates who fail to honor agreements, many recent acts of violence (and the most notorious *levantones* in particular), have aimed to terrify targeted populations into submission. They seem to be more about political control than the drug business (and may, in fact, involve significant risks to that business). How else can we explain why a drug cartel that traffics in hundreds of millions of dollars would expose their operations to massive public scrutiny in order to go after forty-three indigenous student protestors?

Controlling or doing the dirty work of corrupt politicians is nothing new for organized crime, of course. Hubris and thuggery are not in short supply in this racket, either. Nor would it be the first ill-conceived or botched operation by a bunch of *sicarios* ("hit men")].[14] But Ayotzinapa was not an isolated incident.

The 2010 San Fernando massacre provides a horrific example of this new logic. As Valdez Cárdenas recounts in chapter 4 in the section titled "The Pueblo of the Dead," seventy-two migrants, most of them from Central America, were kidnapped at gunpoint from a bus in the state of Tamaulipas on their way to the US border. They were taken to an abandoned ranch, blindfolded, gagged, interrogated, extorted, beaten raped, and then executed. Some elements of the massacre show traces of a darker but familiar history of Cold War violence. In the days leading up to the massacre, the US Drug Enforcement Administration (DEA) uncovered new ties between the Zetas (the dominant drug cartel in Tamaulipas, which is made up of former Mexican soldiers) and members of the Kaibiles, US-trained Guatemalan special forces implicated in a multitude of atrocities during the Guatemalan Civil War, including genocide in the Petén jungle.[15] But the killing of the migrants after they had been robbed of their belongings and after their families had paid ransoms for their release, when many of them were doubtless still in debt to smugglers controlled by the Zetas, made little business sense—at least in a business capable of imagining a time horizon longer than a few hours or days. In a confidential cable, a US intelligence officer admitted: "It remains unclear how these deaths benefit the Zetas."[16]

The same dissonance with the logic of protecting a black market can be seen in the repeated massacres of impoverished migrants or devastating attacks on patrons at casinos, bull rings, and rodeos, or the highly publicized interrogation and killing of kidnappers and petty criminals by drug cartels acting as vigilantes.[17] Political scientist Guillermo Trejo explains: "In states like Guerrero, Michoacán, and Tamaulipas, organized crime has . . . entered a new phase in which one of its great objectives is to take local control—taking over municipalities and their resources to extract local wealth through forced taxation."[18] In the state of Michoacán, organized crime takes 30 percent of public revenues and 20 percent of the salaries of all public officials.[19] In the state of Tamaulipas, the Zetas use municipal infrastructure to facilitate the theft of gasoline and crude oil, kidnapping for ransom, and migrant smuggling.[20]

One can massage explanations out of these practices that relate to competition between rival organized crime groups, but their primary goal seems to have been on controlling particular civilian populations. This kind of power mimics that of a state, to be sure, but its purpose and time horizon are much more limited. Unlike the territorial mafias of the 1980s, the smaller, nimbler cells that make up contemporary drug cartels in Mexico use violence to terrify a population into submission, extract as much as they can from it, and then discard the remnants and move on to the next opportunity. They're not just trying to protect the illicit drug trade, and they're not building a business for the long haul.

Such is the case with many everyday acts of violence in Mexico, including the most common *levantones*—whether they begin as carjackings, kidnappings for ransom, or attempts at blackmail. While they may be carried out by persons affiliated with organized crime, they often have little or nothing to do with protecting the illicit drug trade or even advancing the interests of a particular cartel or faction. Many of these are plainly opportunistic. Some take advantage of the infrastructure of organized crime. In chapter 2, for example, in the section titled "Death Assured," we meet a group of state troopers (or perhaps gangsters posing as state troopers) who use their weapons, vehicles, and mafia contacts to start a highway robbery and kidnapping ring. Others take advantage of the prevailing climate of impunity to pilfer petroleum from national pipelines, steal cars, rob houses, and assault sex workers.

Illicit drugs are one of the most important determinants of violence in many towns and cities in Mexico, but neither international trafficking nor the handful of powerful cartels that control it are necessarily involved. The dramatic rise of domestic drug consumption and street-level dealing in Mexico over the last five years correlates directly to a rise in homicides, particularly the murder of young people. Drugs have become ubiquitous in schools, dance halls, nightclubs, and street corners. Territorial disputes among street gangs, low-level dealers, and addicts have turned cities like Acapulco, where seventeen armed factions vie for control of the streets, into war zones.[21] According the nongovernmental organization Semáforo Delictivo ("Crime Traffic Light"), which has contracts with government agencies across the country to monitor crime data, as much as 80 percent of contemporary violence can be attributed to low-level drug dealing.[22] While this violence is related to a black market, it has nothing to do with prohibition or drug enforcement in the United States, it captures very little of the retail value added to wholesale drugs that interests transnational drug cartels, and it is layered into a complex web of different kinds of violence and social dysfunction.

Other acts of violence demonstrate a toxic mix of personal and social pathologies with the violent memes of the drug war. In the spring of 2015, a group of adolescents in Chihuahua tortured and killed a neighborhood boy while playing a game of "kidnapping."[23] The previous fall, primary school kids in Tamaulipas held down a classmate at her desk, lifted her skirt, and assaulted her while play-acting a gang rape.[24] Privileged university students in Acapulco operated a kidnapping ring that resulted in the death of three dozen of their classmates. After the leaders were arrested in 2013, they admitted that they didn't *need* the money, nor had they been coerced into it. They just wanted to be gangsters.[25] Beer cans, liquor bottles, marijuana cigarettes, and other evidence of partying have been found with the bodies of many of the women kidnapped, raped, killed, and mutilated in Sinaloa and Chihuahua over the last decade, suggesting that they were killed by groups of men as a leisure activity, rather than by more conventional caricatures of a serial killer or psychopath, acting out some hateful delusion.[26] The examples are endless and grim.

On January 21, 2015, a man in Navolato, Sinaloa, an hour west of Culiacán, accused his wife of adultery. He and his brother kidnapped her from another man's house, tied her hands together, and tethered her to the back of a pickup truck. While his brother drove the truck, slowly parading her through the town square at 10:30 A.M. on a Sunday, the man shouted insults, accused her of being a whore, tore her clothes off, and beat the woman savagely. After knocking her unconscious, the two men cut her loose, peeled out of town, and left her lying in the gutter. The husband knew that no one would intervene or call the police, and no one did. He was finally arrested several days later, under pressure from a group of women's organizations and female officeholders in Culiacán, but then released in short order after the victim "pardoned" him and refused to file charges.[27]

Some in Sinaloa will blame the *narcos* for popularizing and trivializing this kind of spectacular violence or corrupting the local police such that they won't intervene to protect the victims. Others will attribute it to rural patriarchy and misogyny and lament the use of the *narcos* as an excuse for everything that goes wrong in their state. Both sides, however, are also likely to explain that people don't intervene in these kinds of affairs in Sinaloa precisely because such a confrontation is likely to result in guns drawn, if not worse. There's a lot of truth in both realities, and neither has much to do with protecting a black market for drugs.

Rather than a "drug war" or a "war on drugs," from the perspective of ordinary citizens, Mexico is facing a situation of chronic violence with multiple and overlapping determinants. The key to understanding and developing solutions to chronic violence is its social articulation—how and why practices filter down from elite drug traffickers to everyday life, how they creep up from dysfunctional social relationships into the voids created by reigning corruption and impunity, and how they affect different subjects differently, leaving complicated legacies of trauma and alienation in their wake. A coherent understanding of this kind of underdetermined phenomena of violence requires a careful, qualitative approach, one that gives us a detailed, human portrait of a range of individual cases. That's exactly what Javier Valdez Cárdenas delivers in the stories that follow. And while they are richly textured and full of local character, they also add up to something larger than the sum of their parts.

There are three key contexts necessary to appreciate the collective significance of these stories: we need to understand what exactly it means to talk about violence that amounts to a "war" in contemporary Mexico, how this "war" is intimately tied to the history and politics of Sinaloa, and how one tells the story of how a classic black market regulated by an authoritarian state evolved into a much broader free market for violence and exploitation.

BEYOND THE BODY COUNT: THE "DRUG WAR" IN MEXICO

Following the bluster and the body count, most accounts of the present "drug war" in Mexico begin in 2006, especially those that explore its impact on ordinary civilians. At the national level, the homicide rate declined by nearly half from the early 1990s to 2007, to levels lower than most American cities.[28] This decline was part of a relatively steady downward march dating all the way back to the 1930s, and one which avoided the marked escalation in homicides across the United States and urban Latin America from the early 1960s through the early 1980s.[29] By this indicator, Mexico was one of the safest and most stable countries in the Western Hemisphere for most of the twentieth century.

Beginning in late 2006, change was dramatic. As President Felipe Calderón (2006–12) initiated major anti-drug operations across the country—including partial military occupations of the states of Michoacán and Baja California—the homicide rate shot up, with annual increases of 58 percent in 2008, 41 percent in 2009, 30 percent in 2010, and 5 percent in 2011. Homicide declined in 2013 and 2014, but the rate still remains near historic highs. Exactly how many of these murders are directly attributable to the illicit drug trade and organized crime is a matter of some contention. Rigorous studies from government agencies, academic researchers, and news organizations estimate that 40–60 percent of Mexico's recent homicides can be attributed to organized crime.[30] The breadth of the definition of "organized-crime-related homicide" accounts for most of the variation, depending on whether it attempts to capture only murders directly attributable to organized crime members or business interests, or all those facilitated by the environment they create. There is little substantive variation in the data, and there is little disagreement that killings related to organized crime account for the lion's share of the dramatic increase in homicides since 2007. A wave of killing rolled over Mexico, massive by historical standards. More than actual drug trafficking or drug enforcement operations, this is what the term "drug war" conjures.

But by comparison to other places in the world, the body count alone does not amount to a "war" that has touched nearly every aspect of Mexican society, nor does it justify the intense media coverage that the most spectacular acts of violence and the most infamous gangsters have generated. Despite the dramatic rise since 2007, Mexico's overall homicide rate remains slightly lower than the regional average for Latin America. For the entirety of the present "drug war," homicide rates in neighboring Guatemala and El Salvador have remained more than twice as high as in Mexico, and in Honduras it has been four times worse.[31] Mexico's homicide rate is also considerably lower than that of other large middle-income countries in Latin America, including Colombia, Brazil, and Venezuela.[32] On the other hand, in particular cities and regions within Mexico, the homicide rate is high by any standard. One of the most striking features of the explosion of homicides after 2007 was their geographic spread from a small number of regional hot spots across the country. In border towns like Tijuana, Nuevo Laredo, and Ciudad Juárez, or regional organized crime hubs like Culiacán and Acapulco, intense violence began at least a couple of years earlier, complicating any simple association with the war on drug cartels declared by the Calderón administration but validating the broader association between a series of conflicts involving organized crime and a dramatic rise in murder. This general trend repeated itself in micro as the conflict spread and the murder rate shot up in previously peaceful areas.

Still, a skeptical observer might point out that the average homicide rate in New Orleans for the period 2007–12 was about the same as that of Culiacán, the home base of the infamous Sinaloa Cartel and the scene of much of the action in this book—62 and 61 per 100,000 inhabitants, respectively.[33] The recent homicide rate in New Orleans, of course, is a statistical outlier in the United States, especially in the chaotic aftermath of Hurricane Katrina, as racial tensions flared and police and politicians scrambled to limit the exposure of deep-seated patterns of corruption.[34] Furthermore, throughout the period in question, the murder rate in Ciudad Juárez, Mexico's most dangerous city over the last fifteen years, was significantly higher than it was in New Orleans—more than double at its peak of 206 per 100,000 in 2010 (and higher than almost any other city in the world, for that matter). It's a similar story with Acapulco, which currently ranks as the third most dangerous municipality in the world. At particular moments since 2007, the homicide rates in Monterrey, Nuevo Laredo, Culiacán, Torreón, and Chihuahua have far surpassed the highest rates in US cities.

Still, there are cities in the United States where the long-term homicide rate is comparable to all but the most extreme cases in Mexico during the height of the "drug war." Detroit, for example, averaged 46.7 homicides per 100,000 in 2007–12, worse than Tijuana or Morelia, where violence got so bad that the government deployed thousands of soldiers and marines to occupy the streets. [35] But the homicide rate alone does not explain what ordinary people mean when they describe "the violence" associated with the present "drug war" in Mexico. Nor does it correlate with the fear, grief, frustration, and outrage that it provokes. The impunity enjoyed by the vast majority of the perpetrators and the bloody spectacle accompanying many of the crimes have magnified the social impact of each individual murder in contemporary Mexico. Nowhere in the United States has experienced anything like it.

The homicide clearance rate in Detroit—the percentage of cases in which a suspect is arrested and indicted—was 92.5 percent in 2014. At its very worst, in 2012, it was 38.5 percent. In New Orleans, the clearance rate was 64 percent in 2014, up from a low of 25 percent in 2010.[36] According to the FBI, the US national average was 62.5 percent in 2012.[37] By comparison, a suspect is detained and charged in fewer than 2 percent of reported homicides in Mexico. In two states, Hidalgo and Tlaxcala, there wasn't a single suspect indicted for the 148 murders committed there in 2012. In the states with the most murders that year—Guerrero, Estado de México, Chihuahua, and Sinaloa—more than 98 percent of reported homicides did not produce an indictment. In Sinaloa, the impunity rate was 98.2 percent in 2012. This staggering level of impunity magnifies the social impact of any individual murder, breeding generalized fear and mistrust.[38]

Impunity for homicide translates directly into generalized impunity for organized crime in many areas of Mexico, particularly in Sinaloa. According to Semáforo Delictivo, 67 percent of homicides in Sinaloa (and 51 percent in Mexico) are targeted assassinations carried out by organized crime. During the period at the heart of this book, 2010–12, the figure was as high as 91 percent for Sinaloa. Factoring out homicides related to organized crime, Sinaloa goes from one of the most dangerous to one of the least dangerous states in Mexico (and would be considered relatively safe by global standards).[39]

It is not just that crimes go unpunished. Anyone who tries to speak up for the victims and demand justice can be targeted. On August 16, 2008, a dozen gunmen in three trucks rolled up to a popular meeting hall in the picturesque mountain town of Creel, Chihuahua, and opened fire, killing thirteen young people, one of them only eighteen months old. After the massacre, the victims' parents organized a series of protests, blocking highways and a train route popular among tourists, and they inundated local and state officials with petitions demanding justice for their children. In response, they received anonymous threats that their tongues would be cut out if they continued to complain. The following spring, Daniel Parra Urías, the father of one of the victims, was kidnapped by armed men in the town of Cuauhtémoc. A couple of days later his lifeless body was discovered by the side of the highway leading to Chihuahua City.[40]

Aligning with national or international solidarity networks has failed to protect parents and activists in similar situations from harm. On November 28, 2011, in the central plaza of Hermosillo, Sonora, Nepomuceno Moreno Núñez was gunned down while protesting the disappearance of his son at the hands of the state police. "Don Nepo," as he was known, joined the poet Javier Sicilia's national Movimiento por la Paz con Justicia y Dignidad, after his eighteen-year-old son and three friends were kidnapped from a rural highway in the Yaqui Valley in 2010 and never seen again. Thanks to his participation in the movement's "caravan of peace,"

Don Nepo had spoken eloquently about his loss across the country. In a formal event at Chapultepec Castle in Mexico City, he had handed a copy of his son's file to President Felipe Calderón, who embraced him and promised to look into the case.[41]

The anonymity of social networks has proved equally inadequate for those demanding justice. In Reynosa, Tamaulipas, a prolific blogger named "Felina" active in the popular citizen journalism network Valor por Tamaulipas ("Courage for Tamaulipas"), denounced murders, robberies, and kidnappings carried out by the Zetas and Gulf Cartels and pleaded with local victims to report crimes to the authorities. On October 15, 2014, her Twitter account @Miut3 read: "FRIENDS AND FAMILY: MY REAL NAME IS MARÍA DEL ROSARIO FUENTES RUBIO. I AM A PHYSICIAN. TODAY MY LIFE HAS COME TO AN END." The last tweets on the account took the form of two photographs, one of a woman holding her hands over her face and the other of her lifeless body sprawled out on the pavement, with a bullet hole in her temple. Family members and coworkers confirmed that Dr. Fuentes had been kidnapped from the hospital where she worked earlier that day after receiving increasingly ominous threats. Using her phone, the killers added a generic mea culpa and a warning to others.[42]

Many of the most infamous cases are from Ciudad Juárez, and they are related to a series of crimes predating the current drug war. An epidemic of rape and murder targeting female factory workers in the booming border town dating back to 1993 was subsumed by the current drug war, but women's bodies continue to appear in the desert. One of the victims was sixteen-year-old Rubí Frayre, killed in 2008. Her mother, Marisela Escobedo Ortiz, tracked down the apparent murderer in Zacatecas. The well-known assassin was arrested and charged but then released on a technicality. Escobedo took her protest to the state capital in 2010. On the evening of December 16, she was holding a placard in the Plaza Hidalgo, when a gunman jumped out of car, chased her across the street, and shot her in the head on the steps of the statehouse. The whole thing was captured by security cameras and posted on YouTube.[43] Advocates for truth and justice in the Juárez femicides are well organized, they have enjoyed considerable international solidarity, and, most important, they began their work long before the country was engulfed in the present drug war. Indeed, the original catalyst for the killing of women—the rise of the Juárez Cartel in 1993—preceded both NAFTA and the current drug war. But the intensification of the drug war certainly exacerbated the risks facing the workingwomen and girls most often victimized and their advocates. The result is a terrifying but underdetermined phenomenon. Some femicides have been blatant acts of political persecution; others reflect a broader climate of violence and impunity. Police discovered the mutilated body of prominent activist and poet Susana Chávez on January 11, 2011. For years, Chávez had worked with the families of murdered women and girls in Ciudad Juárez to raise awareness of the crimes and prevent further killings. By most accounts, the killers were drugged up gangsters, who had no idea who she was and attacked her at random.[44] Once again, it wasn't just the presence of more armed criminals struggling over territory. In June 2015, an indictment implicated Mexican soldiers, stationed in the Valle de Juárez (just outside of the city) to fight the drug war, in the kidnapping, rape, and killing of more than a dozen women there.[45] It was the first time authorities had been implicated in all phases of the femicides, from the initial kidnapping to the cover-up, and it reinforces the idea that impunity in contemporary Mexico is something far more sinister than a lack of punishment.

American cities with homicides rates similar to drug war hot spots in Mexico haven't experienced anything like the reigning impunity. And Latin American places with similar levels of corruption and higher homicide rates than most Mexican cities—Caracas, Río de Janeiro, and San Pedro Sula, Honduras, for example—haven't experienced anything like the other defining aspect of the current drug war in Mexico: the strategic display and mass mediation of torture, killing, and mutilation.

Spectacles of violence sow terror and hopelessness beyond the body count. Most analysts trace the practice to a gory scene from Michoacán. In the wee hours of September 6, 2006, a group of twenty commandos stormed into a popular nightclub in sleepy Uruapan. They shoved their way through the startled crowd, fired automatic weapons into the ceiling, and ordered everyone on the ground. The gunmen shook five severed heads out of a trash bag and rolled them onto the dance floor, along with a message scrawled on a piece of cardboard, attributing responsibility to La Familia ("The Family"), the dominant drug cartel in the state at the time: "La Familia doesn't kill for money, doesn't kill women, doesn't kill the innocent. Only those that must die will die. Everyone should know this. This is divine justice."[46]

Over the next couple of years, decapitation and other forms of mutilation replaced the practice of destroying the bodies of murdered individuals in vats of acid—known as *pozole* ("stew"), managed by *pozoleros* ("stew makers"), in the patois of the drug trade. Before 2006, there was little recent history of beheading in Mexico. The practice spread quickly—despite the paternalistic limitations promised by La Familia—and it became both a grim announcement of the arrival of intensive violence to areas previously unaffected by the drug war and a new medium of communication.[47]

On August 28, 2008, children discovered the naked and headless bodies of eleven men in a rural area just outside of Mérida, Yucatán, along with a series of cryptic notes. The victims turned out to be police officers from neighboring Quintana Roo. Along with the discovery of the headless body of a local drug dealer a few days later, the incident was tied to a dispute between drug cartels over valuable transshipment routes for South American cocaine (the dominant Sinaloa Cartel was moving in on Gulf Cartel territory).[48] Over the next few weeks, the carefully choreographed display across the country of banners attributing responsibility for the killing, counterbanners in other places, and the eventual display of the missing heads in a video posted on the Internet, confirmed that the decapitations reflected a dispute between Mexico's two most powerful drug trafficking organizations. As historian Paul Eiss reveals, the competing displays also reflected a dispute among politicians connected with the two criminal organizations. The potential revelation of these relationships provoked aggressive intervention by both the DEA and President Felipe Calderón. Their joint Operation Mérida flooded parts of Yucatán with military and law enforcement personnel. Fortunately for the people of Yucatán, things did not spiral out of control, and the intensity of violence there never reached the levels experienced elsewhere during the drug war. Neither, however, were any of the public officials implicated in the drug trade ever seriously investigated or punished.[49]

The widespread Internet dissemination of images of acts of torture, forced confession, execution, and mutilation began around the same time. The birth of *Blog del Narco* in January 2010 is a useful marker. Concerned that Mexican politicians were downplaying the extent, ferocity, and danger to ordinary civilians posed by the growing violence of the drug war, a group of young journalists and computer scientists set out to document the violence in graphic detail and in real time, in a way that neither print nor television media was willing to do. By posting gory photographs and links to torture and execution videos produced by the perpetrators, *Blog del Narco* and a series of less scrupulous imitators developed huge audiences and became central points of reference and contention in the drug war. *Blog del Narco* became the ESPN of the drug war, where the players wanted to be seen—and seen at their most fearsome, where they could taunt rivals and imitators, and where followers needed to see their latest exploits to stay current at the water cooler or the cantina. Spectacles of violence developed a language and logic of their own, as rival criminal organizations traded atrocities and competed with each other for the ferocity and gore of their displays, but also for the size of the audience they reached. Once this propaganda war began, criminals also targeted bloggers who posted materials inconvenient or unflattering to their operations. At least two *Blog del Narco* collaborators have been murdered and several other have gone into hiding or exile.[50]

The posting of pictures of mutilated bodies and threatening banners was soon accompanied by videos of torture, forced confession, and murder filmed by the perpetrators. In perhaps one of the more gruesome cases (if such a magnifier can still be applied), in June 2013 a Zetas cell posted a video that shows the hacking to death of four women. The video opens in a cornfield field on a dark gray day. The victims are kneeling on trampled stalks with their hands tied behind their backs, three of them stripped naked from the waist up, with about a dozen masked men crowded around behind them, pointing machine guns at their heads.

A man in a black cap standing directly behind them barks out a series of what seem to be rehearsed questions, eliciting their names, their job titles, the names of their bosses in the rival cartel, and the details of various operations, while periodic slaps and thwacks with a machine gun barrel speed up any hesitant answers. Throughout the interrogation, the head of an axe wielded by a man in the second row occasionally sways into view between the silhouettes of the armed men. The interrogator looks up at the camera and delivers a harangue against the Gulf Cartel, accusing them of messing around in Zeta territory and not having "enough balls" to do their own dirty work, sending a bunch of "innocent women" to do it for them. On cue, the four gunmen directly behind the women kick them face down. Three of the others rush in with knives, slitting three of the victims' throats simultaneously, while the man with the axe begins to hack away at the fourth, and the interrogator joins in with a machete. The camera never moves, and all of the butchery remains in the frame. This particular massacre was apparently an act of revenge. One of the victims, a Gulf Cartel assassin known as La Güera Loca ("Crazy White Girl"), had posted a video of her beheading a Zetas commander and peeling his face off with a box cutter a few months earlier.[51]

Even much less graphic episodes have a dialogic, tit-for-tat quality to them. In August 2013, the Gulf Cartel killed and hanged a young couple (they look to be teenagers) from a pedestrian bridge in Fresnillo, Zacatecas, after forcing them to confess that they were lookouts for the Zetas and then posting the confession on YouTube. In retaliation, the Zetas killed and hanged two other young people, alleged Gulf Cartel operatives, from another bridge two days later. Likewise, they posted confessions on the Internet. Since torture and execution are not part of the videos, these incidents remain accessible on a number of mainstream websites, where their beating or killing would have been immediately censored.[52]

The inability of the government to protect ordinary civilians, its active complicity in criminal violence, and the pornographic spectacle of torture, murder, and mutilation to which the general public has been forcibly exposed have affected Mexican society to a far greater degree than the homicide rate or similar data points might suggest. From the perspective of ordinary civilians, an oppressive uncertainty and powerlessness is what makes the experience comparable to that of war and what demands that those who have declared war accept responsibility for its true cost. This is also, however, fairly recent. Before this brave new drug war, there was an older, more conventional drug war, and it began in Sinaloa.

THE DRUG WAR AND STATE VIOLENCE IN SINALOA

Sinaloa is the cradle of modern drug trafficking in Mexico, the birthplace and sentimental homeland of a majority of its most infamous drug traffickers and the home of its most powerful drug cartel. Roughly the size of West Virginia at 58,000 square kilometers (22,000 square miles), Sinaloa occupies a wedge of territory between the towering mountains of the Sierra Madre Occidental and the Gulf of California, south of the border state of Sonora and north of the beaches of Nayarit. Five major rivers flow southwest from its remote eastern highlands along the border with Chihuahua and Durango, irrigating a rich coastal plain, with large swaths of productive agricultural land in a country where only about 10 percent of the land is arable.[53]

Cut off by the mountains and inhabited by large autonomous indigenous communities, Sinaloa remained relatively isolated from most of the rest of the country until the twentieth century. Remote mountain redoubts, secluded tidal marshes, and coastal islands made perfect hideouts for rebels, bandits, and contrabandists during the century of military coups, foreign invasions, and civil wars that followed Mexican independence from Spain in 1821.[54] And when the central government has made its presence felt in Sinaloa, it has often been as an invading force, whether in brutal counterinsurgency campaigns against the Yaqui Indians in the last quarter of the nineteenth century, anti-Catholic rural education campaigns in the 1920s, or in successive waves of militarized drug eradication efforts since the 1940s.

Thanks to its natural deepwater port at Mazatlán, Sinaloa was more closely tied to San Francisco and even Hong Kong than Mexico City. Since colonial times, Sinaloans have enjoyed cosmopolitan interactions and consumer goods unavailable elsewhere in Mexico—from Chinese spices, opiates, and textiles to American radical literature, blue jeans, and rock music—often as contraband. As historian Froylán Enciso explains, "Sinaloa lived globalization before the term existed."[55] This mix of isolation and cosmopolitanism produced a culture highly distinctive from the rest of northern Mexico. From its thundering and brassy *banda* music and the cults of the bandits Heraclio Bernal and Jesús Malverde, to a rich regional dialect, redolent of criminal slang and a modern literary tradition that's celebrates it, Sinaloa's culture pushes common elements of regional Mexican culture to greater extremes.[56] Border towns like Tijuana and Juárez have their patron saints with criminal backgrounds and their winking celebration of vice and illicit entrepreneurship, but they also demarcate clear social divisions. Cultural elites on the border tend to embrace neither the bandit past nor contemporary cultural institutions designed primarily for foreign leisure or subversion. Instead they celebrate their regions' connectivity, hybridity, and creative adaptability as signs of cosmopolitan sophistication.[57] In Sinaloa, on the other hand, the unruly past and present are widely embraced as essential elements of local rural culture, endless fonts of tragic authenticity, even among boosters and glad-handers. And the aggressive, flirtatious physicality of interpersonal relations in Sinaloa makes the aloof cowboy cultures of Chihuahua or Coahuila seem positively Scandinavian by contrast.

The modern drug trade in Mexico dates back to the Prohibition era (1920–33) in the United States, and Sinaloa played a pivotal role in its development. Chinese merchants imported the first opium seeds and pioneered its cultivation and consumption in and around Mazatlán over the last half of the nineteenth century. But by the time of the Mexican Revolution (1910–20) and the first prohibition of opium trafficking in the United States (1914), the trade was neither particularly large nor particularly Chinese. Local *gomeros* ("gum collectors"), who lance the bulbous green-black pods after the flowers bloom, so that the creamy opium gum oozes out, have been a fixture of highland society since the turn of the twentieth century. Indeed, officials in Sinaloa criminalized opium in the 1920s largely as a pretext for a broader wave of repression and exclusion targeted at the local Chinese population. Anti-Chinese agitation was the hyper-nationalist stepchild of a comprehensive suite of top-down social reforms.[58]

Despite the presence of charismatic gangsters and a local tradition of celebrating them as Robin Hood types, drug trafficking organizations in Sinaloa have their roots in opposition to land reform during the 1930s. During the presidency of Lázaro Cárdenas (1934–1940), nearly a third of the Mexican population received land or access to it, the percentage of land in cultivation and its productivity shot up, and feudal relations of production all but disappeared. In Sinaloa, however, large landowners hired *guardias blancas* ("white guards") or private gunmen to harass and intimidate local campesinos and agrarian communities from making land reform claims. Many of these landowners had gotten into the opium and marijuana business, and their private armies killed on the order of two thousand campesinos to prevent land reform and the exposure of their illicit businesses during the Cárdenas era. While violent resistance to land reform was common enough in rural Mexico, the role of the drug trade exacerbated rural violence in Sinaloa and effectively blocked large-scale land reform, particularly in the sierra.[59]

The outbreak of war in Europe in 1939—especially as it affected the Balkans, Turkey, and other parts of the Middle East—shut down the main pipeline bringing illegal drugs to the United States. While there is a persistent myth that US officials openly encouraged opium production in Sinaloa as a counterweight to Japan's control of opium-producing areas in the Pacific Rim, there is little evidence to support it. The war did create illicit business opportunities. Bugsy Siegel, the intrepid Brooklyn mobster who helped Lucky Luciano conquer the New York underworld, convinced the Italian-American Mafia to begin large-scale operations on Mexico's northern Pacific coast. The cultivation of poppies and the export of opium were already thriving in Sinaloa at the time, but by providing credit to growers and cash to politicians on an unprecedented scale Siegel built a veritable drug-trafficking empire. Along with his girlfriend, the actress Virginia Hill, he hosted lavish parties in Mexico City to woo celebrities and the political elite. So much money and influence was moving around, in fact, that the operation attracted the attention of the FBI.[60] The FBI's role in Mexico, in turn, expanded dramatically during World War II, fueled by fears that "fifth columnists" or saboteurs might use Mexico as a staging ground for attacks on the United States, perhaps with the complicity of fascist sympathizers in the Mexican government.[61]

Under related pressure from Mexico City, Sinaloa governor Rodolfo T. Loaiza initiated a poppy eradication campaign, and he targeted Siegel's suppliers. Months later, on February 20, 1944, Loaiza was assassinated while dining at the lavish Hotel Belmar in Mazatlán, with a beauty queen on his arm. The assassin, Rodolfo Valdés Osuna, aka El Gitano ("The Gypsy"), was an infamous pistolero who began as a *guardia blanca* and was recruited into the drug trade by Pedro Avilés Pérez, a doctor from Badiraguato who pioneered the local marijuana and opium trade.[62] Some local historians believe that Loaiza was involved in drug trafficking himself, and that he was killed for breaking a deal with corrupt military officers protecting the opium racket in the sierra. Others see it as an act of vengeance for the assassination of Loaiza's political rival, Alfonso Tirado, in Culiacán six years earlier.[63] Whatever the precise motive, it is clear that the opium trade was financing an expanding mafia in Sinaloa, a growing army of pistoleros to do the dirty work of politicians and other power brokers. And the federal government's response would follow a similar pattern. After the assassination, President Manuel Ávila Camacho sent federal troops to dismantle the *guardias blancas* and occupy a large chunk of southern Sinaloa.[64]

Beginning in the 1950s, Sinaloa experienced something akin to the "Bulldozer Revolution" in the American South or the postwar boom in the Central Valley of California—the construction of highways, dams, and irrigation networks, coupled with new rural credit mechanisms and large-scale labor migration.[65] The result was an agriculture boom and the dramatic growth of Culiacán, headquarters of agribusiness and mining interests in Sinaloa. From 1950 to 1990, the municipality nearly doubled each decade, growing from 49,000 to 605,000. By 2010, the city of Culiacán had about 675,000 people and the municipality totaled 860,000. Like Sacramento, it is both a political and an agribusiness capital, and it has a similar feel. Sparkling truck, tractor, and agricultural machinery showrooms line the roads leading into Culiacán, in between fields of tomatoes and soybeans, and modern production facilities. On the outskirts of town, one can find entire communities of migrant laborers from Oaxaca and Chiapas, more than 1,500 kilometers (930 miles) south.[66] Also like Sacramento, the city of Culiacán boasts dozens of glass-and-steel corporate headquarters, high-end housing, and consumption options that seem out of proportion to its provincial economy. In Sacramento, these are the accoutrements of the power brokers from the defense, technology, and entertainment industries, and the political apparatus of a state with the eighth-largest economy in the world. In Culiacán they have another source.

Over the course of the 1950s and 1960s, demand for opium and marijuana in the United States soared thanks to its growing popularity in minority and bohemian enclaves and later to the expansion of university campuses and counterculture movements. The opening of the Pan-American Highway along the Pacific coast in 1950 made Sinaloa an ideal source, and the opening of a highway from the highland growing region of Badiraguato to the state capital in Culiacán facilitated a massive expansion of the business.[67] Landowners, suppliers, and intermediaries large and small made overnight fortunes, and the broader agricultural boom provided convenient cover. They built houses in Culiacán, invested in legitimate businesses, and settled their families there. Long after some of these original families from the sierra branched out to other parts of Mexico and joined rival organized crime networks, they continued to keep homes and families in Culiacán, and many of them are buried there, in grandiose *narco*-mausoleums with fountains, original art, air conditioning, and wireless Internet access.[68] As Diego Osorno puts it, Sinaloa was a "microcosm of the good and the bad of the Mexican Miracle."[69]

Sinaloan Pedro Avilés, aka "The Lion of the Sierra," was the first to traffic illicit drugs in small planes, and he set up distribution arrangements in cities all along the border with the United States in the 1950s. He built a network of local growers throughout the sierra, and he also cultivated relationships with powerful police commanders throughout the state to protect the business from prying eyes. Police and soldiers not on the payroll entered the sierra at their peril. As the trade grew, Avilés increasingly played a cat-and-mouse game with US law enforcement, and he carefully crafted his image as a wily Mexican outfoxing slow, heavy-handed gringos.[70]

Powerful politicians throughout the state were clearly involved in the drug business during the postwar heyday of the PRI (Partido Revolucionario Institucional), but the precise degree of coordination between them has yet to be documented. The prototype of the PRIista power broker in Sinaloa was Leopoldo Sánchez Celis—president of the party (1951–53) and then governor or Sinaloa (1963–68). Like other skillful party leaders, he built a political machine by co-opting the leaders of local cooperatives and rural credit associations—trading government investment for loyalty and ruthlessly smashing any opposition. He also bragged that he had protected Sinaloa from the disastrous military interventions of the 1940s by rigorously policing the drug trade with state and local law enforcement. That policing, however, seems to have been not so much about prevention as it was effective management, making sure that the government got a proper cut of the revenues, set the terms of the illicit trade, and kept violence out of the public sphere.[71]

Before the 1980s, drug traffickers directed very little violence at ordinary civilians or people who were not directly involved in the trade or its regulation. As Avilés famously put it, success in the drug business required "mixing in the smallest amount of blood possible." Much of the violence that did target ordinary people or noncombatants was carried out by the government on the pretext of drug enforcement, rather than by the drug traffickers themselves. It is part of an important legacy of state violence and one that intensified during the 1970s.

In 1975, the Mexican government initiated Operation Condor, an intensive aerial eradication program, coupled with search-and-destroy ground operations, modeled on counterinsurgency warfare. Condor targeted Sinaloa, and a smaller sister operation targeted Guerrero. At the time, poppies and marijuana were growing on the hills immediately surrounding Culiacán, in full view of the city, and press conferences kicked off the campaigns—they were anything but secretive. Badiraguato and the villages up in the sierra along the Sinaloa border with Chihuahua and Durango depended heavily on marijuana and poppy cultivation and suffered mightily during military incursions and occupations.[72] Planes doused anything or anyone in the targeted highland fields and valleys with chemical defoliants. Small units of soldiers swooped into remote areas by helicopter, reconnoitered local settlements, and then manually destroyed small poppy and marijuana plots, often in front of the helpless rural people who had cultivated them.[73] US and Mexican officials waffled between buoyancy and angst in assessing their ability to destroy Sinaloa's poppy crop.[74] But they never wavered in their definition of success. In a 1977 report to President Carter, US drug czar Peter Bourne lauded the opium eradication efforts as "100% successful . . . the most persuasive evidence being the extreme, visible economic distress that has developed in Sinaloa, Durango, and Chihuahua (the prime opium growing areas) among farmers and merchants since the eradication program went into full effect."[75]

And it wasn't just physical or economic distress. The same operations also displaced hundreds of rural communities in their entirety. Recently declassified documents from Mexican and US archives detail a systemic pattern of abuse committed by occupying Mexican soldiers against the civilian populations they encountered in Sinaloa, including arson, theft, rape, torture, and murder. The commanding officer for Operation Condor in Sinaloa was General José Hernández Toledo, an old paratrooper infamous for his role in the 1968 Tlatelolco massacre and the military occupation of the National Autonomous University (UNAM) in Mexico City.[76]

Not all of this abuse was simply a matter of harsh tactics, undisciplined troops, or poor military leadership. On the pretext of drug enforcement, the army and federal law enforcement targeted a variety of dissident groups for torture, murder, and disappearance, in what came to be known as Mexico's dirty war. Collateral damages among local civilian populations included rape, extortion, and murder. An official investigation by the Mexican government, released in 2006, documents 797 reported disappearances, from 1971 until 1978, 436 of which can be verified with near absolute certainty in federal security archives. It also includes the list of ninety-nine verified extrajudicial executions, most of which were carried out under the jurisdiction of the Federal Security Directorate (DFS), Mexico's secret police.[77] The overlap between counternarcotics and counterinsurgency operations wasn't seamless, but the data show that Sinaloa and Guerrero were primary targets for both. Sinaloa bore the brunt of eradication efforts, whereas Guerrero suffered the most disappearances and extrajudicial killings.[78] In 2012, Guerrero's official Truth Commission identified 512 additional forced disappearances in the state between 1969 and 1979 and a pattern of rape, torture, and murder that seems to have been more about suppressing political dissent than sustaining either counternarcotics or counterinsurgency operations.[79]

Aggressive enforcement put pressure on family businesses in Sinaloa, and violent feuds broke out. As a result of the intensive crackdown, local drug traffickers took their business elsewhere, and cultivation spread to new areas in Jalisco, Guerrero, and Michoacán. Sinaloan traffickers Miguel Ángel Félix Gallardo, Rafael Caro Quintero, and Ernesto Fonseca Carrillo founded the Guadalajara Cartel, which operated as a nationwide federation and was the closest to a classic clan-based mafia that Mexican drug traffickers have ever created. Félix Gallardo played the role of godfather and was the architect of the cocaine traffic from Colombia, by way of Honduras. Caro Quintero and Fonseca Carrillo coordinated the production and sale of marijuana at properties dispersed across Sinaloa, Chihuahua, Durango, Michoacán, and Guerrero. Pedro Avilés struck out on his own, starting what would become the Tijuana Cartel. It should be noted that cocaine trafficking was relatively new. Even in Colombia, it barely existed before 1970, and the pioneers in the business were from the Chilean Andes. The first to transship South American cocaine through Mexico were Cuban gangsters, in exile after the 1959 revolution. The meteoric rise of the Colombian cartels in the 1970s paved the way for their Mexican counterparts in the 1980s.

After 1977, under President José López Portillo (1976–82), Mexico largely abandoned aggressive drug eradication and enforcement operations. Part of this was the result of pressure to keep the border open for trade and investment. Some of it was the cost—maintaining a fleet of aircraft with multi-lens cameras was indeed expensive, and Washington offered much less support than it had under Nixon and Ford. Finally, the impending fiscal collapse of the Mexican state, which defaulted on its foreign debts in 1982, diminished both the will and the capacity of the state to undertake aggressive drug enforcement operations. Drug traffickers and illicit investment capital flooded back into the highlands of Sinaloa and the "Golden Triangle" areas along the border with Chihuahua and Durango. With cash from their new regional hubs and the

expanding market for illicit drugs from the United States, drug traffickers rebuilt many of the communities devastated by the Mexican armed
forces, and they expanded and modernized both poppy and marijuana
production.

After the Dadeland Mall massacre in 1979 and the Wild West violence
of the cocaine boom in Miami, the United States concentrated drug
enforcement efforts on southern Florida and the Caribbean.[80] Colombian drug traffickers increasingly relied upon Mexican traffickers to move
their products into the United States, and Mexicans gradually claimed
a larger share of the trade. By 1982, Mexico replaced Colombia as the
largest supplier of marijuana to the United States. Quality improved as
well, as the Sinaloans used sinsemilla varietals, fertilizer, irrigation, and
insecticides. Mexican drug traffickers gradually took a larger portion of
the profits and began to supplant Colombians in both production and
smuggling to the United States. By 1985, about one-third of the cocaine
arriving in the United States passed through Mexico, much of it arriving
from Colombia, Ecuador, and Peru unrefined, and Mexico surpassed
Colombia for the first time as the world's leading producer of marijuana.
Coupled with the financial collapse of the Mexican state, which was left
with few resources to invest in rural communities and little credibility,
the new drug boom in the area reinforced the idea that drug traffickers
were the true local leaders—the ones who paid for new schools, health
clinics, and roads, but also local people who grew up poor and made
their mark on the world (however infamous that mark might appear).

Félix Gallardo was a classic mafioso godfather. He started his career in
the state police and then moved into the drug trade after serving on the
security detail of Governor Sánchez Celis. Diego Osorno relates an incident in which the famous drug trafficker read a story in the local paper
in Mazatlán about a child murderer. Incensed, he called the police chief
and offered whatever resources were necessary to capture the killer. He
also parlayed his wealth and reputation into a powerful diplomatic bar-
gaining chip. In 1982, for example, he secured a permanent tourist visa
so that he could visit the United States whenever he wanted, despite the
fact that he had been on the DEA's list of known drug traffickers since
1977.[81] Other sources claim that Félix Gallardo was a major contributor

to the Nicaraguan Contras and that this protected him from US drug enforcement.[82]

However benevolent they were with some of their social investments, the drug traffickers ruled the highlands of Badiraguato and Mocorito with an iron fist. They tolerated no opposition, they enforced contracts with extreme violence, and they often battled among themselves. Joaquín Guzmán Loera, aka El Chapo ("Shorty") a rising local trafficker brought into the business by Avilés and mentored by Caro Quintero, was notorious for executing his own men if they arrived late with a delivery or for a meeting, even if they had a seemingly legitimate excuse (like the collapse of a road). He and other highland drug bosses also imported forced laborers from other parts of Mexico, tortured and killed politicians, journalists, and human rights activists whose work threatened to reveal their operations or political connections, and sought to corrupt or kill any law enforcement agents or soldiers active in their territory.[83]

As the Guadalajara Cartel grew, the stakes behind the business and the political connections necessary to maintain it grew enormously, and violence followed almost inevitably. On May 30, 1984, one of the better-known journalists in Mexico, Manuel Buendía, was gunned down after leaving his office in Mexico City. He had a syndicated daily column in *Excélsior* and was a well-known public figure. Buendía had a lot of powerful enemies. He had accused the Petroleum Workers' Union of corruption, he had accused the CIA of collusion in Mexico's "dirty war," and he was rumored to be working on an investigation implicating the defense minister and various generals in the drug trade. And at the time of his death he was preparing a column on José Antonio Zorrilla—then head of the DFS—and his involvement in drug trafficking. At the direction of Interior Minister Manuel Bartlett, the murder was investigated by the DFS, the institution likely responsible for the murder.[84]

The connection between the DFS and the drug trade was an open secret, one of the many unseemly realities US officials tolerated in the name of the "greater good" of maintaining Cold War alliances. When new DEA agents arrived in Guadalajara, their Mexican liaisons would show them the safe houses that the Guadalajara Cartel and the DFS shared in the city—where they held meetings, conducted illicit business, and hosted huge bacchanals. One of these mansions was only a few blocks from the prosecutor's office and around the corner from the DEA field office.[85] DEA agents did not know that the head of the DFS from 1978 to 1982, Miguel Nassar Haro, was a highly valued CIA asset. When the US attorney in San Diego tried to file charges against Nassar, after accumulating a considerable body of evidence, officials in Washington pressured him to drop the case. The CIA, in turn, also knew that the Guadalajara Cartel was linked to Juan Ramón Matta Ballesteros. The Honduran drug trafficker acted as the middleman for the Medellín Cartel for the shipment of Colombian cocaine to Mexico (and on to the United States). American officials tolerated Matta Ballesteros and his cronies in the Honduran government as a lesser evil, while they used Honduras as a base of operations for the Contra War against the Sandinista government in Nicaragua to the south, the brutal counterinsurgency regime in El Salvador to the west, and the military dictatorship responsible for genocide in Guatemala to the north.

On February 7, 1985, undercover DEA agent Enrique "Kiki" Camarena was kidnapped by armed gunmen, tortured, and murdered. Two months earlier, the DEA and Mexican officials had raided a massive marijuana cultivation and processing complex in Chihuahua called El Búfalo, operated by Rafael Caro Quintero. Perhaps seven thousand campesinos worked at the complex, where five thousand to ten thousand tons of high-grade marijuana worth $2.5 billion was found and destroyed. *Time* magazine called it "the bust of the century." In 2013, two former CIA field officers would reveal that they had participated in the kidnapping in order to maintain their own cover, so that they could continue to procure funds to support the Nicaraguan Contras.[86] Caro Quintero and Fonseca Carrillo were both arrested in April 1985 and sent to prison for orchestrating the murder. Félix Gallardo went underground and used his political connections to avoid arrest until 1989.[87]

In the interim, Sinaloa became the most infamous and violent state in Mexico. In 1986, the federal government deployed 1,300 police and soldiers to Sinaloa, in search of weapons caches and stolen vehicles. Several high-ranking government officials resigned in order to avoid prosecution for their ties to drug trafficking.[88] Sinaloa also played a prominent role in a moral panic over Mexican drug traffickers in the United States that overlapped with the crack cocaine epidemic. In the hysteria, the

US Senate debated imposing economic sanctions on Mexico, and US media outlets alleged that ten thousand Mexican officials were involved in the drug trade.[89] Anticipating the diplomatic and law enforcement crackdown that would follow and ultimately lead to his 1989 arrest, Félix Gallardo tried to orchestrate a peaceful distribution of territories among the families that made up the Guadalajara Cartel.[90] A loose federation would allow for greater local control, easier coordination, and a lower profile with law enforcement.

Sinaloa went to El Chapo (Guzmán) and Ismael "El Mayo" Zambada. (The allocation was actually somewhat more complicated, but their leadership was the critical part). They quickly allied with Eduardo "El Güero" Palma, a seasoned trafficker from Sinaloa who had served eight years in an Arizona prison and had a falling out with Félix Gallardo. This alliance signaled the Sinaloans' independence but also a brewing conflict with the Tijuana Cartel—El Güero's archenemy and the murderer of his wife and three children was working for Félix Gallardo's nephews, the Arellano Félix brothers, who ran the Tijuana Cartel. El Güero was a volatile character but incredibly ambitious, and in El Chapo he found a brutally efficient and tireless operations manager. Together they transformed the Sinaloa Cartel from a producer and wholesaler of marijuana and opium into an international drug-trafficking syndicate. They established transit routes throughout northern Mexico and beachheads up and down the US border. In particular, they made a name for themselves by building increasingly sophisticated tunnels for smuggling drugs into the United States, often in collaboration with the Tijuana and Juárez Cartels but sometimes in direct competition. El Güero's personal feuds proved costly to the growing enterprise. When human rights activist Norma Corona opened an investigation into the murder of three Venezuelan students that El Güero had ordered in an act of vengeance in early 1990, Palma ordered her assassinated by members of the Federal Judicial Police on his payroll. Corona's murder in May 1990 sparked massive protests in Mazatlán and Culiacán and ultimately inspired the Salinas administration to establish the National Human Rights Commission (CNDH), with offices in all thirty-one states. It also sparked a massive law enforcement operation against the Sinaloa Cartel.[91]

In 1993, jealous of El Chapo's rising influence and eager to maintain their own dominance, the Arrellano Félix brothers carried out an elaborate assassination attempt against him. They sent group of Southern California gangbangers to intercept him at the Guadalajara airport. The bumbling assassins riddled Catholic cardinal Juan Jesús Posadas Ocampo with bullets instead, after mistaking his car for that of El Chapo.[92] The cardinal's killing pressured the Mexican government to go after the drug traffickers, and the noose tightened around the leadership of the Sinaloa Cartel. El Chapo was arrested on the Guatemalan border in 1993, alone and unarmed, and El Güero was arrested after a plane crash in 1995—he was disguised as a Federal Judicial Police commander and accompanied by a security detail of actual Federal Judicial Police.[93]

El Chapo continued to manage the Sinaloa operation from behind bars in the prison at Puente Grande, just outside of Guadalajara, and it would appear that he quickly eclipsed El Güero. In addition to El Mayo Zambada, El Chapo relied on his brother Arturo Guzmán Loera and the Beltrán Leyva brothers, a close-knit clan from Badiraguato, Sinaloa, to run things while he was locked up. The Beltrán Leyva brothers proved able managers, expanding Sinaloa's production and trafficking capacity, particularly in Sonora. They also tolerated a proliferation of parallel criminal enterprises, including a nationwide kidnapping ring, a deviation from El Chapo's laser-like focus on the drug business that attracted considerable pressure from law enforcement.[94]

The drug enforcement efforts of the 1990s in Mexico were mired in corruption and overlapped with murderous political repression. General José de Jesús Gutiérrez Rebollo participated in several high-profile actions in the takedown of the Guadalajara Cartel, and he continued to lead eradication efforts in Jalisco, Guerrero, and Sinaloa into the decade. In 1996, he was appointed Mexico's "drug czar," director of the Instituto Nacional para el Combate a las Drogas (INCD), where he had access to intelligence, resources, and equipment from Mexico and the United States, and where he had command-and-control authority over drug eradication operations. He was apparently using these resources to help the leader of the Juárez Cartel, Amado Carrillo Fuentes, to weaken his enemies and grow his own illicit empire. The general became fabulously wealthy, so wealthy that he was investigated for corruption and fraud. General Gutiérrez Rebollo was fired, arrested, and sentenced to thirty years in prison (and a subsequent forty more years after a second trial in 2007). His immediate subordinate in Sinaloa, Brigadier General Alfredo Navarro Lara, was arrested on bribery charges a month later.[95] Similar scandals took down important leaders in the Federal Judicial Police and many state police forces in this period.[96]

The involvement of the highest-ranking law enforcement officers in the country in the drug trade was part of a violent political soap opera that included the assassinations of presidential candidate Luis Donaldo Colosio; the sitting president of the ruling party, and brother-in-law of President Carlos Salinas, José Francisco Ruiz Massieu; human rights activist Digna Ochoa; and more than seven hundred organizers for the Party of the Democratic Revolution (PRD), a leftist opposition party created in 1988.[97]

This is the corrupt Mexico that seethes beneath an all-encompassing yellow hue in Steven Soderbergh's *Traffic* or the materialist dystopia lurking across the border in Cormac McCarthy's *No Country for Old Men*. Soderbergh and McCarthy depict violence as the inevitable consequence of personal greed (for wealth or power or both), to the point that it's basically transactional: you get too greedy in their Mexico, you get cut down. There's a clear moral choice. They cannot accommodate either corruption that is more about coercion than greed, or people who are killed fighting for truth and justice except, perhaps, as collateral damage. State violence melts into criminal violence. Soderbergh and McCarthy also don't convey that violence was at a historic low in Mexico in the early 2000s, when their caricatures became iconic. The overall level of violence declined from 1990 through 2006, to the lowest levels in Mexican history. Obscured abroad by the antics of "drug lords" and high-profile politicians, this relative peace shaped the expectations of an emerging civil society in the middle of a democratic opening and their experience of the wave of violence that has touched nearly every social sector in nearly every part of the country the country since 2006. This is a very different story than that of the old drug war, and one that needs to be told differently.

A NEW KIND OF TESTIMONIAL LITERATURE
FOR A NEW KIND OF DRUG WAR

> They were all headed for the same,
> like Judas in the garden!
> They killed the man who lit the flame
> and gave them life and pardon,
> refusing to herald and proclaim
> the apparition of a star in the skies,
> and refusing to hear the selfsame
> voice that spoke true and wise,
> and not wanting to look, for shame,
> into Gabriel Leyva's eyes
>
> "Por siete caminos de sangre: corrido de Gabriel Leyva."[98]

Sinaloa's classic *corrido*, a ballad lamenting the treacherous murder of local hero Gabriel Leyva by agents of a corrupt government, recites a common refrain in the *corridos* and other popular media to emerge from the Mexican Revolution (1910–20). Even in more playful and innocuous favorites, like "La Adelita," "La Valentina," and "La Cucaracha," the threat of death on the battlefield, or at the hands of enemy captors, is a central conceit. Almost all of the *corridos* named after particular revolutionaries relate the execution or assassination of their namesakes, many by *la ley fuga* ("the law of flight")—where they are shot in the back on the pretext of an escape attempt.[99] The villains are almost always corrupt generals, government officials, or their henchmen, bad guys with the trappings of authority. With blood flowing from the land along "seven paths"—a play on the name of the town where Leyva was killed and the seven paths on which the enemies of the righteous will flee (Deuteronomy 28:7)—and death riding hard on the hero's heels, the ballad reminds listeners of the inescapable fate of anyone who challenges corrupt officials in Mexico

But the *corrido* also has the clear, even exaggerated, moral compass of a tragic romance. More than just the obvious treachery of an ambush and shooting a man in the back, the killers themselves are ashamed—they can't look Gabriel Leyva in the eye, even after he's dead. And the "star" they dimmed, the "voice" they silenced momentarily, was not of one man, but rather "the voice of the people," a moral community that witnessed his betrayal, recognized his sacrifice, and will keep singing his song until justice is done or Judgment Day arrives.

This basic recognition of injustice, the ability to say it out loud and have it acknowledged by a community, even if that community is more or less powerless to stop it, is precisely what is missing when it comes to the quotidian violence of the drug war, *levantones* in particular.

Throughout the Cold War, testimonial literature provided some of the most accessible and insightful scholarship and pedagogy on the experience of state violence (and the popular resistance it produced). The genre revealed that people who couldn't read could still write and in fact had a lot to say. First-person narratives from representatives of subaltern and oppressed groups humanized conflicts previously presented through abstract strategic and ideological perspectives, and they revealed yawning gaps in the analytical frameworks through which policy makers and scholars examine social movements and civil conflicts across Latin America.[100] Generations of students have explored the meaning of rural insurgency and repression in Guatemala, for example, through the writings of Rigoberta Menchú. Her work, in turn, inspired a whole generation of indigenous and women's testimonial literature.[101] *Memory of Fire*, Eduardo Galeano's sweeping five-hundred-year history of the Americas, attracted a massive readership and democratized historical inquiry by translating key documents and ideas into an epistolary or testimonial form.[102] Galeano's grand narrative is a work of fiction, albeit an extremely well documented one. But the structure of the book—a series of suggestive headlines and datelines—suggests the possibility of using a collection of pieces of journalism, both to invite a larger audience and to achieve a deeper understanding of the underlying social reality. By definition, the experience of violence is subjective, and we can't fully understand it without examining how it operates on individual subjects. At the same time, the trauma and fear it causes disrupt the narrative of an individual's life and isolate individual experiences from each other, even if they look similar to an outside observer. Reestablishing a historical narrative and putting accounts of individual experiences of violence together, where they can dialogue with each other can thus create both a better understanding of the social reality of violence and mitigate the articulation of the underlying harm.

The central figure in this historical narrative and the protagonist in the most popular *corridos* about the drug war is, without a doubt, Joaquín "El Chapo" Guzmán Loera. Taking advantage of Mexico's democratic opening, increasing integration with the United States, and the deregulation of firearms and financial markets, he built an unprecedented drug empire, headquartered in Sinaloa. Because it focused on the drug business and generally avoided the worst excesses of violence against ordinary citizens, his Sinaloa Cartel often avoided the most aggressive law enforcement and military operations, particularly under the Calderon administration (2006–12).

El Chapo's escapes from prison, in particular, have fueled a vibrant myth about the scope of his power and turned him into a folk antihero who thumbs his nose at the corruption and inefficiency of the Mexican government.

After seven years behind bars, El Chapo escaped from Puente Grande prison outside of Guadalajara in 2001, then spent thirteen years on the lam. He was rearrested in Mazatlán, Sinaloa, on February 22, 2014, in an operation spearheaded by the DEA. On July 11, 2015, he escaped from the Altiplano maximum security prison outside of Mexico City—right under a security camera, through a tunnel nearly a mile long (one and half kilometers), complete with lighting, ventilation, and a motorcycle-tram. Within thirty minutes of entering an escape hatch hidden underneath the toilet in his cell, he was on a private plane headed for parts unknown. El Chapo was rearrested in Los Mochis Sinaloa on January 8, 2016, after a prolonged firefight with Mexican marines. As of this writing, he sits in a maximum security prison in Ciudad Juárez, awaiting extradition to the United States.

El Chapo's 2014 arrest had seemed to be a feather in the cap of President Enrique Peña Nieto.[103] The "telepresidente"—charming and polished before the cameras alongside his soap opera star wife—had promised new economic opportunities and drug enforcement that would protect ordinary people, with a wink to the paternalistic mafia ties of the old ruling party. In the wake of his tone-deaf response to the Ayotzinapa massacre, however, many questioned how much of the apparent reduction of violence under his administration was real and how much was simply a question of visibility. While the homicide rate dipped, the number of forced disappearances skyrocketed, acts of censorship and violence against journalists increased, and new allegations against the armed forces surfaced on a regular basis. In this environment, El Chapo's 2015 escape was a defiant statement of what many people already felt: the government was irrevocably corrupt and totally incapable of protecting ordinary people. There were parades and marches celebrating his escape, along with defiant placards and t-shirts. Within five days, one of the many *corridos* about the escape would receive more than 200,000 hits on YouTube.[104] The minority who actually celebrated the escape—and it was clearly a minority; most Mexicans were outraged and ashamed— were celebrating the mythical figure of El Chapo showing up the mockery that the government had made of Mexican democracy, not the actual man or his crimes.

The real El Chapo had sensed his own possibilities for Mexico's democratic opening more than a decade earlier. The election of Vicente Fox of the Partido Acción Nacional (PAN) to the presidency of Mexico in 2000, the first candidate from an opposition political party to hold that office since 1929, threatened a dramatic shakeup in the structure of political power and the mechanics of corruption related to the illicit drug trade. While many honest government officials and members of civil society saw an opportunity to rid the country of corruption once and for all, ambitious organized crime groups saw an opportunity to expand their influence. The dismantling of the old regime left a power vacuum. Pistoleros, electoral fraudsters, and other cronies scrambled to find work in a newly competitive marketplace. Stripped of their informal cadres and authority, the institutions that managed the system and acted as a check on excesses of corruption and violence were irrevocably weakened. The bold and the rich could bypass the paternalistic hierarchies of the one-party state and seize power directly. Perhaps the most ambitious crime boss, El Chapo, smelled opportunity and orchestrated his 2001 escape just after Fox took office. There's some debate as to whether he escaped in a laundry cart or simply walked out the front door, but it's clear enough that he had most of the guards on his payroll and had lived a relatively pampered life behind bars, conducting his romantic and business affairs as if he were in a hotel suite.[105]

As soon as he got his bearings, El Chapo went after new territory far beyond Sinaloa, attacking the Gulf Cartel in Nuevo Laredo, the Arellano Félix Cartel in Tijuana, and the Carrillo Fuentes Cartel in Ciudad Juárez. In each of these cases, he used the networks of corruption laid out by the Beltrán Leyva brothers to buy off, intimidate, or kill local police, members of political machines, and leaders of military garrisons. El Chapo sent the Beltrán Leyva brothers to Tamaulipas in 2003, to conquer territory, transit routes, and access points to the United States from the rival Gulf Cartel. Massive shootouts, the takeover of entire local police departments, and a wave of assassinations followed.[106] The Gulf Cartel responded by attacking Sinaloa Cartel territory, and Ciudad Juárez was caught in the middle. As Valdez explains in chapter 3, the war with the Carrillo Fuentes family, a family from the same part of Sinaloa as El Chapo, officially began on September 11, 2004, with the assassination of Rodolfo Carrillo Fuentes, aka El Hijo de Oro ("Golden Child") outside of a movie theater in Culiacán, Sinaloa, but a gradual escalation had already been well underway.

Meanwhile, the expiration of the US assault weapons ban in 2004 made automatic weapons easier and cheaper to procure, and an arms race ensued.[107] Outgunned local and state police officers came under enormous pressure.[108] Local and state police also faced a variety of new armed groups vying to control Ciudad Juárez and its surroundings. The Juárez Cartel responded to incursions from the Sinaloa Cartel by forging alliances with the rival Gulf Cartel and its fearsome enforcement wing, the Zetas, by recruiting prison gangs such as Los Aztecas and arming them, and by strengthening its enforcement branch, La Línea ("The Line" or "The Border"). Before their 2003 alliance with the Juárez Cartel, Los Aztecas (also known as Barrio Azteca) were independent, run from prisons in the United States and Mexico. In 2004 they started to carry out assassinations and other enforcement operations for the Juárez Cartel on a significant scale, which allowed them to expand their local drug dealing and prostitution operations in Ciudad Juárez.[109] For their part, the Gulf Cartel recruited gangsters from the United States and members of the Kaibiles and sent them to Juárez. The Sinaloa Cartel responded by hiring special security squads from as far away as El Salvador and deploying its own special assassination team, known as Los Antrax ("Anthrax").

Just after taking office as president in December 2006, Felipe Calderón announced the "Permanent Campaign against Drug Trafficking," which would result in the deployment of 50,000 Mexican soldiers, sailors, and marines in counternarcotics operations over the next six years. Calderón deployed heavily armed soldiers, marines, and federal police to occupy parts of Michoacán in 2006 and Baja California beginning in late 2008, arrested much of the leadership of the Tijuana and La Familia Cartels, and seriously disrupted their operations. What had been a set of more or less stable regional cartels going back to the 1990s quickly devolved into a series of chaotic and overlapping national archipelagos. Alliances were made and broken more quickly than ever before, the competition for local territories (known as *plazas*) grew increasingly violent, and many previously peaceful areas were pulled into the conflict.[110]

In the winter of 2008, the Beltrán Leyva Organization split from the Sinaloa Cartel. On January 21, 2008, Alfredo Beltrán Leyva, known as El Mochomo, was arrested by federal law enforcement agents in Culiacán. His brother Arturo, El Barbas, started to organize an elaborate paramilitary operation and bribery campaign to free his brother, but El Chapo vetoed the plan. Rumor spread that he had made a bargain with federal authorities to reduce the visibility and public violence associated with the Sinaloa Cartel (and perhaps to betray El Mochomo), in exchange for the government leaving its most profitable operations alone.[111] After the split, the two remaining factions fought vicious battles to retain their conquests. In this struggle, the Beltrán Leyvas forged an alliance with the Zetas—at the time, the security arm of the Tamaulipas-based Gulf Cartel, the second most powerful criminal organization in Mexico, based on the Gulf Coast. Ciudad Juárez was ground zero in this conflict, and it turned into a war zone. The Sinaloa Cartel retaliated against incursions on its turf by attacking Beltrán Leyva, Zeta, and Gulf Cartel territories across the country.

The Zetas had been founded in 1999 as a special security force for the Gulf Cartel, which dominated the drug trade in the states of Veracruz and Tamaulipas. Gulf Cartel leader Osiel Cárdenas Guillén recruited a group of thirty-seven special forces operators from two elite units within the Mexican armed forces and deployed them in aggressive attacks against rival organizations, law enforcement, and anyone else perceived to be in the way of Gulf Cartel operations. The Zetas grew from there into a sizeable mercenary army, with its own arms-trafficking, recruiting and training apparatus. Thanks largely to the bold and ruthless Zetas, the Gulf Cartel expanded dramatically, consolidating its control over eastern Mexico and developing new operations across the country. After Cárdenas Guillén was arrested in 2003, the Zetas began to operate more independently from their home base in Nuevo Laredo, although still in partnership with the Gulf Cartel.[112]

Over the course of 2008 and 2009, as the Gulf Cartel and the Zetas embarked on more ambitious operations—in the states of Nuevo León and Zacatecas in particular—rivalries and disputes emerged among the leadership, which led to a formal rift in the winter of 2009–10. In many other places throughout the country, the battle between the Gulf Cartel and the Sinaloa Cartel to fill the vacuum created by law enforcement operations against the Tijuana, Juárez, and Michoacán Cartels turned increasingly violent, and it became increasingly difficult for the civilian population to escape it.

Then the Zetas formally split from the Gulf Cartel and initiated a reign of terror in Tamaulipas and Veracruz. Five separate drug trafficking organizations were now fighting for territory in northern Mexico—the Sinaloa Cartel, the Beltrán Leyva Organization, the Juárez Cartel, the Zetas, and the Gulf Cartel—and these organizations hired a motley crew of street gangs, mercenaries, and corrupt police officers. To make matters worse, since this violence threatened access routes to the United States that traffickers from elsewhere in Mexico had paid to use, organizations like the Knights Templar from Michoacán and Guerreros Unidos (hundreds of miles away) were pulled into the struggle.

On August 25, 2011, masked gunmen working for the Zetas attacked a crowded casino in Monterrey, Nuevo León. They opened fire on civilians with automatic weapons, poured gasoline on the exit doors, and then set the building ablaze, killing fifty-two people and wounding dozens more. It was the worst attack in the history of this prosperous and modern northern city, and the civilian population was besieged by shootouts, assassinations, and kidnappings for the next eighteen months. Monterrey went from being one of the most peaceful to one of the most violent municipalities in Mexico, and it has never fully recovered.[113]

This is the environment in which organized crime branched out into human and arms trafficking, money laundering, and holding local governments hostage. It is the environment that made the San Fernando, Ayotzinapa, and Tlatalaya massacres possible. Below the surface of these spectacular acts of violence, those who were mobilized to fight in this conflict committed all kinds of parallel crimes using the weapons, vehicles, safe houses, and police connections at their disposal—from lucrative highway robbery, kidnapping for ransom, and auto theft rackets to more personal crimes like domestic violence, rape, and murder. This is the environment in which the individual stories in this book unfolded. While many of these cases have ties to earlier relationships and waves of violence, most of them took place at the apex of the violence of the drug war—between 2009 and 2012—in the headquarters of Mexico's most powerful drug cartel and the sentimental homeland of Mexican drug trafficking—Culiacán, Sinaloa.

This book is divided into five chapters, each of which presents the current conflict from the perspective of a different subgenre of survivors. The first chapter focuses on the psychology and internal suffering of those who are taken, who have absolutely nothing to do with the drug trade or any of its subsidiaries. In addition to the random, opportunistic quality of the violence they present, these stories show how the drug war operates along and exaggerates existing vectors of social inequality, whether of race, gender, income, or politics.

The second chapter explores cases involving dirty cops, criminals posing as law enforcement, and the murky moral terrain that ordinary people are forced to navigate in going about their daily lives amid a complex, multiparty armed conflict. These stories act as cautionary tales beyond any simple narrative of "good guys versus bad guys,'" but they also demonstrate the courage, solidarity, and creative adaptation of ordinary people in the face of fear and injustice.

The third chapter explores kidnappings and detentions related to the recruiting, training, and career trajectories of *sicarios*, the gunmen and enforcers for the drug cartels. They show the greed, machismo, and megalomania familiar to any story about drugs and gangs. But they also reveal a dark underbelly of addiction, dependence, surveillance, and coercion at the lowest levels of criminal organizations, a ruthless subculture that produces many ordinary acts of theft and violence against the civilian population that have nothing to do with the drug trade.

The fourth chapter narrates stories of the persecution, detention, and disappearance of journalists who have tried to expose drug violence and official corruption. More than just reinforcing the danger of speaking truth to power, these stories delve into the perils of trying to define truth or power in a conflict where impunity means something much deeper and more profound than a mere lack of punishment.

The fifth and final chapter relates the stories of the disappeared through family members and civic activists who have fought tooth and nail to bring their fate to light and the perpetrators to justice. These are stories of tragedy and hope that demand empathy and solidarity. Strikingly similar to stories about the "dirty wars" of the 1970s and their aftermath across Latin America, these stories beg for comparison and for an approach to the conflict that includes not just security, but also truth and reconciliation. At the same time, without a Duvalier, a Videla, or a Pinochet to blame, like the rest of the stories in this book these stories underscore the moral complexity of the situation and the inadequacy of either Cold War categories or cops-and-robbers morality plays for addressing it.

There is an inherent risk of exploitation in writing explicitly about violence. The risk increases manyfold when the writing emphasizes the underdetermined, multifactorial quality of the violence in contemporary Mexico rather than a singular agent or cause, and when the individuals involved have lost faith in the institutions to which they might have turned to denounce, punish, and redress acts of violence. Violence allures with primordial force, and representations of it often veer into voyeurism, especially when the trail is lit by a thousand and one Technicolor stereotypes. There's little doubt that proclaiming "chaos on the border" and "violence in Mexico" is a booming industry. Facing a multitude of violent actors with a diverse array of motives and no obvious saviors on the horizon, the powerlessness of an individual victim can transfer to the reader, and empathy can melt into apathy.

Most of the literature on the drug war has focused on the biggest players, the most spectacular incidents, and the perils of trying to get close to them. By recounting the exploits of drug cartels and their enemies, and by presenting them in the form of war dispatches (where the messenger might be killed at any moment), they implicitly accept the very logics that have justified a massive escalation of violence. Even setting aside the coherence of these phenomena, there's a problem of scale. The high politics and crime dramas of the drug war create a promise of causality (and thus potential solutions). But the institutions to which they pin blame—the Mexican government, the drug cartels, the US consumer, corruption, imperialism, et cetera—are so large and amorphous as to make any kind of incremental change illusory at best. The better studies certainly offer critical insights and empirical findings on the larger processes at stake, and one can only hope that policy makers are paying attention. But they don't have much to offer to the people most affected by the violence of the drug war in Mexico or those who wish to stand with them. They don't suggest a place to start, some way to recover the human dignity and moral community fractured by chronic violence that is not contingent upon overthrowing the government or radically changing Mexico's relationship with the United States. Indeed, the existing literature tends to treat the victims either as the products of their own choices (even if their suffering is disproportionate to those choices and the author is plainly sympathetic) or simply as collateral damage—the dead and their aggrieved loved ones.

Javier Valdez Cárdenas preempts apathy first and foremost by presenting the individual stories that follow together. Violence ruptures an individual's self-narrative and isolates survivors in pain and self-doubt. The simple act of telling these ordinary stories of violence alongside each other reveals patterns and commonalities that victims and their friends and families cannot see. The stories reveal many small acts of courage and solidarity, often done at considerable personal risk—a bus driver who helps a kidnapped man to get home, a young woman who shouts a warning to a stranger about to be jumped by hit men, an older brother who trades himself to kidnappers in exchange for his little brother's life, and municipal employees who go on strike to save a colleague from corrupt officials who have targeted him for murder. The chronic violence of the drug war has forced people into impossible moral choices and corrupted institutions that previously anchored the moral compass of the broader society. Small acts of courage show that individual members of society still retain the capacity to be good and do good.

This is no small thing to people grappling with the kinds of moral compromises that characterize the everyday experience of the drug war—pretending not to hear or see someone kidnapped in order to protect your children, ignoring a cry for help out of fear for your own life, or looking the other way during a robbery or extortion so that you won't be targeted. These are not film noir moral compromises of those who "suffer in style" and pave their own paths to perdition with greed, lust, jealously, and revenge.[114] These are stories about survival. The recognition of a common experience and collective moral capacity, in turn, creates the possibility for incremental change, small things that ordinary survivors and their allies can do, right now. In the field of peace-building, we call it "active presence"—listening to survivors and helping them to tell their stories, documenting how those stories fit into a collective experience, so that some kind of justice can be done, and helping the survivors to heal. While it can begin before the larger determinants of the conflict are resolved, this process is not a mere palliative, done in lieu of substantive social change. It is a necessary precondition for any kind of meaningful social change.[115] In the absence of individual and collective healing, alienation, vengeance, and clannishness will breed further violence and tyranny.

In a conflict marked by massive shootouts with .50 caliber machine guns and rocket-propelled grenades and beheadings on the Internet and mass graves for an audience no longer shocked or awed by massive explosions or body counts, *The Taken* offers a fresh and gripping human perspective. In addition to physical violence and death, it presents the experience of soul-searing interior violence—the fear, uncertainty, and guilt suffered by survivors and witnesses of a conflict with no clear boundaries. In addition to the victims and the dead, it presents the survivors—the ordinary individuals trying to make a meaningful life amid chronic violence and impunity. Without using any academic or policy jargon or hyperbole about "revolution" or "insurgency," *The Taken* makes a quiet but indelible statement: whatever we call it, living through this conflict is like living in the crosshairs of a multiparty civil war. It is exceedingly difficult to define a clear moral compass in the middle of any of the situations this war presents, even for the most principled individuals. But it is well worth the effort. And no matter what happens, the wounds this war has inflicted will take a long time to heal.

With Hell inside You

TWENTY-FIVE METERS OF CLOTH

Twenty-five meters of cloth, twelve daughters, and a promise of three hundred pesos a day (about twenty-five dollars): that's what brought this Lacandón Maya to the mountains of Sinaloa.[1] We'll call him Ramiro— Ramiro the survivor, Ramiro the migrant worker. He had crossed the country south to north in a bus. And now, in the highland region of Choix, with his eyes wide open in fright, he stepped over bodies— splayed arms and feet and hair—that had been planted there by bullets. The shootout was long over. It had been several days. And in the middle of thirty-odd cadavers, Ramiro forgot about the cloth and the money. He remembered his daughters, his homeland, and he wanted to return.

Ramiro had been taken from Chiapas by a man who had offered employment to him and twenty-four other indigenous men in an unspecified agricultural area. He'd arrived first in El Fuerte and then in Choix.[2] And there, as if he'd just taken off a blindfold, he realized that he was surrounded by armed men. He and the others asked when they would begin working and where the fields were. In response they were tied to chairs and locked in a dark room. Then the exchange of bullets began.

April of my hopes

Ramiro has twelve daughters. His Tata Dios ("Holy Father") blessed him with them—and with the six pregnancies from which they came.[3] At the time, the oldest pair was sixteen, followed by pairs who were fifteen, thirteen, eleven, nine, and just four years old, and what he earned was simply not enough to support his family. In his hometown of Los Montes Azules, Chiapas, he earned between thirty and forty pesos a day (between US$2.50 and US$3.25) making and selling arts and crafts and working odd jobs in the countryside.[4]

When he saw the man in Ocosingo, Chiapas, offering employment, he accepted. And when he and the others boarded the charter bus, it seemed as if the majority of Chiapas was making the trip—indigenous men from every region and ethnic group. The labor contractor, who seemed decent enough, promised them agricultural work paying three hundred pesos a day, with food, lodging, and round-trip passage. But he never told them where they were going.

That was between April 12 and 13, when their hopes began, but these things always have an expiration date. In this case it was little more than a week later, when the gun battle began, the harrowing and indescribable screams. Then those hopes died along with so many bodies. The indigenous men who had accompanied Ramiro dropped and faded into oblivion along with their unguarded dreams.

Where should we begin?

The trip from Chiapas north to Sinaloa took about three days. They stopped only to eat, and the man who enlisted them always told them that they should eat whatever they wanted, that there was no problem, and he picked up the bill. They got out at fast-food restaurants and roadside stalls.

The tires of the bus devoured about 2,500 kilometers (about 1,500 miles) until arriving in Los Mochis, the municipal seat of Ahome, Sinaloa, and then headed to El Fuerte, located farther north, about 250 kilometers from Culiacán (the state capital). And from there they continued to the municipality of Choix, in one of the regions disputed between the Sinaloa Cartel and the criminal organization composed of the Zetas-Beltrán Leyva and Juárez Cartels.[5] Those who "contracted" Ramiro's group of twenty-five indigenous men were presumed to be Zetas, according to later reports from the office of the attorney general of Sinaloa.

The disconcerted men asked where the work was, where the agricultural fields in which they would earn their pay were located. Don't despair, answered the labor contractor. There's steady work, pay from the first day, food and lodgings for all. The bus climbed up into the mountains until they arrived in Choix. And then they passed through various villages and climbed higher yet. They finally stopped in a small hamlet, and there they were led into the back room of a large country house. There were three doors between them and the outside.

It was then that they began to question in earnest when they would begin and where the work would be. Distrustful and tired, despair tore at their chests. They saw armed men. Ramiro wavered, but he kept it together. As he says in halting, meager, deliberate, and discrete Spanish, "[*Anduvo*] *a ciegas desde el principio*" (I went in blind from the beginning). But Lacandón Mayas are robust and don't succumb easily. He continued asking the man who brought them what was going on, why hadn't they begun to work. It was then that the armed men decided to tie them up. They put them in chairs and took seven of them to "go ahead" of the others. A person they hadn't seen before, and who seemed to be the boss, chose them by pointing his finger: "That one, that one, and that one there." They were never seen again.

It was the end of April (2012), according to his calculations. The battle and the shouts began. It lasted for days. But from the moment the bullets began to fly, nobody came to the room where they were held. And thus they passed eight days: locked up without time, in the middle of a darkness beyond the night, and very close to death.

War dispatches

On the eve of April 27, a commando unit, dressed in military-style outfits from the Policía Estatal Preventiva (State Preventive Police), raided the mountains above Choix. Versions of the story from these commandos and the army indicate that some of the armed groups entered through Chihuahua, which borders this Sinaloan municipality. The objective was to attack the group led by Adelo Núñez Molina, known as El Lemo or El 01, a deputy of the Sinaloa Cartel in that region.

The aggressors were made up of a cell of the Beltrán Leyva brothers, the Carrillo Fuentes Cartel, the Juárez Cartel, and the Zetas. The intervention of Mexican army personnel in El Potrero de los Fierro, El Pichol, and other communities in Choix and El Fuerte—right up to the Chihuahua border—extended the firefight for at least four days. The official tally was twenty-two dead, among them one soldier and local police officer Héctor Germán Ruiz Villas. But the municipal authorities had a different figure.

After the first encounters, in a preliminary statement, Mayor Juan Carlos Estrada Vega hurried to say that the fatalities amounted to between thirty and forty, the majority of them civilians. Eleazar Rubio Ayala, the municipal president of El Fuerte, located less than fifty kilometers from Choix, backed him up: "They've just informed me that they shot down a helicopter over there, and I cannot verify with certainty everything that's been said, only that some thirty people have already died in these encounters between armed groups. I hope that there is a prompt resolution to this, because it appears that the Army is already on the scene, and the municipal police of El Fuerte are supporting them, since they asked for this support," he said in a news bulletin published on April 28.

The attorney general's office reported that four of the dead civilians were from Sonora and Chihuahua. As a result of police and military actions, the authorities recovered several cloned military-style vehicles, two of them made to look like State Preventive Police (and three of them armored), two Barrett .50 caliber machine guns, fifteen AK-47 rifles, an AR-15 carbine, eight pistols, and 118 clips and 5,823 rounds of live ammunition. The bulletin sent by the National Defense Ministry (SEDENA), whose local operations run out of the Ninth Military Zone, headquartered in Culiacán, indicated that the recovered weapons and vehicles were handed over to the federal attorney general's office, headquartered in Los Mochis.

Within a week another confrontation involving the Mexican army took place in Bamoa Station, in the municipality of Guasave. On May 2, 2012, a group of soldiers arrived at the Hotel Macurín there, where they were met by shots from a group of *sicarios* ("gun men") from the same group of Zetas and Beltrán Leyva and Carrillo Fuentes Cartels, this time led by Isidro Meza Flores, known as El Chapo Isidro ("Shorty Isidro").[6]

Ten of the *sicarios* were struck down, and one of them was incinerated in what appeared to be an armored pick-up truck. Two soldiers died as well.

Eight days, many nights

Ramiro has no idea why they wanted him and the others. Now he knows that it wasn't for anything legal. They told him that they were going to work in the countryside, but it could have been planting marijuana or poppies, or cultivating and harvesting them. Perhaps they wanted to enlist them in the ranks of the *sicarios*. The only thing he knows is that he's alive, and that nothing good was waiting for him if he had stayed there. He realized this when they chose those seven men and took them away, never to be seen again.

When the shots first rang out, Ramiro asked what was happening outside. They answered that it was nothing. He and the others were already tied up and ordered to be quiet. They passed eight days that way, without food or much water. It took only two or three days before his companions, whom he barely knew by sight, started to drop off, slumped in the chairs with their heads hanging limp. They seemed to have fainted. Starvation, dehydration: their ravages always move quickly once they set in. In those eight days, nobody came in. Nobody left. They were eternal days without time or light, a heavy, hallucinatory waiting between the whistling of bullets, pitiful voices, and rhythmic shadows of the raised scythe. They were nights of terror. The silence had a deep and painful edge.

Not for Ramiro. He stayed awake, intending perhaps to disentangle if those shouts were of pain or pleading, or last gasps of life. When silence came, he was listening for words—or the guttural sounds of death. He was paying attention when the soldiers kicked in one of the doors, and then another, and finally the third one. It was dawn on May 2.

"There are people here!" shouted one of the uniformed men.

"But at that point," Ramiro remembers, "we were all still tied to the chairs when they entered and a great light lit the place up. I don't know what time it was exactly, but it was early morning. Everyone had passed out except for me. They attended to them first. 'They look bad,' I heard them say."

Ten of the soldiers remained with them and the rest left to continue their operation in the highlands. Someone with a commanding voice told those soldiers: "You guys continue, keep going. Catch up to the troops." The ten remaining soldiers untied them and tried to give them water and saline solution. It was not until the sun came up that they realized Ramiro was conscious. "That one's alive," one of the soldiers said, and an officer approached to ask if he'd been given food and water and to find out how he'd managed to remain conscious.

"'No,' I told him. 'What's going on is that we are Lacandones, we are indigenous, and we are stronger." Ramiro explained that Lacandón Mayas are tough and used to suffering.

"He took the rope off of my hands and told me, 'You need to eat, you need water. What else do you need?' And he asked me, 'Do you know this man over here?' . . . 'The other companions who are here,' I told him, 'I don't know any of them, but they too are from Chiapas.'"

The soldier asked if they were like him. He answered that no, that there were Tzeltales, Tzotziles, and others whose ethnic groups he couldn't discern, but they weren't all the same. They asked him for his papers. For the first time in his life, Ramiro had carried his birth certificate. It was his first time outside of Chiapas, where he never needed it. He didn't have a voter registration card or any other kind of identification, though. In his hometown, he didn't need them. "With the way that we speak you know that we are Mexicans," he argued.

After examining them, they returned his documents, and the soldier who had dealt with them confirmed that they were in order. They asked him if he wanted to go to a hospital or home. The others who were with him were sent directly to receive medical attention, as they appeared to be on death's door. They were carried and loaded into a truck where they had laid out some cushions to make it more comfortable. Ramiro waited. He asked if they would let him return to Chiapas.

They were all loaded up except for Ramiro. Since he was conscious, they left him waiting. The same officer told him, almost advised him, that if he wanted they would put a blindfold over his eyes. He asked why. The answer: outside there are many dead bodies. The soldier didn't say how many, but he wore a serious expression. Ramiro declined. The Lacandón thought that there wouldn't be so many. But his eyes, which opened to the abyss and a breathtaking display of death, told him that he had made a terrible decision. In the short distance to the truck he passed nearly thirty bodies and tried not to step on them even though it was inevitable. An obstacle course of hair, arms, legs, and blood.

"It was some ten meters. . . . I kept stopping every little while, trying not to step [directly] over them. There were women and men. They seemed larger than life. I saw women, something like six of them among the thirty. Grown people, [ordinary] adults, twenty-five or thirty years old . . . a lady, of the last ones that I saw, face up, fifty-some years old. I bowed my head and I climbed up into the truck."[7]

Ramiro's companions were taken to a hospital, and he was taken to Los Mochis (down from the highlands to the tropical northern coast of Sinaloa). He doesn't know what became of them, but he knows that they were in a bad way. The officer suggested that he try the social welfare agency called Family Development (DIF) or the local government for help in getting home.[8] The former gave him a voucher and the latter nothing.

Ramiro went to the central terminal to take a bus to Culiacán, two hundred kilometers to the south. The driver told him that the voucher given to him by the DIF was worthless, that it wouldn't even pay for half of a ticket. Another driver spotted him and approached. Furtive but generous, he told him in a soft voice: "Wait a little bit until the inspector isn't paying attention, and I'll take you to Culiacán."

Tamales

In Culiacán, the driver advised him to try the Women's Hospital, near the bus terminal, where they would surely give him a place to sleep. The local office of the DIF was next door.

It was Saturday, May 5. That day and the following he stayed there in patios, hallways, and corners waiting for Monday morning when they would open the doors to the offices where he would ask for help in getting home. A woman who sold tamales in one of the entryways to the hospital saw him several times and chatted with him. She asked him where he was from. She figured out right away that he didn't eat meat and that it was no use inviting him to eat some tamales, even though they were not hers to give away.

"You are very peculiar. You don't eat meat, you don't eat sweets—none of that," she told him with a sympathy that pierced Ramiro's thick skin. She took out some fruit and a little bit of water and offered it to him. As difficult as it was for Ramiro to say yes, he accepted a ration of fruit and vegetables that day and the next. That's how he held on.

The farthest away

Sofía Irene Valdez, director of the state office of the DIF, put Ramiro in the care of a social worker who would try to acquire a bus ticket that would get him as close as possible to his home. She thought about sending him straight through to Mexico City. She told her boss that she had managed to get a free ticket as far as Mazatlán. Her boss sent her to try again. They argued that there weren't enough resources, but she said that even if it came out of her own pocket, she would help him.

Ramiro remembers it well. He knows it from memory because it is a history often told in his homeland, in his life as a Lacandón Maya: "I spoke to [officials from the state of] Chiapas, but in Chiapas if you tell them that you are Lacandón then they don't help you. If you say that you are Tojolobal, Zoques, Coloteques, Chamulas, they help you, but they don't help Lacandones. When Valdez returned, she asked the social worker, "What have you managed?" and the response was the same as before: "There are no resources." "Look for them, look for them!" she urged the social worker. "Look for a bus connection with the ADO line, from here to Mexico [City] and from there to Chiapas, even if I have to pay for it with my own money.'" But they couldn't find one on ADO: "There are many problems with the connections."

Finally they managed to get Ramiro a trip to the state capital and a meeting with Congressman Armando Ochoa Valdez. At the capitol a staffer of the legislator sent Ramiro to Leonides Gil Ramírez, chief of the Commission for the Development of Indigenous Pueblos in Sinaloa. He and Crescencio Ramírez, an indigenous activist from the area, were able to support him with sufficient funds so that he could make it back to the Lacandón jungle.

Twenty-five meters

Ramiro is forty-one years old, and he remembers everything, even the man who enlisted them to work, a man he never saw carrying a weapon and never saw at all after they were tied up. Sometime before that, seeing that Ramiro was very quiet and didn't curse him, that man gave him a Bible. But it was in Spanish and the Lacandón can't read it. He barely speaks it. On a piece of notebook paper he has written a few symbols. These he does understand. These he wrote himself.

"The man took his Bible, which he carried in his backpack, [gave it to me], and I brought it here. He told me, 'Look, sir, I have not heard you speak or complain about anything. I am going to give you my Bible, and I hope that you will keep it,'" he explained.

Ramiro can describe him, this man who behaved well and never mistreated them. He also has in mind the seven who were selected and separated from the group, and all the rest. He carries them in his head. He doesn't even know their names. It doesn't matter. He hopes, he trusts, he believes that they will return to their homes.

Ramiro has a backpack. It looks stuffed and heavy. During the interview, he places a leather hat on top of it, adorned with necklaces made of seeds and stones. There's a peacock feather in the front, and hidden behind it is a stone that looks like a talisman. He advises that there won't be any photos of his face, but he permits pictures of his hands and arms. He nods his head. Expressionless, gentle. He looks like an ancient wise man in front of a bonfire in the middle of nothingness and above it all. The reporter tells him that he would like to take a photograph of his hat. "I don't recommend that you do it," he answers. He doesn't explain much. He repeats three or four times, "I don't recommend that you do it," to the insistent reporter. But his phrase sounds categorical. The hat is a relic; it has a very special value.

"Because my hat is a relic of us Lacandones, I don't recommend that you do it, but it is up to you. I am going to tell you that as a habit we have many things that we like to present and many things that we don't. Yes, we are very peculiar . . . and thus when I eat, when I stop in a place, I take off my hat out of respect for my race, for my culture," he declared.

End of discussion.

He explains that the forest is his home, and it gives him everything. He pictures himself sitting outside, on the patio of his house, where he soaks in the surroundings: a jaguar, monkeys, macaws, toucans, deer, and other animals. The animals make a happy racket. They are among their own. There's no hunting and no mistreatment. The Lacandón Mayas don't eat meat, only fruits and vegetables. On Thursdays, they do eat the fish and shrimp they catch in the Suchiate River. There are barely seventy-two members of their ethnic group in Los Montes Azules: long-lived, tough, parsimonious, strict, and proud. He explains that they have difficulty in accepting food given to them by others. In a cavernous voice, he says that if they have enough to eat it is because they worked hard for it, and one should never take food away from anyone else. His voice rings of that eternal ancestral peace, that of his father and his grandparents, of a millennial generation. For that he weeps, an ancient and tender flood of tears. His teary eyes sing when he speaks of his twelve daughters, the six pregnancies that brought them, his Tata Dios who blessed them and loves them, and who has set aside more experiences for him to live after his rebirth, after being the survivor of the dense darkness of drug trafficking and violence in the mountains of Sinaloa.

"I could have been among those who were chosen. I could have gone with them. But my Tata Dios had other plans for me. I have twelve daughters, and I came to work in this pueblo only to be able to buy twenty-five meters of cloth. . . . The dream that I used to carry turned into nothing."

He has not spoken with them. He doesn't know kilometers or highways. There's no way to get to the forest that is his home except by walking, and this takes two days from Ocosingo. He misses them. He doesn't talk about anything but them, his land, his skin: the belly of his entire being.

All of this has weathered and seasoned him, and his entire race. His mother is the youngest of her generation, and she is 85 years old. Another person is 118. Of those Ramiro's age, there is no one left. The best of prior generations died of old age, none out of illness: "Everything comes in time, and when they are going to die, they die. My papa died at 125 and his papa at 143."

He knows very well that there won't be another chance to buy that cloth. It's already late; it's May and there's no money. Perhaps he'll continue this way, with that skinny chest that swells up when he speaks of his homeland and the jaguar and his daughters. With that chest that sticks to the back of a body dried out by sadness, frustration, and misery.

He explains how the DIF people spoke to officials in Ocosingo to ask for help and advice on Ramiro's situation. But he's sure that they don't want him. They don't like Lacandones. He doesn't say why. Perhaps it's that toughness, that stubbornness, persistent and untamable like the rain that falls in the Lacandón jungle.

He confesses that he's desperate to leave. His voice cracks, but his words don't falter, they fly, diaphanous, strong, winged. His cheeks flush. He cries again. He again thanks his Tata Dios, who is immense and loves his race, Ramiro assures.

And like a bipedal pachyderm, upright and dignified, he speaks as if this moral chasm that he managed to escape with his life was the beginning of the end. But he's hopeful despite the crumpled dreams that might have been: "The hope that the Lord had in me, he repaid me twofold, by giving me the opportunity to continue living. What more could I ask for? I know that when I arrive my daughters will ask if I brought the cloth. They'll be the same whether I bring it or not. They are the ones who care that I make it back. If I can't buy them clothes this year, it doesn't matter. . . . What I intended to do is over now. I know that my daughters will understand. I know that if I don't bring them the cloth for their clothes it won't really matter. I know that if I don't have it, I don't have it. The important thing is that I am going to return. That my Tata Dios permitted me to return in order to die in my own land."

THE FORTUNE TELLER

The cards were on the table. The young woman wanted to know on that January day in 2011 how the year was going to go. In love, in business, et cetera. The woman told her that she should warn her people that the shit was a about to hit the fan, that soldiers were coming for them, and that they should get all of the marijuana and weapons out of there, because the property was about to be raided.

She got up and grabbed the phone. She passed the message along to her people. Doubtful to the point of mockery, they nevertheless proceeded to get everything out of there before any uniforms showed up. A few minutes later, the place was full of soldiers searching for drugs and firearms in all of the rooms. They found nothing.

Afterward, the owner of the house and the merchandise sent for the fortune-teller. Two men were waiting for her outside of her office, located on the main square in Culiacán, a few meters from Obregón Avenue and right next to the municipal market. They asked if she was the fortune-teller. Come with us. She said that it was fine but asked that they allow her to let her make a call first. She dialed someone on her cell phone: they're taking me, and I don't know where.

In her work space, there are effigies of La Santa Muerte.[9] One of them sticks out right in the middle of the doorway, like the head of a welcoming committee. Inside there are candles, dangling ornaments, Rosary beads, unguents for erections, magic powders, cards with images of the saints on them, syrups, and plastic bags full of dried herbs. She doesn't sell them; she's just a fortune-teller. She reads the cards, gives good luck, and advises on friends and enemies, money management, love, et cetera. The products belong to the owner of the space. She sees a client and tells him, you've got something. Just by looking at them, she can tell that some of them are in a bad way, that they should be careful. "You bring tidings of death, *muchacho*. She's close by." She shows them the cards, and they pray for good luck.

She's seated on the other side of a narrow table. There's a decorative tablecloth on top of it. She's wearing wool slacks and a blouse with a flower print. She's not quite thirty-five, short and slight, and intelligent in dealing with her clients. Many of them, whom she knows are drug traffickers, triggermen, or otherwise "heavy" people, she doesn't charge. They are always offering to pay her with favors, but she never accepts. She attends to them, for sure, but asks for nothing in exchange. It's her work, she says, her calling, her virtue, and she feels privileged to be able to help. She's a simple woman of few words. But when she speaks they strike like stones. She hurls them and these stones don't fly by, they lodge themselves in the forehead and nest between the eyebrows. She speaks to them, the heavy people, about envy, about jealousy and death, about destruction and infidelity. She passes along business tips. "You're going to save a lot of money," she tells one of them. "Just don't despair, and don't go around telling everyone, and don't pay attention to those who say that you're not doing well. You're moving forward and not looking back. To a hundred. To two hundred. You heard it from me, it's going to go very well." The man thanks her. He takes out his wallet. She gestures to him and says, "No, listen, it's nothing. Take care of yourself, and God bless you." The man almost kisses her hand. He leaves there, jubilant. She bids him good-bye with a smooth, warm hand gesture as if she were blessing him. She sits back down.

That's how she works, despite the surrounding gale, in a violent city, the capital of a brutish state: the gale of assault rifles, drugs, shootouts, decapitations, corruption, and impunity. *El narco* on the streets. *El narco* everywhere. *El narco* in charge. In that January 2011, Jesús Aguilar Padilla finished his term as governor of Sinaloa, a six-year term marked by "normal violence," as he himself assured in an unfortunate statement.

In total, in those six years there were 6,616 homicides, the majority of them related to clashes between the drug-trafficking cartels. Barely forty-eight hours had passed in 2010 before sixteen homicides had been registered in the state. It was our fate, and it continues to be so. The year ended with 2,238 violent deaths, the highest figure in the history of the state, closely followed by the 2,200 recorded between 2008 and 2009.

She was lying on the floor of the car, face down. She couldn't see. They placed a hood over her head as soon as she got in the car, which she couldn't have identified anyway as she doesn't know much about the different makes or models. Turns, bumps, sudden braking. The engine roared. The men didn't speak. There were four of them. She heard her own heavy breathing and theirs as well. Little wheezes escaped from their lungs and noses. Everyone there was afraid. Nobody knew what was going to happen.

They arrived at a large house. She realized this when they took her out of the car and removed the hood. It had a wide driveway and a garage in front. A girl of about fourteen took great pains to snort the neat lines of white powder from a wooden table and quench her thirst with a beer. Two men sat nearby drinking Buchanan's whiskey, and two others stood guard. There was a kitchen and a dining room that nobody had bothered to clean in a long time, with the outlines of food scraps and stains from drinks that nobody seemed to notice on every surface. Oblivion has its nests, and one of them was here. A refrigerator full of spoiled leftovers, green, gray, and black, stains, foul smells. It was like a coffin.

Two men with guns in their waistbands took her to see the boss. In a low voice he asked her who had warned her about the military operation. "I told him 'nobody,' that I dedicate myself to reading the cards, and from there it all came, and thus 'I told the girl to whom I was attending, who is my client, that she should advise you guys,' that's how I answered," she remembered.

He was a man of fifty-odd years, dark, tall, and somewhat large. He looked at her as if he wanted to search her, as if he were leaning into that halting voice, those eyes that didn't dodge his gaze. Again and again, the same question. Fifteen times. She held firm. A surgical serenity adapted her responses, those same words, to the tone of the questions. The certainty of the hunter, of the sharpshooter enveloped her eyes, controlled her breathing, holding her gaze on that of her interrogator.

He told the gunmen, "Take her away and bring her back in a little while." The men seated her in the living room. There were two handguns on a nearby table. She thought, "If I grab one of them and shoot at them, I'll take one or maybe two of them, but I'll never leave here." She thought a lot and a little. She decided to keep her hands to herself, in her lap, under the table.

Two other killers played cards, and another one looked her way now and again, keeping vigilant. She got up. She wasn't nervous, per se, just a little anxious, and she had to do something, at least to find a way to distract herself in the middle of this confinement, between drugs and druggies, gunmen and a death that brushed against her skin, cold and aloof, and that capo who didn't believe that she wasn't somehow involved. She

got on her feet—she wanted to be spontaneous—and she walked pur-
posefully toward the kitchen. She took a rag and washed it and cleaned
everything in sight as if it were her own. She threw out the trash and tied
up the plastic bag. She looked for and opened cans, rinsed off vegetables,
chopped, and diced. She switched on the gas valve and with a lighter she
found nearby, lit up the burner, and prepared *chicarrón ranchero*, beans,
and *machaca*.[10] She heated up tortillas.

The smell brought the girl, who insisted on snorting powder without
knowing that it accelerated her heartbeat and her expiration date, along
with the four gunmen and the boss. "*Oiga*, well done." She responded
with a smiling thank-you. Some ate in the living room, others in the
kitchen, and the boss upstairs in the bedroom.

They returned to take her before the boss. They sat her in a chair in
front of him: "Who told you, how did you know, and who do you work
for?" "Nobody," she repeated ten more times. He looked at those killers
and ordered them, "Buy gasoline and burn her up." She said, "Why, if I
haven't done anything, if I've actually helped you?"

"I don't know why they didn't react. The *patrón* didn't realize that I
really wasn't interested in any of that, that I had only done it to help
them. I think it was the drugs, that they were so gone that they didn't
know who they were talking to," she declared.

At that moment, the young woman for whom she had read the cards
came into the room. She was the boss's lover. She realized what had happened, and she asked if the woman was okay. She ordered the men to
take the fortune-teller back to the living room. And then she shut herself in with the *patrón* for a shouting match. "From where I was, downstairs, insults, *fuck this* and *fuck that* and *bitch*, could be heard. For me,
the truth is, at first it scared me. Maybe they're going to kill both of us.
But later I took heart. *Be calm, at peace*, I told myself, and that's when she
came out."

The young woman emerged in semi-darkness, after having it out with
the boss. She addressed herself to the gunmen and ordered them to
take the person they had held captive back to her home. She offered her
apologies, and the woman responded that there wasn't a problem. The
bodyguards turned to the *patrón* and he assented with a nod of his head.

"The girl told me, 'Those *pendejos* aren't going to do anything to you,' whispering in my ear."

Her stomach and legs were still shaky. The fresh air loosened and relaxed her muscles, once she was outside. They drove her away in a pickup truck. At an intersection, they swerved and blocked a taxi in. They gave the driver a five-hundred-peso bill and shouted, "Take her wherever she wants to go."

After they left, "The diver was terrified and had no idea where to go. 'Listen, I can't do it. I can't drive,' he told me. Then, since the taxi driver was so nervous, he intercepted a colleague, another driver, and he gave him the bill . . . he told him, 'Here, I'm placing you in charge of this passenger. This thing's a real bitch.' And he took off."

It was four o'clock in the morning. Approaching the front door of her house, alone, with the street receding and sun about to rise, she dropped her courage and opened herself to a flood of tears. Death was once again far away. Safe and sound, she had come back to life.

YOU HAVE FIVE MINUTES

That February 26 was not the worst day in María's life, but those two hours certainly were. She got home, in Infonavit Humaya, in northern Culiacán, after having worked a ten-hour shift at a supermarket.[11] It was 9:30 P.M., and she'd never forget the next two hours.

Her neighbor intercepted her. Some boys that she didn't know had taken María's son away. And that's how she said it. María thought that perhaps they were his friends and that they were cruising around the neighborhood in one of the cars she sometimes saw around. But the neighbor insisted that she look for him or at least call him to make sure that he was all right.

She dialed and no one answered. She tried again a few seconds later. It rang until the voicemail picked up. She waited twenty minutes. A growing anguish started at her feet, gradually climbed up through her stomach, and threatened to keep rising. She called again, and this time he did answer. They greeted each other casually, but then he continued in a fragile, wire-thin voice: "Mom, you have to find Sergio, tell him to bring the jewelry, tell him that they took me." And then he hung up.

Where?

María asked where she should look for Sergio. She knew about him and knew who he was because he was one of the guys who hung out with her son the most. He would show up sometimes and take him to breakfast. She didn't like him because he didn't have a job, and she questioned where he got his money. But her son liked him and it appeared that Sergio treated him well.

She remembered that Sergio had been the boyfriend of a girl who lived nearby. She sought her out and confronted her. "Please, it is very important—it is urgent," she said to her. The girl gave her the cell number of the young man, and she called him. She told him: "You have to come, bring the jewelry, my son was taken."

I am going to kill him

She called her son again and heard a strange noise. The phone was snatched away from her son, and a man with a voice she didn't recognize took the phone. "You have five minutes," he threatened. "If not, I kill him."

"I didn't know that man, I didn't know who he was, but he sounded like someone older, not like a kid. He was the owner of the jewelry, and I thought that there must have been a bunch of it, but that wasn't the case. He told me that I had five minutes, that if I didn't hand over the jewelry, he was going to kill my son. I remember that before hanging up he told me, 'If you don't go through with it, I'll kill your son and leave his body where I grabbed him.'"

She didn't calculate that the time he had given her to recover the booty wasn't going to be enough. She only realized it after she hung up the phone. She again called the young man who supposedly had the jewelry, and he arrived very quickly. Once again she called her son's cell and the unknown man answered. She didn't miss a beat and asked the man for more time. The "that's fine" that he uttered gave her a sense of relief, albeit a fleeting one; then she decided to pass the phone to her son's friend. She listened as he explained that he had pawned the jewelry and asked for time to hand it over another day.

"As my son's friend listened, they beat my son, and [my son's friend] said, 'Listen, wait, don't hurt him—tomorrow I'll hand them over without fail, I promise.' Suddenly he hung up and handed me the phone without saying anything [at first]. As he ran off, he shouted that he'd be right back. He returned with a plastic bag containing a few pieces of gold jewelry. Then we called again."

That same interlocutor warned that he would kill all of them if they contacted the police. Then he gave instructions to María. She was directed to a nearby hotel, and then he told her to walk two blocks away. There she received another call: he was behind her, a few meters back, and he told her not to turn around or he would kill her and her son, and then he asked her to leave the jewelry in a flowerpot in front of a store.

She did as he said. Then she asked him what was going to happen to her son. He responded, "I'm going to let him go, but don't call me and don't call the police."

"I told him that I really didn't want any problems. The only thing I want is that they return my son." The man hung up. She called. She called again. He answered. "Come and get him." He was sitting on a bench in the middle of the principal boulevard of the Bugambilias neighborhood, located in the western part of town, a few meters away from the Municipal Public Security Ministry and in the middle of several school buildings.

It was almost midnight.

Rebellious and inexpressive

She was born in Guadalajara, and she'd been in Culiacán for a little more than fifteen years. She came there because her ex-husband was from this city. Now she lives alone with her son in a rented house. Rent eats up almost half of what they pay her at the supermarket. At forty-seven, this dark-haired, slender woman appears resigned to a life of routine and yawning toil. Or so it may have been until those two intense hours came along, in which she thought the worst and that she will never forget, which jolted her out of the slow death of that rusty life. And they almost killed her, as might have happened with her son.

He is fifteen. He left high school, he once explained, because "it's not for me." He loves the Internet, watching television, going out with his friends. He is a rebel. A child in transition, inexpressive, who doesn't appear to enjoy speaking with his father, and when he does it's because every once in a while his father calls him. They talk. He makes faces; he wants to hang up. She doesn't know what they talk about, but she does know that he's not happy. It doesn't bring anything out of him to talk with this person. A stranger, a neighbor, a random countryman. Somebody else. But not his father. That's what he seems to say with those facial expressions, that posture of *I don't give a damn.*

He doesn't say what he wants to do when he grows up. He doesn't appear to want to study. According to his mother, he's not on a wayward path, even though she has occasionally spotted him selling cell phones that were perhaps stolen. She doesn't know for sure. "He'll be sorry if he gets mixed up in that business, because then he'll learn what real problems are. And here in Culiacán they kill you even for looking ugly."

He's serious, with a strong character. But María says that if he were to head down the wrong path, she would know because he would start wearing new clothes, brand-name stuff, that costs a lot. If he showed up with another cell phone instead of the little "burner" that he uses now, or new sneakers, sunglasses, or a bunch of money. He's got none of that. She barely leaves him twenty pesos a day, or whatever she can, so that he can buy some chips, an iced tea, a soda, or a couple of hours at the cyber café in the neighborhood, near their house.

He already killed him

It was February 27, the morning after her son disappeared. María had been up only half an hour when she found a friend who had a car. She explained the situation in a flurry, and the friend agreed to take her. They went off, sharing their fears, erratic and shaky. They went thinking the worst: fatality, the end, nothingness.

"When the man told me that they'd left him on a bench, outside of a school in Bugambilias, I thought that they'd left him dead. *He already killed him*, I thought. It is the truth. One thinks the worst."

"He didn't tell me where or give me any signs to look for." Before she could ask for more, he hung up. She took Emiliano Zapata Boulevard, which is called Airport Road in that part of town because the airport terminal is only about a kilometer away. She was just approaching the central boulevard in the neighborhood when she saw her kid walking slowly, trying to make his way against the wind, with barely a breath of life in him, approaching a gas station.

"Get in! Get in!"

She hugged him, but he didn't hug back. He was stone-faced, immutable and cryptic. Serious, stoic, and inexpressive. He had been beaten all over. Cheeks battered and eyes lost under the swelling. His arms, chest, and back all worked over, heavily bruised. The butt of a rifle had made symmetrical marks all down his back. He only related that they had covered his face with his shirt, that he hadn't seen their faces, that they had slapped him around until they grew tired of it, that they had kicked him in the abdomen, and that rifle butts had rained down upon him from all sides.

A timid, "I'm fine, I didn't do anything." That's the only other thing that came from his disjointed mouth. He didn't cry, and he didn't plead. He didn't say anything further about the business, he won't, and he never will. Now she knows.

The mother managed to learn that a young man who had accompanied her son that day had somehow escaped. He didn't appear to have had anything to do with the men who took her son, but he got away, nonetheless. A few days later, the kid who had kept the jewelry and had to return them fled as well, leaving the neighborhood, the city, and the state of Sinaloa for good.

"From what little he has told me, I gather that the man who put the pistol to his head told him, 'You don't know who you are messing with: this house belongs to El Chapo Guzmán.'" Joaquín Guzmán Loera, boss of the Sinaloa Cartel.

When they released him, they threw him out like a sack of potatoes in a vacant lot. He was left, face down, waiting to hear the sound of bursts from the AK-47 rifles and feel the hot projectiles burning him from the inside, draining him of blood. Dying.

Two minutes. He heard them leave and stopped hearing voices and other sounds. Then he got up, dazed and nauseated. He struggled forward. He walked who knows how far until his mother caught up with him.

She doesn't believe that he did anything wrong or that he participated in a robbery. She believes him even though sometimes he drives her up the wall listening to *narcocorridos*. She knows that he doesn't like guns. He's inexpressive. Nobody can penetrate that cold gaze, that strong character. He keeps it all to himself. He doesn't complain or cry. Sometimes, very seldom, he'll give a hug. And when they ask him about the time he was taken, he answers hurriedly, "It's not so, it's not true."

But it is and she knows it. And she knows it well. It wasn't the worst day of her life, just the worst two hours. She knows it so well that she cries and cries when he "plays dumb." She doesn't forget. She can't.

I DON'T SEE ANYTHING, I DON'T SEE ANYTHING

The man's shouts drew her eyes toward him. Two young men armed with *cuernos de chivo* ("goat horns")—AK-47s—were beating and kicking him, trying to get him under control so that they could get him into their vehicle. She had just stepped out of her house in a downtown neighborhood and heard all of this. At first she'd thought that there was some kind of domestic dispute, the verbal row that took place every morning in that particular household, and thus she hadn't paid much attention. But when she heard the shouts and saw gunmen who were trying to subdue him, she couldn't help but take it in.

"The man said, 'It wasn't me, *compa*. I didn't say anything. I didn't speak. On my mother's life, I swear to God,' he repeated shouting, and crying," remembered Rebeca, the neighbor woman, long afterward as she passed the spot where it had gone down—on Escobedo Street, a few meters from Nicolás Bravo Avenue, very close to a well-known Chinese restaurant called China Loa, in the heart of the city.[12]

The man bellowed like an animal being dragged to the slaughter. He wept, begged, and thrashed about, clinging to the railing of his front porch and then grasping for the plants his wife had been growing in the garden in front of the house.

One of the men hit him on the face with a rifle butt, and then the other one kicked him twice in the stomach. When they thought he'd finally given up the struggle, they grabbed his hands and feet and tried to carry him off wriggling, but it was in vain. He weighed too much, and they weren't strong enough.

"Don't take me. Listen, please. It wasn't me—I didn't say anything," the man told them. Rebeca says that those two murderers didn't appear to listen. Like beasts, they beat their victim, hitting him with the butts of their assault rifles and kicking him. The only thing that mattered was subduing him and getting him into the waiting car.

"Shut up, *pendejo.*"[13] The neighbor clung to the poles and wire of a chain-link fence, grasping at freedom, at life. "Don't take me, please." In response, they ordered him to be quiet and threatened to kill him then and there. One of the killers, the one who appeared to be the younger of the two, took out a handgun and cocked it. He pointed it at the man's head, yelled that he was serious and that the man should calm down and get into the car.

"He was a fat guy, around three hundred pounds. He was wearing a tank top and blue pants. He had a mustache . . . chubby cheeks and stubbly beard," Rebeca recalled.

The men beat him. They couldn't manage his heft. He lay on the ground looking defeated, but when the hit men tried to lift him, they failed once again.

Rebeca tried to distract herself so that she wouldn't hear or see what was going on. She had her two kids with her, and she tried to distract them, tried to chat with them so that they wouldn't pay attention to the shouts or the weeping, and she blocked the violent scene from their view with her body. "One of the children asked me what was going on. 'Nothing, my child. They're just fighting, they're men who are having an argument, who are trying to solve their problems. That's it, don't worry.'

The truth is that that's all that occurred to me to say. I was just trying to get out of there safe and sound."

She said that she got the kids in her car, swung into the driver's seat, and backed quickly out of the garage. She accelerated away, without looking in the rearview mirror, muttering, "I don't see anything, I don't see anything," in a barely audible voice. From afar, that horror scene of rifle butts, kicks, and grappling was still going on. The two gunmen were joined by the one who was waiting for them in the car.

Others passed by there. They did so in buses, in cars, and on foot. Everyone fled. They passed by and hurried away. They pretended not to see. They would pretend to forget. "That already happened, it's already over." They beat a hasty retreat, barely realizing what the three trigger-men were doing with that man who they tried to illegally deprive of his liberty. "Don't turn around; they are taking someone." That was the order of the day, the banner of survival, the daily dose of "I don't see anything, I don't hear anything, I won't say anything."

The woman pounds on the steering wheel, trying to distract herself. She thought that she'd be able to remember a song in order to escape more quickly. Or to make a little bit of music and surround her children with it, her children whose eyes were open wider than usual and who had fear on their faces. She searched the dial for the news station that she listens to every day. She wanted to cancel out the memory, the shouts, the weeping, the begging. She sped away, shivering despite the summer heat, under an ill-humored sun that at nine o'clock in the morning already cast its insufferable blazing rays over the heads of the *culichis*.

As she sped away, with the image of the men struggling to subdue her neighbor stuck in her mind, she couldn't help but think: "I'd better gain some weight."

SURUTATO

On September 25, 2011, an armed group arrived in San José de los Hornos, a community located in the highlands of Sinaloa, near the

Chihuahua border. Since July, men in climbing helmets with AK-47 rifles had made incursions in the area, in commando units of fifty or even eighty. The unknown men carried off Jaime Acosta Parra that day. He was with his wife and daughter. That's when the screaming began.

Since then, Doña Juana has harbored no illusions. She is one of the three hundred people from fifty-six families who now live in Surutato, a medium-size town in the foothills about twenty kilometers (six and half miles) to the south of Los Hornos, after fleeing their highland communities in the face of violence, threats, and the presence of heavily armed groups.

Like the majority of those who have fled, she left her chickens, her pigs, her land, and her personal belongings in San José de los Hornos, an hour and a half drive up that dry, dusty, and serpentine road, with its rough, unforgiving stones. Now she sells ice cream bars—mango, coconut, and other flavors. She makes barely enough to survive. She ekes out a maximum of four hundred pesos a week (about US$30). Her husband cuts firewood up in the mountains and sells it. You have to pay for everything here. It's not like in their hometown, where all you had to do was hold out your hand and it would be full of corn or tomatoes. They have to get enough together to pay the rent on a small house, which they initially borrowed but now costs five hundred pesos a month. Here there's never enough. There's unemployment and drought. There is a lot of open, exposed space but few houses. If it weren't for the generosity and help of their neighbors, they would have completely lost hope.

They rushed out of their hometown in terror. About an hour outside of town, you reach the border between Sinaloa and Chihuahua, and below there sits Surutato, in the municipality of Badiraguato.[14] On a late July day—they don't remember the exact date—an armed group burst into town. It was before dawn. Nobody dared to investigate who they were. In the morning, the body of an unknown man was found lying on one of the main streets in San José de los Hornos. He didn't appear to be from the community but rather a member of the armed group. Nobody knows who killed him. That's what planted the seeds of fear and anxiety, that bleeding itch in your chest that never rests: terror.

The acts of aggression continued, and three houses were burned down. Another person was taken and then shot to death nearby. The armed men travelled in a half-dozen trucks. Their constant incursions fed the adversity, the feeling of being threatened and vulnerable, and the urge to pray, but above all else to flee, to save oneself before it was too late. Thus, many decided to leave their homes behind. The violence was repeated on September 25, and then everybody else, everybody, left to live in the bush.

Risking your neck

Emeterio is also from up there. He notices the reporter writing down his name, his rare last name, and the number "40" for his age. He asks that his identity not be published. He's on his haunches, constantly looking over his shoulder. He doesn't want to be overheard by anyone except the man in front of him. He's afraid, very afraid.

"Listen, here the guy who's willing to risk his neck plants marijuana or poppies." That's the reason he's afraid. He believes that the armed men who've invaded his town belong to "Los Mochomos," as they call the Beltrán Leyva cells that operate in the area, who are now enemies of the Sinaloa Cartel. Apparently, others relate, they suspect that some of the townspeople work for Joaquín Guzmán Loera, El Chapo, the boss of the Sinaloa Cartel.

"It's the dispute over *plazas* (territories). All of the time he knew what it meant, that they wanted to be in charge, to have everything to them-selves, to control all of it," Emeterio explains. He left his community in July. He felt sad leaving his cows and his house, running away with his kids and abandoning everything. Many others did the same in neighbor-ing communities like Ocurahui, Alamillos, and El Potrero, all of them small rural communities that were now completely abandoned, ghost towns up on the sierra.

Despite the turmoil, soldiers never appeared. "Before, I remember, they were around, very near our towns, but just when these conflicts began, they quit patrolling the region."

"The *guachos* (soldiers) have to be careful around these guys. They stay in their barracks. But the scoundrels know the lay of the land, and if they want, they come—they kill some poor fucker and leave as if nothing had happened."

He's a mechanic and has three children. Luckily, only the youngest one—who is nine—missed the rest of the school year when they fled their community. The others, sixteen and seventeen, enrolled in the Surutato college prep school, "because there, in San José de los Hornos, there isn't one."[15]

An aunt loaned him the house in which he is living, and there are three trucks in the patio with which they share the small space. The vehicles are waiting to be fixed. A few days earlier he sold a Lincoln Marquis that belonged to his father, who died a while back. It pained him to have sold something that reminded him of his father, but he got ten thousand pesos for it, a considerable sum, and he needed the cash.

"All of us left there thanks to that breed of men who run around in gangs. They brought chaos upon us. They killed two people, burned down at least four houses, and busted in the doors and windows of all the rest, destroying everything. And they said that if we didn't leave, they were going to kill us," he declared.

A lot of pressure

Omar Gilberto Ortiz is the *síndico* (popular representative) of Surutato, that community up in the heights of the Sierra Madre Occidental, about 150 kilometers (ninety-three miles) north of Culiacán, the capital of Sinaloa. He had worked in the timber industry, but that ended when they closed the sawmill about ten years back. Now they want to make the space a tourist destination, with cabins and restaurants, but it has many deficiencies: the highway and the streets are in bad shape, water is scarce, the local clinic has only one doctor in training and two nurses, and the violence generated by organized crime is all around. Groups of gunmen growing drugs submit the residents and neighbors of this town and other settlements to constant stalking, beatings, banging on the door at all hours, and other indignities.

The *síndico* reports that he's helped the displaced population with various vouchers and dispensations, and that the state government, by way of the social and human development ministries, has given other support, such as subsidizing the laying of foundations for new houses and building thirty-six greenhouses for the cultivation of mini bell peppers for export. "The idea," he explains, "is that right away they would begin growing and shipping to the market in the United States, and the people would begin to earn a little bit of money. We've helped them with dispensations; we've been in solidarity with them. There are houses that have three or four families [packed into them]. It is difficult, but we're trying to move forward from there. The greenhouses are going to generate 150 or 200 jobs. First we've got to place those who are from here and then the displaced."

"But that's discrimination," the reporter interjects.

"No, of course not. Nothing of the sort. The federal government is going to place others, some 120 of them, in temporary labor programs. Moreover, the construction of the greenhouse will give work to forty more, and they'll earn two hundred pesos a day."

Ortiz explains that nearly 1,300 families live in Surutato, 300 of which have sought refuge there out of fear of the violence. "That," he warns, "has put enormous pressure on the place. For one thing, there's not enough water, despite the nearby reservoir that supplies us. Some residents tell how cold it has been over the past year, but it didn't rain. Now, we've got heat of more than ninety-seven degrees, it continues without raining, and the water, even in the wells and springs, has evaporated."

"It's a lot of pressure. Listen, this had changed everything, but basic services above all else."

The *síndico* grumbles that he's asked the government to put a real doctor permanently in the clinic, that they build another reservoir, and that they improve the highway and the access roads. "Surutato," he insists, "depends not just on the people who live here, but on at least twelve other nearby communities." "In the summer, when those who go to school in nearby cities return, it will only get worse."

Numb, with pain in their bones

María del Rosario Núñez Barraza lives with another family, in a rented house. Two families, six people each, share the space. The house is made of wood, with two bedrooms, one of which is in the middle of what looks like a living room full of mattresses and pillows, next to the kitchen.

They don't have electricity, except for what they get from a car battery attached to the front wall. They don't know why the pipe quit supplying water a week earlier, and now they've only got the water from a big plastic jug, which is for drinking only.

She and her children wandered in the mountains for more than two months. Out there she, her husband, their two eight-month-old twins, and her pregnant daughter slept in the pitch black, among the weeds, trees, thorns, insects, and every kind of animal. Lighting a lantern, making a fire, cooking up in the hills—these were suicidal acts. Things that could give them away. During the day, hiding as best they could, they came and went from the houses in San José de los Hornos, looking for food and clothes. And when they heard an engine or the noise of a vehicle, they knew it was time to run or to hide.

Her daughter, Brenda Guillermina García, twenty-four, gave birth during this exile, in the city of Guamúchil, the municipal seat of Salvador Alvarado. Now the family is homeless, without a hearth, without anything. They're barely making it, surviving as long as there is water in that plastic jug that they hope to refill.

"We scavenged what we could and survived by the skin of our teeth in the forest, cut up, splintered, and scratched, between sticks and cow shit. One time an animal bit me, and we were good and scared for the babies, there in the dark. We don't even know what it was. We couldn't sleep. I remember that my leg went numb and my bones hurt," recounts María del Rosario.

Now she feels bad. Her green eyes can't hide the shadows that loom above them. She's nostalgic for the corn and beans she cultivated in her parcel of land and for her chickens. Above all, she didn't used to be this way, always nervous. Now the sadness makes her feel spent and sick. And death wears on her mind.

"Sometimes somebody would chat with me, but other times I would cry and it would feel like my body was moving, trembling, and the slightest thing would set me off, make me nervous. And, the truth is, I didn't used to be like this," she says.

There in that fragile dwelling, there were seven families right after they arrived. The kids alone amounted to sixteen. They accommodated everyone as best they could, in the patio, in the two rooms, in the kitchen. There were so many people that the last of them had breakfast at two o'clock in the afternoon. Slowly they moved out and settled into other houses. But the situation remains dire. At the edge of the hills there is still a small house sheltering twenty-three people behind its thin walls.

There's nothing sadder

Doña Juana was already gone. She carried an umbrella and a bag. She set them to one side when the interview began. She's next to her brother, on the patio in front of the house that they rent. Behind her bifocals, moisture wells up. Teardrops bud but then dry. Their glimmer is incomplete, like everything here, and she can't hide her grief.

In the state of Sinaloa, the register of displaced families reached 1,200 in May 2012, according to the state government. Among the municipalities with the highest incidence of displacement due to the violence is that also named Sinaloa, where Juana is from. Recently, Juan Ernesto Millán, secretary of social and human development, warned that this figure could rise to three thousand families affected by violence, families who have decided to abandon their hometowns. The phenomenon is growing, getting ever more complicated, and involves Sinaloans from at least ten of the eighteen municipalities.

The Commission for the Defense of Human Rights in Sinaloa, an independent nongovernmental organization, warns that the number of displaced people could rise to 30,000, as it involves 6,000 families in eleven, not ten, municipalities. Óscar Loza Ochoa, one of the directors of the commission, laments that the government hasn't studied the phenomenon and that federal officials are worried more about the image of Mexico abroad than resolving the issue. Thus they haven't asked for help from international organizations that have experience dealing with the problem of displaced people, organizations like the Red Cross or the United Nations.

Héctor Orlando Ortiz, a high school teacher, explains that over the last two years there has been recurrent drought in the region. And now with the displaced people, the dynamics of coexistence have changed. Despite the increased pressure on already scarce public services, "the people have put solidarity above [self-interest], and each is helping the other."

He knows of forty or so young people who—due to the violence— were accepted as new students in the classrooms of this community and at least three elementary school teachers who used to work on Ocurahui, one of the abandoned communities.

"There's nothing sadder than leaving one's home. Living somewhere for so many years and then leaving from one minute to the next," Juana says. She was born in La Joya de los Martínez, where a group of soldiers fired upon some people in a truck, causing five deaths, three of them children (the other two were local schoolteachers). The victims didn't have any weapons or drugs on them. The soldiers, drunk and high on drugs, claimed that the truck didn't stop at a supposed roadblock, and that's why they fired. This massacre occurred in May 2007.

That's why they don't have any confidence in the soldiers. That's why they left La Joya de los Martínez after that massacre.

In order to get to Surutato, you take a left at the fork in the road in the city of Badiraguato, the municipal seat. It's about twenty-four kilometers of unpaved road from there, out of a total of seventy, and about a three-hour drive if you leave from Culiacán. The countryside doesn't recover its lush green at altitude, despite the pine trees. The trunks of many trees are gray, and they suffer with the parched ground. The carpet over the hills is black, burned and sinister-looking thanks to the drought, a rapacious scorching. It is very hot, and some stretches show loose, brown sand. It blows around on the surface, like a devious mist. It is ground that deceives, that's in disguise. It is so light that tires or even footsteps raise a thin cloud of dust, rebellious and irreverent. That's when the stones emerge, sharp and haughty on this rugged ground.

Juan remembers September 21. It was nine o'clock at night when the masked men arrived and took away Jaime Acosta Parra, thirty-eight. He was in his house with his wife and daughter, a girl who screamed at them, imploring them with a flood of tears not to harm her papa.

"The little girl cried 'Leave my papa alone! Don't hurt him!' His wife also begged them. They hugged each other, they stayed there, hoping to ransom him, but they couldn't do anything. They could only watch how they took him away, how they beat him as they went," Juana remembers.

That night they heard screams. It seemed they were torturing him. Then a slow burst of sound, with distinct echoes, coursed through the mountains and nested itself in the hearts of the wife and child and in everyone in San José de los Hornos. Many asked why it was him that they took. Jaime didn't go out drinking, barely interacted with the rest of the townspeople, was a serious man, and had "never had problems during the time they knew him in those communities . . . he was one of the calmest guys around." If it was about planting marijuana, well, many planted it there. That he would have *broncas* (problems), that they would come to get him for that—it just didn't make sense.

The next day, nobody got up the courage to go and search for him. The men glanced at each other, pale and unsure of themselves. They looked around as if to say, "Now what?" They shrugged their shoulders, twisted their mouths, and bent their heads, resigned. "Who is it?" someone asked. Silence. It was the women, headed by the widow, who hadn't given in yet. They walked around in the woods, on seldom-used paths and through pines still pale from lack of water. They found him, shattered, a few meters from there. That kicked off the exodus: "All of us headed for the hills."

In the photograph distributed by the family as a memorial to the deceased, it says: "My happiness remains with you, who've known me well before I had to depart. Live with love and happiness as I did. God almighty needed me and I had to depart. To my family and my friends, take my departure with peace and resignation. God, our lord, gives you blessings and love. Amen."

But there's no peace, no resignation. Nor is there a desire for vengeance. There's plunder and dust, dirt on their skin and beneath their fingertips, and images of violence burned on their brains. Juana and her family wandered in the forest for more than a month, hiding under the trees, trying not to make a sound.

"From that day until now, we haven't had any peace of mind. I don't yet have any. I don't even have the illusion of it. I am sad. The truth is sad. You know why? Because nothing belongs to anyone."

Juana sits down underneath her ice cream sign, in that dry place, and she can barely muster enough energy to cry.

PSORIASIS

"'What did you do?' my son asked me. 'What did you do so that this would happen to me, Papa?' I told him nothing, that I didn't owe anything to anybody, that I've been good for all of my sixty years, forty of them as a taxi driver. And it's true. I don't owe anybody," confessed the corpulent taxi driver. A dark cloud comes over his face and it appears to envelop his entire existence.

It is the middle of 2011. The taxi driver hunches over, searching for a beige cloth trapped between the seat and the gearbox, next to the hand brake. He reaches it. He struggles desperately until he's able to bring the rag up to his face and smell it, then he wipes his forehead. He imagines that each bead of sweat is a shard of glass scraping his face. He's a taxi driver at the Culiacán International Airport. He gets in line, like all the rest, until it's his turn to pick up a client. But there's little moving this May evening. The passenger asks him how business has been, and he concedes that it's been slow, that he's only the third fare of the day since six o'clock in the morning. That means that he got up at four in the morning, had a coffee with his wife, and maybe a little bit of bread—who's hungry for more than that at such an hour?

His son was a taxi driver just like him. His only son. And his wife waits for him at home, she'll be there for him after eighteen or twenty hours behind the wheel. He mentions her, and his face softens, like a lullaby. That woman still inspires him and sustains him and occupies his thoughts. He confesses to his more than fifty years by her side. It is a constant goal: to remain, to be, to live together. And he doesn't like to wake her up when he rolls in at two or three in the morning or that she should get up and put supper on the table for him. The last ride is a mirage: it's the same whether he arrives at eleven or at midnight or at dawn. It's a biblical sentence: he's always late.

He pauses while eating the *coyotas* he buys to calm his guts, the only thing he's eaten today, and his wrinkles deepen, interminable and dark, when he thinks about how tough it's going to be to get the five hundred pesos he must turn in to the boss to rent the taxi daily. He buys those little sweet rolls that they call *coyotas* in this part of the country, always chewy and crusty, with a filling of sweet paste, not sickly sweet. These days they sell them on the Pedro Infante outer belt, one of the two routes to get from the airport to downtown Culiacán. The seller passes by with a basket of three *coyotas*. Just seeing them whets anyone's appetite.

The taxi driver pouts. He's a baby without a mother, this tall, heavy man who barely fits into the white Nissan Tsuru, with cobwebs instead of hair, looking out of his bifocals. He's a street kid, in despair, unprotected, alone and sad.

His son, he relates, is sick. "What do I do? Listen, what do I do? I can't help him, nor can I help myself. And when I drop by his house to be with him, he gets embarrassed. And he cries. It's been months, mark my words, since this shame began. Now he doesn't know what to do. Those men, those *cabrones*. They have no idea the harm they've caused a good man."

His son picked up a person, it was one more fare. The passenger told him, "Stop here." Just like that, suddenly. This happens often enough in taxis: the client tells you to go back, not to take this or that boulevard, to turn here or there, or unexpectedly tells you to stop. That's how it went on this fare. That guy told his son to stop his taxi on a particular corner, and he stopped.

The man paid him and even gave him a tip. Two minutes later, three other men got in. It appeared that they had been following close behind the taxi, and they got in quickly. One of them took out a pistol and gave him several butts to the head, just above his right ear. "They asked him where he'd left his passenger. They shouted, swore, and insulted him. Listen—and they did this to my boy, who doesn't even swear, who didn't know them or the passenger who had just gotten out of the cab," the old driver recalled.

"And he told them [that his fare had gotten out] on that corner. And he described him and explained how things had gone. And they didn't believe him. 'Tell us, tell us,' they repeated as they beat him. And my son told them that it was the truth, that in the name of God he was telling them the plain truth. Until they pointed the gun at him and pushed the pistol into his mouth. And the man shouted, hysterical, pissed off, that he should say good-bye because he was going to kill him."

Finally they realized that he was telling the truth. And so they took him, passing through various sectors of the city, with nothing left and at risk of losing his life.

"But the next day my son didn't want to eat, couldn't sleep, and some kind of hives appeared on his skin, and he went to the doctor. They did some tests, they looked him over. And then they diagnosed psoriasis."

"They are like bumps or a rash. They showed up all over his body, on his face, on his head, everywhere. He can't go outside because the sun hurts him. He's out of work, and his wife is covering all of their expenses, but she doesn't have enough for the medicine: so many damn ointments, pills, and doctor visits."

His father also wants to support him, to give him a little bit of money. "But I don't even have enough for myself, listen." He goes to visit his son, to be with him, to encourage him. But his son hides, he's ashamed: "His kids tell me, 'My papa is there, crying, huddled up in the corner of the patio,' and there I see him, under the fat shadows of his miserable life. All because of his nerves, the fear. For those *cabrones.*"

His son asks him what he's done. Nothing. He hasn't done anything wrong. And more than one man is crying. The father of the man with psoriasis also cries like an abandoned child, and he cries more when he takes out that rag and uses it to wipe sweat off of his brow. "It's been a fucked-up day, without much work," he repeats, trying to conceal the tears. And he declares: "I've been a good man."

It's time to get out. The taxi arrives at the Villa Universidad neighborhood, on the east side of the city. The driver is still sad. He rings up the fare and between prayers says, "I've only got half a *coyota* left."

RUN!

Mother and daughter were walking together that morning. The area was nearly empty, a place used for jogging or walking, and even though the sun was coming up menacingly and you could already feel its ill humor, the temperature was still agreeable and there was a pleasant breeze.

They walked at a regular pace and came upon other people as they approached the wide boulevard, and one after another greeted them. It was a familiar excursion, strolling the old concrete and admiring the facades of the great mansions.

Colonia Guadalupe, one of the oldest residential areas in Culiacán. From some of its heights, particularly near the temple to Our Lady of Guadalupe, better known as La Lomita, the city presents itself below, surrendered at the feet of those who admire it. The stretch here, part of Paseo de la Palmas, is used by many for exercise, and it has been for many years. Now that the pavement is stained with blood, however, and there's no corner or hour of the day that escapes it, people walk and jog in hopes that Jesus is watching over them with every huff and puff of air.

There were older couples. Husbands and wives. A *culichi* December with a morning chill that passes quickly, a cold that is better described as the absence of heat, a time of freshness that gives the sun a rest. Young people passed by, vacationers who'd gotten up early to go for a jog or a stroll along this path up high, without big buildings to block the breeze and the view.

They talked and talked. About a son who didn't want to study, grand-kids that didn't ever visit, about vacations, about a cash flow that wasn't enough for anything. Their sneakers squeaked on the pavement.

A lone man came up behind them, caught up to them, and they barely heard an unenthusiastic good-morning. Still, they responded in chorus, in the key of F.

"There were other young women who came along facing us on the same sidewalk, and they raised a hand in greeting'" recounts Dora, one of the women exercising that morning. That smiling gesture, she recalled, would spoil on their lips.

"There were some jokes, some gossip. We knew many of them, but we hadn't been around all of them before. And we hadn't chatted much, [there's no time to do that] as everyone up there is . . . crossing each other's path, passing one another," she recalled.

Dora stated that one man, about forty years old, came from in front of them, approaching at a slow pace, as if distracted, having crossed from the other side of the street. Behind him was another man, older, familiar to them, who always walked alone. And a little farther back, just a few meters or so, were at least two young men in a black compact car. The car moved slowly and the driver braked frequently, suspiciously, first slowing at the solitary man and then as it reached them, the two women, who maintained their pace.

Dora and her mother had seen the car, and it provoked a chill. It seemed to be predatory: hunting, prowling, its occupants spying from behind its tinted windows. Then the car stopped, and one of the men stepped into the street. The movement startled everyone who was passing.

"One of the walkers dove onto the ground behind a thicket of bushes, in an empty lot. We saw that the fortyish guy continued forward alone and that when he saw the guys in the car trying to get out and the other guy dive into the bushes, he slowed down. He reacted when we shouted, 'Run! Run!' I remember that my mom started to pray. She did it in a low voice, but it was obvious that she was praying . . . and I was just shouting 'Run! For the love of God, run!,'" she declared.

The man who'd crossed the street stopped and looked this way and that. He saw the guys in the car, and it looked like they were hunting him down. There was nobody else in the street at that moment, just parked cars and mansions with giant garages and windows through which nobody was looking. He couldn't figure out whether to flee or to crouch down and try to hide among the cars lining the sidewalk. Indecision. Eternal seconds on the hands of the clock.

The young man who had stepped from the car looked at the man he was going to victimize. He was standing but with his hands still inside of the vehicle. Dora shouted again, to make him react, "Run! Run! Save yourself, for God's sake!"

"Then he took off and ran and ran. He headed in the opposite direction of the guys in the car. They [made a U-turn], accelerated and disappeared behind him, but they never caught up to him. Ahead, since they were going the wrong way, other cars [coming] hindered them. Meanwhile, that guy ran, terrified, trying to save himself," Dora declared.

She finished her story with her sleeves bunched up, covering her face, stammering, "Run, save yourself."

On the sidewalk that day, her mother hugged her, and they remained that way a long time, melted into each other, with the street, the neighborhood, the city immutable. In the distance: the roar of cars, a drowsy siren, and the inevitable honking of horns.

She prays. They both pray. And they will never go there again. Not to pray, not to walk.

THE REUNION

The guys in the patrol car spotted him from afar and circled like a bird of prey. "What have you got there? Are you stoned? Steal something? We'll see, we'll see." They got out and pushed him toward the patrol car, and he remained with his back to them. One checked his pockets while the other examined his documents.

His voter registration ID, a paper with various phone numbers scribbled on it, and a balled-up napkin. "You're stoned," one of the cops insisted to Manuel. "No boss, none of that." "Yes, of course, you smell like pot. We're going to detain you. We're going to take you up to the big house. Nobody there will believe you. We're going to say that you were carrying weed."

"No, boss, no. I just got out of there." Manuel speaks of the Culiacán prison. "I told the cop, 'Give me a break. It's the truth, don't take me there,' but the truth is they weren't listening. They didn't believe me." The one who went through his pockets found two two-hundred-peso bills and one hundred-peso bill. They asked him for two thousand. He told them, "That's all I've got, boss. I swear on my poor mother. Keep the money and I'll die right here."

"Get out of here, then." He had to recover the papers and the ID card that the officers had thrown in the bed of the pickup. Trembling with fear, harried, he gathered up his things and even said thanks to the police who were already back up in their patrol car, who turned their heads to see but not to look at him.

He went along, crouched over, trying to recover from what had just happened. The street, a tapestry of loose stones, waited for the soles of his sneakers, the new ones he'd just been given. His baggy pants fluttered with his movement along with his shirt, which was big enough for two guys his size.

He lifted his face and a few meters ahead he saw several men stopped in the path. "It's no problem if I have to go back," he said. His legs turned to tissue paper when he realized that they were carrying guns. His chest froze. The men were masked, spread out on both sides of the street next to brand-new trucks.

"Mentally, I said to myself, *Nothing's going to happen. Nothing's going to happen. There's no problem. Don't turn around. Act like it's nothing. Don't get nervous. Quit trembling. Calm down. Don't cough. Nothing's going on.*" He walked into the middle of them and one of them said, "Hey, you, come over here." Out of the corner of his eye, he asked if they guy was talking to him.

"The *bato* had a mask on, like the others. He said, 'Yes, you, *cabrón.* Who else? Don't be a *pendejo.*'"[16] Manuel got shaky again, unsure of himself, a wild animal in a trap: "I didn't do anything, boss."

— Come over here. Let's see, what did you say to those fucking cops?
— Me, nothing. Nothing.
— What do you mean, nothing? I saw you chatting with them. What did they ask you about? What did you tell those *cabrones*?
— Well, they wanted to detain me for being on drugs.
— And, what else? Don't play dumb, because you went on for a fucking while with them. And it looked suspicious to me. We saw you from here. Maybe you think we're *pendejos* or that we're fucked up.
— No, boss. Of course not. I'm telling you the truth. They were just trying to get some cash out of me. That's it.

This dialogue left Manuel's throat dry. His tongue turned to stone, and he lost feeling in his lips when that man took out a pistol and pointed it at his chest. "That *bato* told me to quit with the bullshit, and that if I wanted it that way, he'd kill me right there for being a liar."

Manuel drew upon strength from who knows where to answer and to do so without tripping himself up any further, but the masked man asked him again, shouting, if he wanted to die from a bullet, right then and there.

— Do you want it?
— No, boss, please.

With the hand not holding the pistol, the man took off his mask and revealed a crazy smile: it was Luisito, a high school friend of Manuel from the Nakayama neighborhood, a working-class area at the southern edge of the city. He said: "You shat yourself, *cabrón*, am I right?" And then he gave Manuel a two-hundred-peso bill, saying, "To lighten your load."

CHAPTER 2

Assassins with Uniforms

SINALOA STYLE

He is, he was

Rocío sometimes says "is." Other times she uses "was." Alive or dead, this is the crossroads in speaking about Daniel Zavala, her husband. The reporter begs her pardon and asks about her using both tenses of the verb. She responds that there's no problem, because she hopes that he's still alive.

Two years after his disappearance, Rocío, as we'll call this young *culichi* woman living in the United States, gets tripped up: her memories lead her to say "my husband was . . . is" and vice versa. It's a reflection of her wishes, her desires, the stars she shoots for, which never fall from the sky despite a stubborn and galloping heart that insists on disconnecting itself from her mind. The clash of tenses marks the distance between desire (or illusion) and reason. Both heart and mind, in her body, her life, and those of her children, appear not to address the word *muerto* (dead). Dark silences, black holes, a primordial struggle, short circuits stand between the desire of finding him alive and the thought, painful but real, eminently possible, that he is already dead.

That's how her life moves ahead, how she goes on, her trips, her telephone calls with the prosecutor's office, the loving shelter she gives her children, her work, the efforts and lobbying and interviews, her fight: he is, he was, he is, he used to be.

A warning in the chest

Daniel is a US citizen. In the spring of 2010, Dan Zavala, as he is also known, told her that he was going to return to Monclova, a small city on the state of Coahuila, to take care of some business at a seafood restaurant that he had opened with his two brothers, Rafael Zavala Martínez and Rafael Zavala Contreras. He said also that it would be the last trip he would make there, that he had decided not to spend so much time apart from her and their children any longer, and that he was going to settle definitively in the United States.

They embraced. She was pleased by the news; she celebrated it. But when they said their goodbyes, her heart skipped a beat. No one said anything. Afterward she felt a profound sadness that didn't seem to fit with the good news, and she somehow knew that when they parted it had been final. Something large and powerful had happened between them, and it would separate them for good.

"The last photo that we took together, the last day that I saw you, my love, March 26, 2010, that day when I saw that you'd gone away, my heart wept and deep inside I cried out, 'My God, this is final,' and I said 'please give me strength,' and I never imagined that these words would turn into a cruel and cold reality. I love you, Daniel. I will always love you."

This is the voice of Rocío on her Facebook page. It is the written voice that is heard, characters that shout, a sentence that arrives and settles, like what happened that day, squarely in your chest. It leaves a mark, a tattoo. Weeping is inevitable: every tear speaks, every streak of saltwater down her cheeks is an "I miss you," every memory a solid, accurate blow of nostalgia.

Sinaloa style

Daniel had always kept the dream of returning to his home country on the back burner. He told his wife this, and she supported him. The place called to him—his memories, his childhood, his family, his people. His roots pushed, pressed, and beckoned. Now they ache for him and lament his loss: he was disappeared April 23, 2010, with his two brothers, and now his wife and their two children cry for him and clamor for information that will allow them to turn the page.

Daniel had worked for a steel company in Mexico, and they had sent him to various states in the northern part of the country to do business on a regular basis. He'd visited Monclova various times, an industrial city of about 200,000 in eastern Coahuila, where the company had a branch office, and other places nearby.[1] And he'd decided to return. With his brothers, Rafael Zavala Martínez and Rafael Zavala Contreras, all from Sinaloa, in 2009 he opened a "Sinaloa-style" fish and seafood restaurant.

Daniel's wife is afraid of the government. She appears always to be looking over her shoulder and making sure that "there are no Moors on the coast," because she's afraid of reprisals, and she knows that they could come from anywhere.[2] Rocío is not her real name, but she asks that we use a pseudonym and do not reveal her identity or those of her family members because their faces have appeared in the media. She doesn't even have to say it: she's afraid that the internal hell that she's already living through, thanks to her husband's disappearance, will be extended and the wound opened if it should reach another of her relatives. They have shared it with her. They are always close by. They give her courage and energy. They protest and accompany her when she goes to a hearing or asks if there's anything new in the ongoing investigation of Dan's disappearance. In 2010 she informed the Mexican daily *La Jornada* that she would offer a reward, the amount of which she did not reveal, to anyone who gave information that led to the finding of the three men, and she gave an email address so that they could contact her.

The idea at first had been that Daniel would take the first steps in opening the restaurant and that his family would return later to live there. That's what Daniel had told his brothers and what he told his wife. But in Monclova, in March 2009, he had changed his mind about bringing his wife and children to Mexico. Once he was sure that he'd done his part in the family venture, he would leave the restaurant to his brothers and return to the United States for good. It was November 2009 when they opened the doors of the culinary establishment, and after that Dan had returned to his home and family in the United States.

But he had returned to Monclova in the spring of 2010 to tie up some loose ends, and on April 23 he was disappeared. On that date, Rafael Zavala Martínez, a chiropractor by trade, was visited in the restaurant by some unknown men, who arrived in a white extended-cab pickup, a luxury model Ford Lobo, according to information later provided by neighbors, Coahuila State Police, and the office of the prosecutor leading the inquiry. The men all left together, along with Daniel and Rafael Zavala Contreras. The employees and family members who were there thought that they must have been friends of Rafael Zavala Martínez, or patients, because from afar, as he got into the truck, he appeared to signal to them that he would be right back.

"Everything indicates that [the brothers] left there without even closing the restaurant or explaining anything, and when other relatives arrived at the business they found that there were no signs of violence," said a person close to the family.

Dan's wife, sisters, and other relatives filed complaints with the special prosecutor for kidnappings, a joint task force of the state and federal attorneys general, but there haven't been any developments in the case.

"We asked the authorities to investigate, not to let the crime pass them by, to find these three people and their captors, those who have them or know of them, to [make them] hand them over . . . or tell us where they left them," said a family member.

Days after the disappearance, an unknown man arrived to take one of the pickup trucks parked in front of the restaurant, trucks that belonged to the family, and when they asked him where he was taking the vehicle, he responded that "he had orders and that we shouldn't get involved because it would cost us dearly, and so we let him take it away."

Some family members traveled to view the bodies found in newly discovered mass graves left by drug traffickers—*narcofosas*—in Torreón, about a four-hour drive to the southwest, but the brothers weren't among the fourteen victims there. The family members said that a person identified as Ricardo Farías had called them three times to inform them that the brothers were going to be set free, but afterward nothing happened, and finally he called again, claiming that they were alive and on the road home, but again nothing came of it.

Family members said that there was a woman named Ana Patricia Flores, who was apparently the girlfriend of Rafael Zavala Martínez, who said that she could make a statement about the case but that the authorities would have to agree to protect her and her children first. Despite this, she was called neither by staff of the prosecutor's office who were investigating the case, nor by police detectives assigned to the case. No one followed up on the lead, even after other members of the family had repeated it to the authorities. They added that there was an agent of the Federal Police (PF), Jorge Alberto Muñoz, who appeared to be involved.

"We begged them to help us: 'Please, my children are suffering terribly for the absence of their father and also my husband's mother, and of course me too.' We were so ready to wake from this nightmare," said Daniel's wife.

Now she laments the cost that they had to pay for wanting to return to Mexico, even after they had abandoned the idea—blessed land, full of great memories; cursed land, blood-stained, full of wilderness and desert. Welcome to the land of impunity and desolation.

From the wolf's mouth

"There's nothing new. Everything continues the same as it was at the beginning, and two years have vanished." Rocío makes herself heard clearly, despite the two thousand kilometers between her home in the United States and the reporter in Mexico. She doesn't seem tired. She has not given up.

Unofficial sources claim that a member of the family had taken up the case on his own account. He realized, like everyone who lives in this country, that the government wasn't going to do anything. That new investigative offices, programs, special grants to the state or federal authorities would not get them any closer to finding the three men, alive or dead, recovering them in any sense of the term, or detaining those responsible. "Justice," this relative told Rocío, that's what they want. And for that reason this family member began to look into organized crime, carrying out inquiries on his own dime, to see what he might come across.

He traveled in several states, including Sinaloa. He spoke with various people until he found someone who promised to help him for a fee. Other family members noted that this self-appointed investigator, out of desperation, wanted to disguise himself as a homeless man and wander the area near Monclova, asking here and there whomever it was necessary to ask, including drug traffickers and gunmen, about those three disappeared men. But they convinced him not to do it. He opted to hire someone else to carry around photographs of the victims and to track the brothers' route through Monclova, Saltillo, and wherever tips led.

"I am going to find them, alive or dead. I am going to find them," the supposed *sicario* promised that family member. The hired man, whose identity remains unknown, went to the area of Coahuila around Monclova and infiltrated its underworld as a part of the Zetas Cartel, which has an important presence in the region: "He went to the camps and bases of this criminal organization and asked time and again, and showed the photographs. He did this many times over several days."

In one of the camps, he ran into some young *sicarios*. With a coldness that chilled him to the bone, they admitted that yes, they'd had the three brothers there for a few days, but then declared, "We already killed them." He asked them why they had been murdered, what had those Sinaloans done in order to be killed? "For that, because they were from Sinaloa. Because we thought that they were El Chapo's people," people affiliated with Joaquín Guzmán Loera. "That was their mistake, *amigo*. Those *compas* were from Sinaloa."

And, yes, they were from Sinaloa. They were, they are, from the Sánchez Celis Ejido, a plot of agricultural land in El Dorado, a small city about seventy kilometers (forty-three and a half miles) south of the city of Culiacán but within the Culiacán municipality. And straight from the mouth of the wolf from Coahuila, in that extremely dangerous place, they were also from Sinaloa. Rocío had to return to make a statement. The staff person at the Ministerio Público who kept the case file, identified as "Mr. Olivas," told her that she and other family members of the Zavala brothers were going to have to testify again, because the prior interview they had done hadn't been strictly "legal." Nor had they filed it. And nearly two years had passed.

"There's nothing new. Everything continues the same as it was at the beginning, and two years have vanished. There's nothing. Nothing."

She says that she's not looking for vengeance. She only wants to find her husband and her two brothers-in-law. "Vengeance?" she asks, "no, of course not. Because we don't know with whom we're dealing, against whom. I continue the fight, the search."

> — Have any of these programs set up by the government to deal with these kinds of cases, the special prosecutors, for example, helped at all?
> — They don't work . . . they reopen the case and then tell us that they changed personnel, and the new ones who are coming in don't know anything about the file, and they open the archives anew, and the story never ends. It's like returning to the beginning. For many, . . . disappearance is worse than . . . death. There's no body and no live person [either]."
> — It's like a death that never ends, that is prolonged?
> — Exactly. I've been thinking the same thing: an agony that lasts practically forever, because when you don't have news, you don't know if they're alive or dead. . . . We sometimes believe that we are okay, and we smile on the outside and have hope, but the pain that we carry inside—and the hope—is latent. So long as they don't tell us anything, a new lead that suggests that they're not still alive, well, then we are left with the illusion.

Rocío doesn't think it wise to speak out against the presumed implication of the authorities in Dan's disappearance. She avoids mentioning the Federal Police and fears that focusing on its supposed involvement would get in the way of the investigation. She doesn't exactly say it, but she doesn't cast doubt on it either.

"Look, it is not possible for people who are part of the problem to investigate it. They wouldn't know what to say. But in the prosecutor's office in Saltillo [Coahuila] I went to see this guy Olivas, the one who did the initial interview and all the rest, and he said that the interview we had done hadn't been a legal one, that it was just an introduction, and it hadn't been saved or filed away. Imagine how this made me feel. So much time risking our lives, looking for these cops . . . it's like being in the mouth of the wolf and knowing that you didn't do anything, that nothing has gone forward."

Rocío remembers that Dan had told her insistently that he didn't want to go back to Sinaloa, even though his homeland lured him back, and provocatively. Sinaloa, no, because of the violence. And that place, his homeland, his origins, sentenced him to death, without his having done anything to deserve it, he, who was calm by nature, who lived with his kids and was dedicated to hard work. He didn't do drugs and didn't know anything about weapons—that's why he was never afraid.

"He is or was a calm person, peaceful, friendly. He was hardworking, responsible, patient with his kids. He had good work in the United States, he never had any legal problems, he never liked weapons, and he was never involved in illicit activities, like the sale of drugs—nothing. We worked in order to be able to give everything to our kids, and we had a good marriage."

— Did he ever tell you that he was going through any difficulties or that he was afraid?
— No, he never, ever told me that he was afraid. The only thing that he told me the last time that I saw him was that he was only going to stay one more week in Monclova. And I told him that that was good, that I was very happy he was coming back soon.

But he never came back. And *boom*: that conjugation of the verb "to be"—he is, he was—beats in her chest. It squeezes the life out of her.

CADAVERS FOR SALE

One

As if he were closing a deal, offering some kind of bargain, the clerk said "it's yours, take it." But when Eloísa Pérez Cibrián touched the cadaver, she felt nothing. She couldn't find the little mole he had on the small of his back or the other one next to his mouth. The unknown young man lying there was wearing her son's clothes. But her mother's love, her instinct, told her that it wasn't him, that Juan Carlos was still alive.

In Culiacán and in other cities stained by the violence generated by drug trafficking, to disappear is to cease to exist. To die is a luxury in the face of this much more generalized practice, equally macabre and criminal, of stealing a person's freedom, of disappearing them. But "disappear" is a verb that Eloísa refuses to conjugate. Not in that sense, anyway. Not for her. Not for her son. With her gaze and those wiry hands that hold up her son's high school graduation photo, she tries to add weight to her hopes.

They never found her son, Juan Carlos Sánchez Pérez. The government, the police, the staff of the Forensic Medical Service (SEMEFO) have left him for dead, and they continue killing him. They don't investigate. The stream of cadavers handed over to them accelerates cruelly, and they try to divest themselves of his case, one more on a long list of young people killed and disappeared in Sinaloa.

Two

On September 8, 2010, about eleven o'clock at night, some neighbors, young men like him, called on Juan Carlos to go out with them. They thought that the street, outside of their houses, belonged to them. They were mistaken. Among them, there was one whom they called El Güero ("Whitey"). The three of them were standing there in front of the house of Juan Carlos, when two cars pulled up, out of nowhere, one of them a white Nissan Tsuru, called a Sentra in the United States.

Men with high-powered rifles, dressed in black, jumped out of the cars and started to beat one of the young men when he tried to run away. They shot him and then held him down and shot him again until he appeared dead. El Güero and Juan Carlos were shoved into one of the cars. One of the killers yelled, "That's him, bring him!" Another one shouted that if the two didn't do what they were told, they'd put them down, right then and there. Perla, another of Eloísa's children, who'd poked her head out when she heard the shots, couldn't tell if they were referring to her brother.

She wanted to go out there. But the door was blocked, like her throat. Juan Carlos, who heard her there trying to open the door, sensed her presence on the threshold, and shouted her nickname at her: "Vidrio! Vidrio, don't come out!" And she didn't.

On the scene, according to the report from the Municipal Public Security Ministry of Culiacán, "Juan Carlos Manjarrez Esparza," twenty-one, was found dead (a different young man, also named Juan Carlos). The kidnapped young men were identified as Juan Carlos Sánchez Pérez, twenty-one, and José Abel Leones Martínez, thirty-three, a resident of the neighborhood. The agents of the State Ministerial Police found three 9mm shell casings.[3]

Three

Perla, twenty-four, notified Eloísa, who was visiting her parents in Colonia Díaz Ordaz (a residential area southwest of downtown, near a large Pemex complex). Eloísa crossed town as quickly as she could. When she arrived, the street was choked with patrol cars, lights flashing, and there were cops everywhere. She hurried through. She told the investigators that her son had been wearing red shorts, a white shirt over an orange T-shirt, and flip-flops.

From the uniformed men, she learned that a body had been found in a section known as Las Torres, not far from there, in the southern part of the city. She heard them comment that the victim was inside of a white car, and she asked the cops to take here there, but they refused, insisting that if their bosses saw them talking with her, they would have their heads. But in the end they gave in. It wasn't him.

It was a night of the stained scythe and the raised rifle, hot and spitting bullets. Six young people were shot to death in the city, and Eloísa visited all of the crime scenes, looking for her son. In the Felipe Ángeles neighborhood, on the outskirts of La Primavera, here, there, and everywhere. The search ended at about six o'clock the following morning. With the images of many dead imprinted in her memory, disgusted by the bloody and exposed chests, all her hope was shattered—yet she waited to see her son once again. To see him alive.

Four

That same day, September 9, Eloísa showed up at about 2:30 P.M. at the seventh precinct prosecutor's office to file a criminal complaint. In the copy of the file, marked CLN/ARD/13662/2010/D, the mother asks that an investigation be undertaken to find Juan Carlos, who was captured and taken to an unknown destination by various armed men, the night before.

Eloísa says that the young man is "single, a bricklayer by occupation, dark and tall, dark hair, thin, without a mustache or beard, and . . . has a mole underneath his nose, small ears" and that he had neither tattoos nor scars.

Five

Nine days later, on September 18, she received a call from the Forensic Medical Service. She had gone there a number of times, but this time they told her about a new cadaver that they hoped would turn out to be her son. The cadaver had been found near the community of Costa Rica and Rancho Las Flores, about twenty kilometers from the city. The victim was wearing red Bermuda shorts. A light appeared in her watery eyes but it quickly disappeared when staff from the Criminology and Ballistics Division told her that this body had been dead for about ten days, not the eight days that her son would have been dead if they had killed him the night he was taken.

It was a young man. "His face was totally destroyed," she says with a sad and wrinkled face and a voice that breaks. They couldn't take any fingerprints because his fingers had been chopped off. Irreconcilable. The devastation of the body was so bad that at first they didn't want to let her inside to see it. It fueled the fires of the walking hell she'd had inside of her since the attack. Finally they let her go in and touch the body. She didn't feel anything. Her heart let her know, her blood called out to her, announced it. "It's not him," she concluded. "My mother's heart tells me he's still alive," she responded with a firmness that had sometimes abandoned her. And she told them that it wasn't him.

Six

Eloísa has her two daughters and their husbands at home with her, and her grandchildren as well. Juan Carlos: she's used to writing her son's name in his clothes so that they won't get lost when it's time to take things off the clothesline or out of the pile. She stitches it with a needle and thread, letter by letter. Her strokes gradually take shape into letters. Curiously, despite the pounding they take in the wash from the soap and the scrubbing, the letters hold up, even as they fray around the edges. That name, "Juan Carlos," evokes what's most important to her—the one who disappeared, who is absent, taken by the reign of indolence, impunity, and killing. The murdered young man, whose face and hands were smashed beyond recognition, was wearing those same red shorts, the ones with her son's name stitched in them.

That's why they brought her. Neither her heart, nor her head, nor her maternal instincts responded to the body. Then she asked the medical examiner's staff to turn him over. She wanted to look for a birthmark above his rear end. It wasn't there. Nor was the one by his upper lip, just below his nose. His face had been badly damaged, so she had greater confidence in the one on his back. "It's not him, it's not him," she repeated.

Rushed, but deadpan, the employees of the SEMEFO make an offer, as if proffering a terrific bargain: "Say that this is the body of your son, and tomorrow, by eleven o'clock in the morning, you'll have him at your house." Home delivery—death and impunity delivered quickly and efficiently. Satisfaction guaranteed.

"I answered, 'Give me your 100 percent assurance, and I'll take him,' and he responded that he couldn't do that, that he was only 70 percent sure, and I said 'No, I want 100 percent,'" Eloísa remembered. The man made the droll, disappointed face of a failed salesman, and he got hit with another blast of courage and love from that mother.

She asked him if he had kids, and he answered that he did, two of them. "I told him to put himself in my shoes, which hopefully would never happen for real, but to put himself in my shoes. And I asked him 'Let's see; what would you do?' But he didn't answer. He just looked the other way." He turned the body around and left. A few minutes later, another employee arrived to help the mother.

Seven

Colonia Progreso should change its name. Nearby there are mid-range housing developments, and at the back, all the way south, there is that great residential bunker known as La Primavera, king among housing developments, a walled-city unto itself amid the pigsty of what remains of that part of the city. Next to that development, there's a seemingly interminable vacant area of what agronomists might call deciduous scrub forest. It's the city's new clandestine cemetery, a replacement for what El Tule Hill was in the seventies, also located south of the city. Everybody knows it: it's where bodies are tossed, the site of executions, a vast *paredón*—a wall for firing squads. Nobody in the government does anything about it. They simply wait for notice of the latest bodies to appear, so that they can show up and demarcate the latest crime scene. Good work if you can get it.

There's dirt on the plants, the windowpanes, and the desolate faces of the kids who shout in the streets where Eloísa lives, in Colonia Progreso. She and her family do not have regular plumbing—the sewer has only made it a few streets away, so far. But they're charged for it anyway. Her two daughters, their husbands, and two grandchildren live in that little corner, sitting packed elbow-to-elbow on the front patio of a house pieced together with cardboard sheets, wooden boards, spare bricks, plastic sheeting, and miscellaneous rubble—pieces of dreams that are quickly converted into despair. It's almost inconceivable that she and her family live in that little cave under a pile of rubble, that that's where they did their best to make a life for her son.

Street 13, house number 4209. She doesn't want the name of her street to be her destiny or that of her son. She works cleaning houses, and she's done this for nearly nineteen years. The staff at the funeral home, who witnessed her travail in search of her son, found a job for her in one of their branches, where she does the cleaning.

Eight

She carries a photo. She takes it out, sad and proud, and shows it like someone opening her chest to show her beating heart, tired but still working away. The interview with the reporter begins, and she puts the poster-sized photo on top of some heavy contraption covered in plastic sheeting that serves as a mantelpiece. It's a photo of him, his graduation photo in a pressed white shirt, with gel in his shiny, carefully coiffed hair. It's Juan Carlos.

"Why does he seem sad?," she's asked. She responds that he had been crying that day because they told him that he wouldn't be able to continue with his schooling. They didn't have enough money. They couldn't cover the costs, even though he worked for a bricklayer and wherever else he could. His eyes cleared up, but whenever anyone else in the family saw him, they started crying as well, and everyone was sniffing around. "Because he had illusions—and that's how he said it—of finishing preparatory school and enrolling in the law school at the Autonomous University of Sinaloa and becoming a big-time lawyer." The news ended his celebration of having finished secondary school and started a river of tears: it was a look of goodbye, of late afternoon, of the sun setting.

Nine

The woman responds confidently, without doubt. Her son didn't have any problems, didn't going around hiding what he was up to, nor was he nervous, nor were there suspicious people hanging around, looking for him. He didn't buy any fancy clothes, nor did he use one of those Nextel two-way radios or other luxury devices. His clothes were second-hand or bought in the flea market at Huizaches with what money he had earned working as a bricklayer. Before that, he had worked in an HSBC Bank branch and at the Plaza Forum (a shopping mall in an upscale neighborhood). He managed to balance working and studying simultaneously. Still, after combining his earnings with those of his mother and his brothers-in-law, they barely covered the basics.

Ten

José Abel Leones Martínez, the other guy who was taken with Juan Carlos, was released, near the town of Costa Rica, in an uninhabited area. Leaving him there half-naked, the *sicarios* ordered him to lie face down.

And he stayed that way for several hours. When he finally lifted his head, he saw distant lights, got up, and staggered toward them, confused. Some police found him by the side of the highway, but they didn't want to help him. Near a tollbooth, some farmworkers took pity on him, gave him clothes and fifty pesos, and took him to a store called Ley del Valle, near the entrance to Culiacán, where the highway diverges for Navolato. From there he called his family, and they came to get him. He was seen around the neighborhood a few days later, and when Eloísa's family asked him about Juan Carlos, he responded that they had taken him in another vehicle and he didn't know anything else.

Eleven

In November 2010, staff from the state attorney general's office (PGJE) recommended that Eloísa take a DNA test in order to find out if the body (the one with her son's shorts) was in fact her son's or not. They began the formal procedures at the Ministerio Público in the town of Costa Rica and then informed her that the cost would be seventy thousand pesos, but that the government would cover half of the cost, even though it would take three months.

"But if you want it to be faster, it's going to cost you more." Eloísa told them to do it, that she didn't have the money but that she would figure out some way to do it. They promised to call her and to continue tracking the case. As of March 2011, they still hadn't done anything.

Twelve

In the Plazuela Obregón downtown, on Rosales or Ángel Flores, all around the cathedral, there are eight-by-ten posters with the photo of Juan Carlos. It's the same graduation picture. At the bottom it reads "My graduation 2006," and the poster reads: "Missing: if you have seen him, please contact," and then phone numbers are listed. The poster has been copied, thanks to small donations—ten pesos here, twenty pesos there—given by friends, neighbors, and classmates from Salvador Allende High School, collected at sit-in in front of the Autonomous University of Sinaloa, where he wished to enroll.

It is Juan Carlos with a sad smile and eyes about to go dim. His family members say that they dream about him, that they hear him, that he's crying. In her travail, trudging through the offices of the PGJE, Eloísa Pérez Cibrián ran into another woman doing the same thing. The woman, who didn't identify herself, confessed that she was very angry with the abuses committed by the SEMEFO. She had waited for her son, with the hope of finding him alive. Two years after he disappeared, they found a body with the same clothes as that young man. The public servants from the SEMEFO insisted that she accept that dead body as that of her son, and the pressure was such that she finally bowed and said yes. She kept vigil, buried the body, and prayed on the Rosary for that man. On the ninth day of *la novena*, nine days of prayer and mourning, her son returned home on his own two feet. After the shock, surprise, hugs and crying, he explained that he had been kidnapped and forced to work up the sierra, cultivating marijuana and heroin, but that one day, when his captors weren't paying attention, he'd escaped. Now the woman explained to Eloísa that she was there to file a formal complaint against the SEMEFO, but she did not do it in the end, and Eloísa never saw her again. Perhaps she fled in the interest of her safety and that of her family.

In another case, in November 2010, a young man was shot to death in Culiacán, two days after having disappeared. The family went to the SEMEFO to identify the body, but they weren't sure it was him. The brothers weren't convinced, but the mother was: yes, it was him. The forensic staff took advantage of their doubts in order to pressure the family and make some extra cash, according to unofficial sources from within the prosecutor's office. Accelerating the release of the body would cost some ten thousand pesos. Discussion continued until the family decided that it was indeed their relative but advised that they weren't going to pay money to have the body released to them. The Ministerio Público in charge of the case authorized the release of the body, and it finally took place, albeit after much longer that it should have taken.

On October 14, 2010, brothers Armando and Uriel Ríos Aréchiga, twenty-two and thirty, respectively, and half-brother Omar Octavio Ríos Espinoza were taken by unknown men. Days later, three bodies were found, one of them unrecognizable and burned. Their relatives insisted that the burned body was that of Uriel, and there were no doubts about the other two. Without carrying out the most basic scientific tests, the Ministerio Público handed over the bodies, and they were buried the following day in the Lima Cemetery, in Culiacán. But then on the night of October 18, two other bodies turned up near the Los Angeles housing development, located near the road to Imala (a small town northeast of Culiacán, up in the sierra). The family realized that one of these bodies was that of Uriel—his features were intact.

Facing the family's claim, staff from the Ministerio Público changed the initial investigation report and erased the name of Uriel from the document, substituting it with that of Víctor Manuel Espinosa López, the name of the man whose body was already in the grave. The exhumation, exchange of the bodies, and reburial happened quietly the next weekend.

Thirty months of waiting and silence

Since September 8, 2010, Eloísa Pérez Cibrián has looked for her son or any sign of him, anything that leads in his direction. And since then she has waited in vain for the attorney general to turn in the results of a DNA test practiced on a body that could be that of her son.

It's been about thirty months of absence, pain, uncertainty and indolence. What Eloísa and her family want is to confirm whether that dismembered body, found days after the disappearance of her son, in the area around Costa Rica, is his, and to stand vigil for him.

Many others have suffered and died in the interim.

We'll call you

Eloísa indicated that officials did at least one test but they didn't trust the result. According to the PGJE, it wasn't handled properly. After many unfulfilled promises, they finally collected a new DNA sample in November 2011. But when she calls the PGJE office in search of the latest developments in case number CLN/ARD/13662/2010/D, they tell her that there's nothing new, that they'll call her when there's news. "Like they were angry, as if it bothered them that I was calling to find out if there was anything new on the whereabouts of my son and on the DNA tests,

DIRTY BUSINESS

Staff from the Medical Forensic Service (SEMEFO) receive up to sixteen thousand pesos per month in exchange for favors for funeral parlors in Culiacán and ten thousand pesos for the quick handing over of bodies, according to investigations carried out by staff assigned to the state attorney general's office. Unofficial accounts indicate that the attorney general himself, Marco Antonio Higuera Gómez, secretly went to the office of Coordinated Criminal Investigation and Forensic Services located next door to the local office of the federal attorney general (PGR), a few days after assuming his post. One of the first orders issued by the new attorney general was to cut the funeral parlors out of the business of handing over bodies.

"The attorney general found people within the SEMEFO who didn't work there or in the prosecutor's office, who charged for certain 'services,' passing themselves off as employees, but who actually worked for the funeral parlors, and who actually decided who got the bodies in the end," claimed a public servant who had access to the investigation.

Some of the functionaries and employees, he added, received sixteen thousand pesos per month in exchange for working for particular funeral parlors rather than the prosecutor's office. Among the irregularities they found was a delay in the handover of dead people, most of the time those killed in violent incidents, in order to drive grieving relatives to despair and obligate them to pay sixteen thousand pesos to speed the process.

Authorities also investigated cases of impersonation of identity, taking advantage of the bodies of unidentified persons unclaimed by their family members after twenty or more days in the drawers of the morgue. The beneficiaries of these illegal operations were often people in organized crime who had pretended to be killed in order to evade prosecution. These substitutions were carried out with burned bodies or those in advanced states of decomposition.

The sources indicate that in December 2010 citizens located the photograph of a dead person on the website of the state attorney general's office (PGJE), in a section on unidentified bodies. When relatives went to the attorney general's office to identify the body, it had already been "sold" to other people, such that staff had to give them another one without the family realizing it.

"These cases are being investigated to the fullest—this is what I found since the first day I arrived, and these are my orders," said the official from the PGJE. But months have passed, and the investigations have proved a dead end, without formal inquiries or punishment.

they just tell you that there's nothing, that they'll call you when something comes up," she declared, according to a news story published in
Ríodoce, which circulates in Culiacán and other parts of Sinaloa.

She's in her house in Colonia Progreso. The dry dust hits you in the
face and makes it difficult to cry. A stubborn sense of oblivion pervades
the place. There is no development, no justice, and no law in that *colonia*,
or in any other.

She remembers, in her struggle to find out about her boy and not
to forget him, that he was a bricklayer, that he worked in a bank, that
he finished secondary school, and that he cried the day that he got his
diploma, because that same day his mother had informed him that he
couldn't continue with school because they didn't have enough money.
It's May 2012 now, and she hasn't found him yet. But if he were to show
up alive there would be an effort to help Juan Carlos get over that sad
face that his mother and sisters pasted all over downtown. How would
they cheer him up? They would find a way to support him so that he
could enroll in law school.

"I haven't given up hope. I still think that I can find him alive," she
says. She believes that they could have him captive somewhere, working against his will, in the cultivation of illegal drugs, up on a mountain
somewhere, in a laboratory processing synthetic drugs. She recounts how
this has happened to other young people, some of whom have managed
to escape their captors and return to their families.

But the tears win out today—with the sadness of eating and not knowing if her son has enough to eat, the sadness of wrapping herself in
a blanket during the winter not knowing if her son is suffering from
the cold.

Scandal

In the branch of the Ministerio Público in Costa Rica, staff complained
that they didn't understand why there was a scandal in the media about
the disappearance of her son. Eloísa answered them: the only thing she
wanted was to know what happened to her son and to get a DNA test
completed.

"Sometimes it makes me afraid to speak up and, if he is alive, that they will kill him on my account. I'm not afraid that they will do something to me, to us, but rather that they might do something to him," she explains.

Her daughters sometimes protest. They know that the other option is silence. To be here without doing anything. "But it's just as bad to go about it that way. I want to do something, because I don't want them ever to ask me why didn't you do everything possible to find your son?"

She will never forget when she went to the Ministerio Público to lodge a complaint about the disappearance. The public servants who attended to her responded that she should investigate, that she tell them who her son went around with, what kind of people they went around with, where they went. She didn't go in for that. She knows that this is the government's responsibility. Hers is to insist, to demand, to feed her bright if skinny hope, even though it is consuming her life and her health, even though it has meant to die, to never stop dying.

DEATH SQUADS

"Wretched dogs." It's the voice of a mother, drowning in tears. "Dogs, damn dogs." That's what she calls the government types, the *empatrullados*—the police who caught up with her son that day.[4] "Even if he were the worst kind of criminal," she affirmed, "he deserved to be tried." But not this.

On the night of Sunday, June 3, 2012, Jesús Felipe Alvarado Juárez, known as El Pelochitas, was traveling on his skinny, rattletrap motorcycle. He was twenty years old and lived in the Colonia José María Morelos. The police spotted him from afar and intercepted him. Suspiciously, they put the motorcycle in the back of a patrol pickup that they had called for assistance, and they dragged the young man into the back of another municipal vehicle.

He is known in that area. Los Mochis, the municipal seat of Ahome, continues to be a large city that feels like a small town, disrupted by the

shootouts initiated by the triggermen of this or that criminal organization, but still a place where everybody knows each other. When neighbors saw what the uniformed agents had done to Alvarado, they called
his mother. "Listen, they took your son. The police took him."

She is Yadira Juárez. As soon as she left work, in an area near her
home, she went looking for her son. She lived about three hundred
meters from the Municipal Public Security headquarters, on Macario
Gaxiola Boulevard, which leads to the highway to Topolobampo (the
Pacific coast). Acquaintances told her that they'd seen a patrol truck
arrive with the motorcycle, but when she asked about her son, nobody
could tell her anything.

It took five hours for an agent to come forward. After asking that Yadira
not reveal his identity, he informed her that the motorcycle was indeed
there, but he didn't know anything about the young man. Monday rolled
around with the same result. Her son didn't come home. Once again,
Yadira went to police headquarters. There, asking one and then another,
without being seen or heard, she was like a phantasm, a tormented soul,
a mangy stray animal to be ignored until she left. Nobody attended to
her. The woman at the window wouldn't even look her in the eyes when,
like all of the others, she said, "We don't know anything."

With exhaustion weighing on her neck and shoulders, she went to the
local representative of the State Human Rights Commission (CEDH),
located in the northern part of town. The staff there contacted Juan
López Carmona, the judge in charge of cases involving "breaches of the
Edict of Police and Good Government," and he responded that he didn't
have any young man with the stated name or description under his protection. He also permitted the mother to visit the pretrial detention cells
in order to verify that he wasn't there behind bars.

Two days of pain and anguish for breakfast, lunch, and dinner. Of asking here and there. Of waiting rooms that looked like cemeteries full of
open tombs and exposed dead. Expired tenderness, canceled generosity
and compassion. Obsolete justice.

After two days they found him. Dead, with wounds that indicated
that he'd been dragged over a dirt road, savagely beaten, tortured, and
hanged. He was found on the train tracks that run parallel to the highway to Topolobambo. During the wake, patrol cars from the municipal

police were seen along with two pickups belonging to the security detail that protects Jesús Carrasco Ruiz, the official in charge of public security in Ahome. These "security rounds," which served to frighten attendees at the wake, were repeated during the funeral Mass for the body and the procession to the cemetery.

One after another

In Sinaloa, twenty *levantones* were reported in a single day. One after another the disappearances—classified as "illegal deprivations of liberty" —were reported to the offices of the State Human Rights Commission. All of them were young people, and most of them were from peripheral *colonias*, whose families live in poverty.

Four young people were detained by agents of the State Ministerial Police (PME). It was March 29, 2012, in the Colonia Adolfo López Mateos, located in the southern section of Culiacán. The preliminary investigation report CLN/ARD/5373/2012 lodged with the satellite office of the federal Ministerio Público downtown, says it clearly.

The complaint indicates that Jesús Fernando Urrea Vega, twenty, and Jorge Armando Manjarrez, a minor, were working on a car outside of the former's home, when five patrol cars from the PME rolled up.

"The police showed up claiming that it was a routine check, but after checking them out, I guess to see if they had any weapons or not, they pulled their shirts and undershirts over their faces, covering them completely, and took them away in their patrol cars, like that, quickly," said a family member of the minor, who witnessed the arrest.

Jesús Fernando Urrea Vega's mother came outside just in time to see the patrol cars move out and to hear the shouts. She called after the agents, who were wearing masks. They didn't answer, and she saw no more of them. According to the complaint, the same convoy of patrol cars from the Ministerial Police then went on to detain the brothers Luis Eduardo and Jesús Ángel Ontiveros Campos, seventeen and twenty-one. They surprised the former while he was playing soccer on a field near his house and the latter at home in the same *colonia*.

Family members, neighbors, and colleagues from workplaces of the disappeared young men conducted a sit-in in front of the State Prosecutor's Office three weeks later. After much coming and going, making calls and calling in favors to try to get some information about the whereabouts of the victims of this police operation, they did the only thing they could: protest.

The protestors accused police and prosecutors, including the local prosecutor and the Public Security Ministry and the chiefs of various police agencies, of staying silent, denying them access to information, and violating the law. They asked for justice in this and in other cases.

Facts gathered by various human rights commissions indicate that the number of disappeared persons in recent years has reached more than three hundred in Sinaloa. An accurate list of this kind of criminal activity would be much longer, perhaps two or three times as long, even though many families decline to file formal complaints. But the really alarming figure comes from the State Human Rights Commission of Sinaloa, whose directors report that on February 12, 2012, alone, they received reports of twenty different kidnappings in the state. All of these people are still listed as disappeared.

Hitting close to home

Among the reports received by the State Human Rights Commission and the municipal police was that of the disappearance of Édgar Guadalupe García Hernández, twenty-four, who worked as a messenger in the office of Marco Antonio Higuera Gómez, holder of the office of state prosecutor of Sinaloa.

Accounts indicate that commandos arrived at his house in Colonia Progreso, in that capital city, Culiacán, and took him away. Initially the families thought that it was a kidnapping, that the criminals would demand a ransom. But no. And so his relatives and friends set up a sit-in in front of the cathedral in the Plazuela Obregón, located in the center of the city, on May 31. They shouted and clamored, using placards, banners, and flyers, calling for the government to begin an investigation for real, to get to the bottom of it, to find the young man and punish those responsible. It was like throwing stones at the stars.

Cloned patrol cars

Francisco Córdova Celaya, state secretary of public security, warned that this type of act was generally carried out by criminal groups who cloned patrol cars. These cloned cars have been discovered in various operations carried out by organized crime and by Mexican army personnel, in cities as well as in the *sierra*. He dismissed the idea, of course, that his agents or those of other police agencies had participated in these *levantones*, some of which had turned into disappearances. And the worst into homicides.

Accounts indicate that the State Preventive Police and State Ministerial Police, along with municipal police from Ahome, Navolato, Culiacán, Guasave, and other municipalities, carried out a "cleansing" of alleged criminals, hit men, operators, and spies or *punteros* ("pointers"), as they call those who watch a certain place and report to bosses on the movements or presence of "suspicious types" or enemies of the Sinaloa Cartel in northern Mexico.

It is estimated that cells composed of people from the Beltrán Leyva–Carrillo Fuentes Cartel (Juárez Cartel) and the Zetas have a presence and even control important regions in eleven of Sinaloa's eighteen municipalities, working to undermine the operations of Joaquín Guzmán Loera, El Chapo, and Ismael Zambada García, El Mayo, bosses of the powerful Sinaloa Cartel.

This explains at least two of the prisoners found dead, one of them stabbed, in the Culiacán prison, which is now called the Centro de Ejecución de las Consecuencias Jurídicas del Delito ("Center for the Execution of the Judicial Consequences of Crime"), as if it were simply a center for executions.

In this penitentiary, lawyers and relatives of Enrique Alonso Espinosa Hernández warned: "They're going to murder him." They asked the state authorities and those of the Aguaruto jail to take measures to protect him or to transfer him to another prison. But the authorities did nothing. The twenty-six-year-old man entered the jail on Friday, June 15, 2012, at about six o'clock in the evening. The authorities had linked him to the Carrillo Fuentes organization.

His father called lawyers very early in the morning. "I am afraid that they're going to kill my son. What's worse is that he may already be dead by this time," he said. The lawyers sprang into action, but they couldn't do much at that hour, six in the morning. Half an hour later, the young man was found lifeless, hanged in his cell.

Earlier, on May 27, 2012, another prisoner, Francisco Javier Avilés Araujo, who had been arrested in Guasave, had been stabbed to death in the same penitentiary. In response to this homicide in Culiacán, flyers were dropped from a small airplane, with accusations that the governor, Mario López Valdez, known as Malova, had facilitated this homicide on orders from El Chapo, leader of the Sinaloa Cartel.

Coincidentally, Avilés Araujo belonged to a criminal organization opposed to the Sinaloa Cartel, a cell made up of members of the Zetas–Carrillo Fuentes and Beltrán Leyva Cartels.

Questioned by journalists, Córdova Celaya said that authorities in local, state, and federal jurisdictions were investigating the fabrication of law enforcement uniforms by criminals and using ballistics tests on captured firearms in attempts to learn whether they had been used in criminal activities. "All of the patrol cars of diverse police agencies, as well as the agents themselves, have been perfectly identified so that the population can distinguish them from fake policemen or supposed soldiers," he assured. But this was a lie. In the principal cities of the state there are patrol cars with tinted glass, masked officers, covered license plates, and no other identifying numbers.

Convoys of patrol cars circulate with nothing more than the seal of the agency on them, there is no way of identifying one if it is used to commit a crime, and it is necessary to denounce them.

Death squads

The secretary of public security of Ahome does a double take when he sees the reporter. He turns away, stares off blankly, and asks, as if he were talking to someone who wasn't really there: "Death squads?" And he doesn't answer. He gets quiet. Since the secretary's arrival at the agency, complaints have multiplied that officers are doing double duty in the same uniform: *levantones*, disappearances, and assassinations.

Here the case of the disappearance of a young couple who collected scrap metal in the northern part of the city of Los Mochis revealed the double operation of the officers of this police agency. The two were found lifeless near the community of Villa Ahome, some twenty kilometers from the city.

The murders were committed in June, and they fit the pattern: the victimizers were police, municipal police—preventive police from Los Mochis, to be precise—and the victims were neighborhood friends, members of the same clan, as opposed to belonging to the "official cartel," the Sinaloa Cartel.

Sometime between the end of May and the first days of June, the metal collectors, Marcelo Félix Armenta, twenty-seven, and Yolanda del Carmen Araujo Félix, twenty-six, residents of the community of Las Grullas Margen Izquierda, disappeared. The only clue they left behind was a call from a cell phone. "They were being stopped by the preventive police of the *sindicatura de Ahome*, that's what they told us when they called. But, please, we can't say any more. We are afraid," said a person who had communicated with the two before they disappeared.

"After that call," the person added, "their cell phones went dead." Their families filed a complaint with the State Human Rights Commission. A week later, their bodies were found in the municipal cemetery, each showing signs of torture and with a bullet in the head.

"We can't let ourselves fall into playing the game of taking seriously the complaints or . . . conditions made by criminals. If we're going to doubt the actions and integrity of our functionaries and public servants thanks to the allegations of a criminal, then we'd really be in bad shape," Carrasco asserted when questioned by journalists.

And then the secretary of public security continued to be questioned. And he denied a police role in the murder. Then he didn't respond. But his policemen, that was a different story.

Nothing's going to happen to you

Víctor Alonso Gil Aguilar, twenty, was well acquainted with the police, as he had been arrested in 2011 while driving a stolen car. One night in 2012, he and his wife were awakened by no fewer than six officers of the municipal police. The uniformed men, their faces covered by ski masks, kicked in the door, and by the time he opened his eyes, terrified, they had already surrounded him and his wife.

"Calm down," they ordered her, as she took her baby daughter into her arms. "Nothing's going to happen to you," they told her. And then they tied her to the bed. They put a hood over Víctor's head and tied his hands. The officers carried the little girl to a back bedroom, and they later untied the young woman and carried off her husband.

He asked, "And me, *jefe?*" The response was a question: "What do you do for work?" He said that he didn't do anything. The six police officers took Víctor and went off in two patrol cars and a white truck. The license plates had been covered. The residents of Calle Alejandro Peña, in the Colonia Rosendo G. Castro, realized what was going on and went to help the woman once the officers had left. As soon as she could, she called her husband's mother and told her what had happened, and Víctor's mother started the search for her son.

While Víctor's wife fled from home, afraid for her children, and took refuge with her mother-in-law, Dora Alicia Aguilar desperately looked for her son but could not find him. She complained to local media, but only one news channel and one small newspaper publicized his disappearance.

The following day, Víctor's body was found—decapitated—in the Ejido Primero de Mayo. His head anchored a card, on which two words were written: "Sigues Trolo."

El Trolo

According to internal reports from the municipal police and the State Ministerial Police, and according to public knowledge, the person they call El Trolo is the boss of the *Halcones de los Mazatlecos* ("Lookouts from Mazatlán"), as they call a cell of drug dealers who operate in the region at the behest of the Beltrán Leyva brothers.[5] Moreover, El Trolo is responsible for paying for the printing of banners with threatening messages and accusations related to the supposed complicity of state authorities and the army with drug traffickers from the Sinaloa Cartel. On various of these banners the chief of police, Jesús Carrasco Ruiz, and the com-

manders of the State Ministerial Police were accused of serving Joaquín
Guzmán Loera, El Chapo.

Triple

María Araceli Sepúlveda Saucedo, representative of the State Human
Rights Commission in the northern zone, declared that from January to
June 2012, police abuses against the civilian population had tripled, just
as reflected in the complaints.

She claimed that the situation was "worrisome," above all because two
of the cases that began as arbitrary detentions ended in murders. "It's
gone from violations of personal liberty to serious violations against the
integrity of persons, and there's a third case with two deaths in which
there are many similarities, all of them attacks by police," she declared.

"The investigations," the human rights commission officer added,
"have been initiated with the seriousness and speed that they deserve,
but they haven't had the results that the plaintiffs demand." And all
because there are formidable obstacles in the way: the plaintiffs aren't
able to identify the patrol cars involved because these lacked numbers, or
license plates were covered or removed by the same officers, and because
the police covered their faces with black hoods. She stated that when
she had made an official request for information on these cases, the
police chief, Jesús Carrasco Ruiz, had simply denied the participation
of his officers. "He always responds that there was no such operation,
that they didn't detain anyone, and that they don't know anything about
these cases." The complaints filed from January to June 2011 reached
nineteen; during the first half of 2012 they rose to fifty-seven.

The dogs

Yadira Juárez cries over her son. His body is now laid out in a funeral parlor. At the wake the casket had to be closed. They say that he was stabbed
repeatedly with a sharp object and then hanged. Yadira doesn't accept
her son's death. He was young, and if he'd done something wrong, they
should have arrested him and brought him before a judge. The murderers didn't just end his life; they also took a part of her, part of her life,

her soul. Not content, they surround her like beasts, threatening and boastful, during the wake and the funeral Mass.

"Wretched dog, thinking himself powerful enough to end lives. Our damned inept government. Why do we have so many laws, so many jails, ministries, if the police become wretched murderers? If my son were the worst criminal, he would still have the right to a trial, and if he were convicted and put in jail, it would have been just, because he would've been able to defend himself, but with uniformed assassins in patrol cars in the streets, nobody is safe."

Outside the funeral home, young people the same age as her son, with whom he'd grown up, say the same thing: the police stop them now and again, accuse them of being spies and lookouts, ask them where El Trolo is, and then let them go until the next time.

And El Trolo, he's around. Doing fine, thanks.

LIFE INSURANCE

José said, "We can't file a complaint." Despite the insistence of the commissions agent who had come to Sonora and Sinaloa to buy shrimp to send to Veracruz, he remained firm in the thought that he couldn't turn to the local or federal authorities. And when the commissions agent asked him why not, he answered that they had been threatened.

That January day in 2012 José and his truck driver had been intercepted on the outskirts of Culiacán. They had been headed toward the port of Topolobampo, located 215 kilometers (134 miles) north of the city, in the municipality of Ahome, in order to unload about twelve tons of shrimp and ship them to Veracruz.

Between January 8 and 9, the members of a deep-sea fishing co-op and owners of large fishing boats all over the region learned about the intercepted load and the presence of the commissions agent, who appeared to be from Veracruz and was well aware of the high quality of the Sinaloan crustaceans.

As the local marketer, José had received the shrimp and been preparing to send it to the port. That bright morning, the highway was abandoned, four open lanes over the hills. He was successful in this field, knew everyone, and was known in what had been his trade for more than a decade in and around Culiacán.

"Let's go, we've got to hand over the merchandise so it's loaded on time." The port was an hour and a half north of the city. "Let's roll, *compa*," he told the driver, "so we don't have to hurry later on." The tires gobbled up the asphalt, yellow and white stripes tearing by. Ten minutes later an SUV approached at high speed and flashed its headlights over and over. It seemed like a frantic signal that started to entrance them and cloud their vision. It later appeared that they had tried to ignore the vehicle tailing them, perhaps suspecting criminals. In that region, especially in the north, in the municipalities of Salvador Alvarado and Guasave, robberies of this type, assaults and murders, had provoked widespread paranoia, even among people just passing through. This had largely been attributed to organized crime, in particular to cells of the Beltrán Leyva and Zetas Cartels, which operate in the region and count on the complicity of the authorities.

A few weeks later, personnel from the Mexican army, assigned to the Ninth Military Zone, chased a commando of presumed criminals down the same section of the highway. The pursuit followed a confrontation near the Regional Hospital of the Mexican Social Security Institute in Guasave, and it later turned into a manhunt.

Testimony gathered by Paul Mercado, a journalist from the weekly *Ríodoce*, described the terror of civilian witnesses. Alma, for one, was practically paralyzed by fear. "At about 6:30 in the afternoon," she told Mercado,

> I came from my mother's house, taking a back way to avoid traffic. I passed through the Calle Colón and then Revolution. At the top of the hill, near the Hernández Bakery, when I turned to cross the street onto the boulevard called Central por la Corregidora, at the very moment I stopped to see if any cars were coming, I started to hear the explosions. At the same time, I saw that a little girl was running away and shouting. I pulled over into a driveway and ducked my head. . . . When I peeked out, I saw a truck passing by at high speed, with the copilot hanging halfway out of the door firing back at the soldiers who were following them [and] responding with more of the same: bullets. The only thing that I could do,

after freezing for an instant, was to duck . . . , and after hearing the shots a little farther off, I pulled back into the road the same as the cars behind me, waiting to turn onto the boulevard. It was horrible to see the intersection of the boulevard full of cars, . . . [and] I couldn't drive any farther. I was already grasping for my cell phone when my mother called, because she could hear the shoot-out from her house, and she was worried because I'd just left there. She told me not to move from where I was and arrived with some neighbors who stayed with me until the fright subsided a bit. The people didn't know what had happened, and soon municipal patrol cars came by, but something like fifteen minutes had passed by that point. They took me to my house, because I hadn't yet stopped shaking. We tried to take the most far-flung route, but throughout the city we heard the sirens of patrol cars and explosions . . . it was like a war zone, and that wasn't even in front of the hospital, where they tell me it was worse.

She had passed by just as a shootout began that had ended with the death of two soldiers on Boulevard 16 de Septiembre. The shootout had injured one other person, who died later in the hospital emergency room.

On this stretch of road between Culiacán and Los Mochis, a little more than two hundred kilometers, hundreds of tons of corn, beans, fertilizers, and shrimp had been hijacked by commandos since the beginning of 2009. Armed with high-caliber weapons, operating in late-model cars, the criminals demonstrated the capacity to move dozens of tons of whatever product in a matter of minutes. And to hide it all without being detected by local or federal police, or by the army, despite the fact that these authorities had announced a joint operation in 2011 to combat highway robbery, which until then hadn't cost any lives.

We're cops

The shrimp marketer called a friend on his cell phone and told him about the vehicle that was following them. Half-awake, the friend advised him that they shouldn't stop: "They must be scoundrels." And so they kept on. But after the driver of the SUV overtook them, and another man placed a flashing red light on the hood in front of the windshield, as police officers in unmarked vehicles often did, they opted to pull over.

"We are from the Ministerial [Police]," one of them would have said, according to accounts collected by the officials from the federal Ministerio Público specializing in crimes against commerce. Forced into compliance, they would have asked themselves, "What's going on?" Men in the SUV climbed out with their pistols drawn and visible. Two of the four moved toward them, with assault rifles slung from their shoulders.

"Get out. We're going to check it out."

They climbed down from the cab of the truck and asked, "What's this about? We're carrying shrimp, and we have to arrive in Topolobampo in less than two hours, and we're already late."

"Nothing. Don't worry, it's just a routine check. We're looking for weapons and drugs, illegal stuff."

They opened the back of the refrigerated truck and an enormous pillow of vapor escaped. The guy who appeared to be in charge of the operation announced that they were going to confiscate the load of shrimp. The businessman questioned him and asked that they provide an order or show some kind of identification. They answered him with a hard rifle butt in the belly: he was knocked down, mouth open, unable to speak.

Before leaving, one of the armed men shouted at them, "You'll be sorry if you go to the police." As soon as he could, he called the owner of the shipment. He explained everything that had happened and advised that they wouldn't be able to file an insurance claim, because they weren't going to file a police report. The owner got angry and disagreed. But the death threats were persuasive.

Expensive insurance

The shrimp marketer thought that he'd made a long trip for nothing, but that load of almost twelve tons was very valuable. He thought about the loss and the little that he'd be able to recover. The owner insisted that he file a complaint. They could at least try.

Since the crime had been committed on a federal highway, he and the driver had to go to the office of the federal attorney general (PGR) in Guamúchil, the municipal seat of Salvador Alvarado. The officer from the federal Ministerio Público there asked what he could do for them. They told him everything that had happened and that they wanted to file a police report. Hmm . . . He clicked the mouse and typed something on the computer.

They left there, and the driver asked: "Now what are we going to do?" The marketer looked at him and then turned his head to see the owner of the merchandise arriving. "We're going to get some tacos," he responded. While they were eating, four men approached. All of them dressed in black with hoods over their faces. Rifles in full view. "Get up," they ordered.

"What's this about? We haven't done anything wrong!" one of them shouted. The leader of the hooded men answered, "How's that? We told you not to go to the police."

Their bodies were later found about twenty kilometers from there, full of bullet holes, with their hands tied behind them: insurance collected.

THE ENEMY ON THE INSIDE

First a woman arrived. She came with two men. They didn't carry any visible weapons. She appeared to be the wife of the deceased: the man who was lying on one of the slabs of the Forensic Medical Service (SEMEFO). There were not many personnel on hand, only two or three. One of them attended to the woman, who had strangely passed through several layers of security and was there, demanding the body.

It was May 15, 2007, Teachers' Day. Among the cadavers was that of a murderer who had served as a gunman for the Sinaloa Cartel and operated in the community of Costa Rica, in the municipality of Culiacán. As it happens, no one could remember his identity. He had been a gunman of considerable regional fame and in the same way that he had dispatched his assignments they'd finished him off: by way of bullets.

"We already paid. Give us the body," the woman said, in ill humor, with a commanding voice. The staff person was taken aback. But he knew of the problems of corruption within this institution: some public servants charged for the rapid handover of cadavers and for other services. This forensic dentist, who shall remain anonymous, responded that she didn't need to pay, that it was their obligation, and that they received a salary. He said that he hadn't been filled in on the details, but that in any case he needed an order from the prosecutor's office, which was in charge of the case, in order for them to take the body.

The woman said something through clenched teeth. She turned around, without saying thanks, and muttered a "let's go" to her companions. In a matter of minutes, a group of nearly fifteen gunmen arrived. Accounts from other employees of SEMEFO, located in the main building of the Coordinated Criminal Investigation and Forensic Services agency, next door to the state delegation of the federal attorney general's office, indicate that the commando had entered the parking lot in three late-model trucks and stormed into the forensic medicine lab through the main entrance. Nobody asked them "Where are you going?" or said "Stop!" They entered and asked for the man who had attended to the widow. Then they took him away.

Another staff person had observed both episodes. Once the aggressors left, he slipped out the back door and followed them in his car. The unknown men, hooded and dressed in black, carried high-caliber weapons, which appeared to be AK-47 assault rifles. The convoy took the narrow street that merges with the highway to Navolato and veered to the left, toward the western sector of the city. They stuck close together, as if guided by an invisible magnet, and moved along at a considerable clip, weaving through an area with dense rush-hour traffic. The doctor who followed them carried a walkie-talkie and used it to advise the State Ministerial Police that a commando had carried off the forensic dentist.[6] Unexpectedly, the armed men, who by this time realized that they were being followed, stopped near the Culiacán International Airport, and some of them got out. There was a patrol car with agents of the Ministerial Police with whom they spoke and to whom they handed over the dentist.

The convoy of trucks left, and the man who was following them opted to stay close to the patrol car, which set off by way of Emiliano Zapata Boulevard, toward the department headquarters. There they got out and locked the dentist up in a cell at the back of the building. The detained man was said to have been surprised while committing an act of corruption, according to unofficial accounts. "There were direct accusations," they affirmed. But these never materialized in a case file, much less a formal criminal complaint.

The protest

In the Forensic Medical Service there are many problems: a lack of confidence in public servants who are on the front lines, disunity, petty jealousies, low salaries, and long, strenuous workdays. Add to this an abiding fear that commandos, whom no one would dare to stop, might burst in at any moment to carry off cadavers, and morale was low.

But the kidnapping of the forensic dentist changed things such that the staff cast aside everything that had divided them. They organized and came together in front of the ministerial offices, one by one, slowly, until they formed a cohesive group. They demanded that the authorities set the detained man free.

The demonstrators asked if those who had violently entered the SEMEFO were agents of the Ministerial Police or a commando unit from organized crime or both. They maintained that this seizure was directly related to the visit of the supposed widow and the cadaver that she had demanded. "It was a reprisal," declared one of the experts who worked in the Criminology Department, "for not lending ourselves to the corruption of others, but the worst thing here is that we are paying for the reprisals ourselves, not them, those of us who have nothing to do with those kind of machinations [*malos manejos*]."

Among the problems endured by public servants in the state attorney general's office is the stealing of cadavers within the state facilities or on their way there, when they are in transit from a crime scene to the SEMEFO.

"It has happened that they take the cadavers from us en route. They block us in, they close off our way, but they also prevent us from taking evidence, making assessments, in the places where the murders occur. . . . 'Hey, what are you doing here? Go fuck your mother somewhere else,' and they run us off. They don't let us do our work. And nobody, not even the police who are there, close by, protect us," affirmed a member of the Coordinated Criminal Investigation and Forensic Services.

BODY SNATCHERS

On Thursday, October 29, 2009, a commando of around twenty recovered the cadaver of an unknown man from the Forensic Medical Service. Accounts from witnesses indicate that the gunmen entered the SEMEFO at about one o'clock in the morning, armed with high-powered rifles, and threatened and incapacitated the staff of the state attorney general's office, whom they forced to lie on the ground, face down.

"We are at the mercy of the damn criminals," said one of the staff members, who complained about the lack of rights and security for the forensics experts at the various police departments.

The cadaver had been found that Monday night near the community of Campo del Diez in Culiacán, the victim killed by bullets and burned. Accounts from those close to the investigation suggested that the victim might be a member of the Carrillo Fuentes family, the heirs of the late Amado Carrillo, "Lord of the Skies," founder of the Juárez Cartel.

The prosecutor's office announced that it had opened a high-level criminal investigation of the murder (case # 157/2008) precisely because of the possible connection to the Juárez Cartel and informed the federal attorney general, due to the presence of weapons considered high-powered and exclusively for military use (which implied a variety of federal offenses).

The same as reporters, rescue workers from the Red Cross, and even members of various police forces, the SEMEFO people can only approach crime scenes once they've been secured by the military, for their own safety.

The pressures

Aware of the forensic workers' protest, high-ranking officials in the local prosecutor's office began to pressure them to withdraw from the place, to suspend the public demonstration, and to return to their work. But these nonconformists refused to follow the orders and stayed there in front of the holding cells of the Ministerial Police.

Other sources from within the building pointed out that there was neither an arrest warrant nor a flagrant offense, but there were clear signs of corruption within the SEMEFO. Someone had fabricated an account in which the dentist had asked for money from that woman in order to turn over her husband's body.

The authorities promised to set him free, but they didn't say when. The demonstrators remained there, united. They knew that this dentist who came from their own ranks "had busted his balls to get ahead, he's a father with a family, he teaches classes, he has a consultancy, and on top of all this he's a government employee. And above all else, he's an honest man." Nobody doubted his honor, and for that they remained intransigent.

Early the next day the dentist was set free "for lack of evidence." But his colleagues knew that if the staff member hadn't followed him after the armed group made off with him, he would now be dead. And if they hadn't turned up to demand his release at the ministerial headquarters, he would still be a prisoner in the Culiacán jail.

The change

Facing the fear of reprisal and new actions against him, the dentist sought the backing of the Union of State Workers. And he found it: the secretary general at the time backed him up and proposed that he switch to another government agency. The dentist agreed. But officials in the prosecutor's office resisted. They wanted to keep him there. Nobody knows why.

"We know that they threatened him, that he was in danger, and that what we must do as his union is to protect him, support him, be with him, and thus we started to process his change of appointment. His bosses wanted to bring him back and demote him, but we didn't allow it," declared one of the leaders.

The union member, this source added, was afraid that they would kill him, that those armed men would return to finish what they had started.

Now he's among children and their happy shouting. He's no longer in the middle of cadavers and threats. But, yes, he's still in a city that wrecks itself, that falls, exhausted and overtaken. On streets, medians, sidewalks, and corners, the memorials to the dead grow and multiply, traces of the violence, as if Culiacán were a dead city, a giant cemetery.

PATROL CAR 1342

Getting involved in a lawsuit with his neighbor proved very expensive to Luis Alfonso. Old quarrels—something about the trash or that thieving dog or the stubborn dampness that collected on the floor and walls from the bathroom on the other side. He paid a high price. He paid dearly. He lost everything.

His reputation as a punk had served him well: the man could make noise. Many had backed off, because when they had agreed to go out with him to a restaurant or a bar, he had talked loudly about his deeds and almost brandished the automatic pistol that always accompanied him, tucked into his waistband, his shirt always partly open where it met his pants.

For a long time, forty odd years, he had come and gone from the border and farther. Going, he took drugs—cocaine and marijuana. Coming, regularly, he brought money. He had the officer who always attended him check, except that this cop changed his cell phone number without telling him, to get a rest from his shrapnel-like voice. That voice, the officer recounts, always asked for two things: help getting out of some tangle with the police or with other pistoleros or help acquiring a new pistol.

"That guy was all right, truth is. But he was annoying and scandalous. And when I changed phone numbers he managed to get my new number, and when he called me, he complained 'Listen, you changed your number and haven't given it to me,' and I had to make up some kind of pretext, that I hadn't updated all of my contacts, that I was still working on it, that I'd just started yesterday. And that *bato* was always involved in some kind of *broncas* ("mess"), and he always wanted me to sell him a pistol," affirmed the officer from the State Preventive Police, with whom Luis Alfonso had been friends.

When he'd had them, the cop had sold him a 9mm pistol, a thirty-eight, or a forty-five. It was to calm him down. He knew that the next week or sooner he would call again in order to buy another weapon. A thousand pesos, fifteen hundred, perhaps a bit more, that was the price. It wasn't high, because they knew each other, they were comrades.[7]

Let's get them

One night, Luis Alfonso interrupted a marital conversation of the officer with whom he dealt. He recounted to that he'd had to go to Infonavit La Flores, located on the western side of Culiacán, to fix a problem. The cop knew what it meant "to fix something" in the voice and life of that man. He told the officer that when he'd arrived there, they were already waiting for him. There were various men, of whom he'd only known one.

"He told me that the *compa* with whom he'd had problems was there, and that he wanted 'to fix' things, but since there were a bunch of them, he couldn't even consider it. Those *cabrones* surrounded him and started to beat him. He tried to take out his pistol and defend himself, but they snatched it away from him. They surely knew that he carried weapons, and I guess they didn't want him to draw it on them," declared the state policeman.

Luis Alfonso had scarcely finished recounting what had happened when he asked the cop for help. That the police go after them, kick the shit out of them, and recover his pistol. His contact responded that he couldn't do it at that moment, that he was working outside of the city. That he should wait, and the next day they would look into what they could do. But it was just an evasion.

The next day, he changed his phone number again.

Loud and combative

Constantly Luis Alfonso got into trouble. There were complaints, law-suits, arrests for public drunkenness, altercations with neighbors and with officers from the municipal police, conflicts with other drivers on the road. Almost all of these types of encounters ended with him drawing his pistol, even though he never fired it.

"The *bato* was combative, you couldn't be more problematic. When we went to restaurants or bars, after having a few drinks with other friends, he would become absolutely insufferable. He would talk and talk, getting louder and louder, bragging that he was friends with this guy or that guy who was a heavy hitter. He acted as if he was in on things that he wasn't, and I think that's in part why he was always getting into trouble from all sides."

In addition to his fondness for draining bottles until they were empty to the last drop, there was his addiction to marijuana. It was almost a given that he was high or drunk. Or, better yet, both. He was like a trigger or a firing pin for a gun that didn't shoot but always had a bullet in the chamber. And when it finally went off, it made a huge mess.

A dispute among neighbors

Something went down between that neighbor and Luis Alfonso. It was a sequence of disagreements that got progressively worse until they boiled over and multiplied, without division or subtraction: there were already gunpowder and rigid muscles in the way, that little path between his house and that of the man who reported him.

According to the sparse and very preliminary investigations undertaken by the Ministerial Police, that didn't amount to anything. The problem was that Luis Alfonso took out a firearm and pointed it at that man, whose identity, of course, wasn't revealed. The neighbor, disturbed and afraid, dialed 066 (the same as 911 in the United States), and two minutes or so later, maybe a bit longer, patrol car #1342 of the Culiacán municipal police arrived. Its occupants got out and went directly to Luis Alfonso, whose confidence was buoyed and whose rational thinking was dimmed by so much alcohol and weed. Luis Alfonso faced them with his pistol drawn, out in the open, exposed but sure of himself. "I'm not afraid of these *cabrones*," he would have said in recounting the altercation, as he had on occasion dropped code words that implied the backing of powerful men, as any good narco did when he found himself in a tight spot, facing a handful of men in blue or gray uniforms.

But it didn't go down that way this time. It couldn't. Not to him, with his past, his reputation, and that automatic pistol that accompanied him everywhere, and those toxic clouds that led him faithfully to hell. The cost of all this was his life. That's the price he paid. The patrolmen subdued him easily and tied him up. After they knocked him over, face down, they shoved him into the truck with kicks and punches, and they took him away. Some of his family members called the Ministerial Police and headed over to the local lockup and then to where the pretrial detainees of the Public Security Ministry were held, in Bachigualato. In both places they told them that they didn't have anybody with that name or matching that description. This struck them as strange, given that he'd been arrested right there in the neighborhood, in front of various neighbors and even relatives who had known him for his whole life. Nobody had intervened. They knew how things worked, that there was no option but to wait or else risk being arrested by one or another police department.

The discovery

The next day, before twelve hours had passed since his arrest, he was found. He was lying in a vacant lot, empty, like his life. Forty-some years of being a little mad and more than a little stoned, of coming and going in criminal activities, of drunken and smoked-out neurons. He was alone there, with dried blood, flat and dull, on his skin.

The report released by the media claimed that his body was wrapped in a plastic campaign sign for Eduardo Ortiz Hernández, candidate of the National Action Party (PAN) for municipal president of Culiacán. Others claimed that murderers had wrapped him in blankets, that they had "blanketed" him in the argot of the police blotter.

The daily *Noroeste* reported on June 23, 2010:

> An unknown person was found shot to death, tortured, and wrapped in tape, on the back patio of a church in Colonia Buenos Aires. Next to the victim, the authorities found campaign materials for Eduardo Ortiz Hernández, candidate of the National Action Party (PAN) for municipal president of Culiacán. The State Ministerial Police report that the victim was between forty and fifty years old, was 1.7 meters tall, white, with a regular complexion, and short, thick, gray hair, almost woven looking.

At the time of the discovery, the unknown man was wearing gray Wilson warm-up pants, a sleeveless T-shirt, and gray Nike sneakers. Next to the body, they found a matching gray Wilson jacket.

The discovery was reported to the police at approximately 9 am by residents of Calle Cerro de Salto, near the corner of Calle Rodolfo Fierro, in Colonia Buenos Aires.

The body, which belonged to Luis Alfonso but had yet to be identified at that time, bore wounds indicating savage torture. Some accounts claimed that he had been asphyxiated; others claimed that he had been shot to death. They all coincided in the fact that his hands and feet had been tied with strips of hard plastic.

That's how it ended, paying dearly for a dispute that could have been resolved amicably from the start. The solution was finally his disappearance at the hands of those officers. And his death. Two years on, his closest family members haven't asked for justice, nor have they filed a complaint against the uniformed men responsible, nor do they want to stir the pot. Everyone has their peace.

THE LETTER

The two brothers heard noises. It sounded like gunshots. They came downstairs and realized that two unknown men were banging violently on the front door. They got a knife and steeled themselves to confront the intruders, but then they thought the better of it and ran down to stay by their mother's side in her bedroom. She had already awoken. She told them to call the police. Then she went out on the balcony and yelled for help. Nobody dared to poke a head out in response. A police officer who was outside pointed his assault rifle up at her and told her to be quiet.

The men wore black hoods and uniforms from the municipal police of Apodaca.[8] After splintering boards and kicking in doors, they entered the house. It was a middle-class development, and the date was January 11, 2011. The uniformed men entered and found the three clinging to each other, huddled up, not wanting to die. Two of the men stayed with them, rifles pointed at their heads. The others went through the house like industrial vacuum cleaners, sucking up electronics, cell phones, clothing, televisions, perfume, shoes, and jewelry. They took everything, including two pickup trucks.

"It was January, we had the Christmas presents, everything we'd bought on the other side, in Laredo, as we do every year, and that included clothes, perfume, gadgets, many things. And they took it all, including my son Roy," Lety Hidalgo declared.

Once they concluded this ritual of pillage, they directed their attention to the family. They asked who was the eldest son, and, face down on the floor like the others, without turning toward them, Roy raised his hand. "They grabbed him and they took him."

Nobody could truly grasp what had happened. They had taken Roy. They fled the house and took refuge at a neighbor's, who wouldn't even turn on the lights out of fear. Lety and her younger son blindly groped for a phone but couldn't find it in the dark, and thus it wasn't possible to call the army, as Lety had decided to do. "Why not call the police?" one of the neighbors asked. "Because they are the ones who did it."

A patrol car from the municipal police passed by. The officers acted as if nothing out of the ordinary had happened. They barely stopped, and they didn't get out of their pickup, despite the fact that the door to the recently sacked house was wide open. Then they left. And then, in the middle of the darkness, the confusion, and the terror, they remembered Roy. And they called for him again and again.

Lety and her son concluded that they had taken him away. A new stage had begun, another level. Terror and desolation.

The word of Alejandro Fernández

The next day, the mother remembers, the criminals called to ask for a ransom. With the help of other family members, she got the money together, the amount of which she declined to reveal. The criminals also demanded the titles to the two cars, a 2008 Jeep Patriot and a Chevy Zafira compact that her father had loaned her so that Roy could continue his studies. They set the San Benito church as a meeting place.

They told her not to inform the police. They told her that a school bus would arrive, and that she didn't have to say anything, just hand over the money and the documents. She did just as they asked. In two hours we're going to set him free, they told her over the phone. They explained where he would be. It felt like an all-night vigil. Those two hours turned into something outside of time, a bitter and cracked night, a life without a soul, a call they waited for constantly but that never came.

The parents and the other son, just a kid, started to take note of everything. They started with the telephone numbers the criminals used. They already had three jotted down in a notebook. They called one of them. It was six o'clock in the morning the following day. The same person who had given them the instructions for handing over the money answered the phone.

— Ah, yes. We are still working, dealing with *señor*'s vehicles.
— I carried out my part. But you all haven't—
— I'll call you in a little while.
— But please do so. Don't try to fool me.
— No, no. You have the word of Alejandro Fernández.

As was to be expected, they never called back. Two days passed. There were various telephone exchanges, but rather than nourishing their hopes, they had opposite effect. In one of these, the unknown man, who sounded like he was in a cave, told them, "We're going to return your son in little pieces." The family decided to take matters into their own hands. She went to the local offices of Telmex to find out the names and addresses corresponding to the telephone numbers. The employees refused to provide the information, and Lety immediately opened a counteroffensive: she offered them money, and they accepted.

Which one of you is Roy?

The captor answered the phone again. The interlocutor put someone on the line who in a childlike voice said: "Mama, pay them what they ask already," but Lety realized that it wasn't her son and asked to talk to the kidnapper again. The man hung up, but she called him right back and asked him to pass the phone to her son, that she wanted guarantees that he was still alive.

—Who is Roy, you assholes? Which one of you is Roy?

A faint voice chimed in, "I am." And they gave him the phone. In the background, she could hear laughing and joking around.

— Is it you?
— Yes, Mama, it is me.
— What's your brother's birthday?

He answered her correctly. Sobs. An "I love you" remained suspended between the two receivers, along with an "I'm sorry," an "I miss you," and "everything's going to work out." The men started in again with their jokes and guffawing. They took the phone from Roy. The laughing got louder. Roaring like sharp weapons. Voices that cut. A scythe that smiled.

— Do you have the money together?

The man proposed to send other criminals to pick up the complete ransom at her house, but she disagreed. She didn't want to see them again, much less in her house. Then they agreed that it would be the church again: her alone, without police, weapons, or traps.

It would be there, outside of the San Benito church, where there would be a yellow school bus again. The family worried that the kidnappers might try to take her as well or cut one of her ears off as a lesson. None of it came to pass. It was already January 13, and the night that began that day never ended.

GPS

"We began to move. Obviously, we weren't going to the police, not ever." Lety turned to the army, the Seventh Military Zone, and she gave them what she had: telephone numbers and the information she had collected from the phone company. One of the officers who attended to her asked her to file a complaint with the local or state police, but she refused. She knew that officers from these agencies were carrying out kidnappings, robberies, and murders, and that many times they acted on orders from the drug cartels.

"I asked the major who was attending to us what his experience told him was behind this kind of case. He answered that they were bands of active-duty cops—not ex-cops or retired officers or fake officers, but rather part of the departments. They used their weapons, uniforms, military-type or black-and-white camouflage. The officers offered to put out a bulletin in the area, including a photo of Roy," the mother remembered.

In addition, the soldier advised them that if they weren't going to notify the police, they could at least try using the GPS service offered by Nextel, the provider of one of the cell phones that the criminals continued to use. They did exactly that, and they began to track the movements of the phone and to take photos of the locations where each of the calls were supposed to have been made. They took eighty photographs back to the soldiers, of streets and houses where the GPS coordinates indicated that the phone had been used: they included locations just north of Monterrey, in Escobedo, San Bernabé, Santa Catarina, Garza García, and near the municipality of Saltillo, at the edge of the state of Coahuila. They also handed the tracking device and the password over to the soldiers, so that they could continue to track the criminals.

A few days later they were informed that the military had carried out an operation in Garza García, and that they should go to the offices of the federal attorney general, because they had detained three presumed kidnappers and liberated three victims, although Roy wasn't one of them. They offered to let Lety interview the detainees and try to obtain information about Roy.

It was March 7. She went there, and after hours of waiting in anguish she was finally able to hand a photo of her son over to the prosecutor handling the case, and they allowed her to interview the detainees. One of them told her that he didn't know her son, nor did he remember him from among the fifteen kidnapped children, that some had been taken to another place and others had been killed. He told her that they kept track of them by number, not by name.

According to information taken from the criminal case file, the detainees, two men and one woman, testified in front of the Ministerio Público that they worked for the Zetas, a criminal organization with a strong presence in the state of Nuevo León and across the north, one that had been blamed for a dramatic rise in crime and violence.

The last satellite signal made by the phone they were tracking occurred during an operation carried out in the community of Sierra Ventana, considered a "conflict zone." Television news stations reported that the operation was carried out by state police officers, under the name "Operation Razor." Roy's family thought that they would finally get some news. They waited, glued to the television, or perhaps for a call, a name, a face, something. They waited in vain.

That day, right in the middle of the police operation against organized crime in that area, the GPS signal was lost for good.

Automobile insurance

The companies that insured both of the family's cars refused to pay Lety. They told her, with atrocious cynicism, as if the news itself weren't enough, that they couldn't pay out on the policies since she had "donated" the vehicles to the criminals. During the "transaction" involving the family cars, they insisted, there hadn't been any violence or any weapons used, and thus it should be treated as a "gift" that she had decided to give to the criminals.

She spent two months in waiting rooms, arguing and complaining, trying to recover some of the value of the items lost during the police pillaging of her home. On April 7, 2011, she got a call and thought at first that she was finally going to get some money for the cars, but someone explained instead that one of the cars had been found.

The Zafira minivan had been "recovered" by the Mexican army in an operation carried out in El Carmen. The car was at the disposition of the federal attorney general's office, along with a 2011 Mazda, also stolen. They'd also recovered weapons in the operation. The soldiers reported that during their pursuit of three criminals, two of them had been able to escape. In the car driven by the third, whose identity they did not disclose, they had found the keys to four other vehicles, including the keys to Lety's car, as well as weapons, ammunition, and supplies. The detainee denied having participated in Roy's kidnapping, and assured that he hadn't ever met him.

They have the equipment; I have the will

Lety Hidalgo is a teacher. The director of the high school where she works gave her permission to take some time off, given the gravity of the case. On the brink of retirement anyway, she now has a new mission, for which no one will ever pay her: search, search, and search again, until she finds him. If necessary, she assures, she'll give her own life to find him.

"How curious it is: the government has the equipment, the weapons, and the money. All I've got is the will. I, we, the family—we have given them the information they need to get some results, but it's only because we have gotten going. They say that they have detained five individuals, and they believe that I should be happy with that . . . and I tell them, 'What's it to me? I need to find Roy.'"

All of them—the anti-kidnapping unit, the prosecutor Adrián de la Garza, and the mayor. They're all sitting there, and none of them are really searching. Only General Cuauhtémoc Antúñez Pérez, commander of the Seventh Military Zone, has stood by her side and worked for the same cause. A thought strikes her, and she turns her face away: after letters to the president, to Marisela Morales (head of the PGR), "It's just not possible that with five arrests, they haven't found my son . . . that with everything I've given them, they haven't been able to come up with anything, anything at all."

The tears roll. They fall and fall and never dry up. She still has hope. Her son is worth it, that quiet little guy, peaceful, responsible, educated, and enchanting. He had a lot yet to do and to give, half of his life in front of him. She will never give up. She'll never retire from this work.

"I believe that he's alive."

Interview with a Zeta

On the rough roads of her journey, during the respites and sleepless moments of that interminable night into which her life had been converted, Lety got together with a group of other mothers, fathers, and siblings of the disappeared. Together they've carried out various activities, and one day they decided to find a member of the Zetas Cartel willing to talk with them.

"He told us that he was working with them of his own volition and that in the whole strip of the border, including Reynosa, Matamoros, Nuevo León, Miguel Alemán, and in many, many pueblos and ranchos there are boys and girls, women, doing forced labor. They force the women into prostitution, and they have the men planting, harvesting, and packing drugs."

"How do they get around?" she asked. "Why are they never detected?"

The man explained with an account that sounded fantastic but which nobody ruled out: "There are tunnels, that's how they move around. They come and go, they are hidden and are whisked away, even carried on motorcycles."

He told them that the whole thing was organized and controlled, that they knew exactly who entered and exited, who asked too many questions, who they needed to check out, take out of there, or murder.

Embroidering her memories

Lety is an activist. The disappearance of her son took her to various plazas and street corners, offices, and sidewalks, where she had found many others with whom to share her grief. She was no longer alone. Some of them formed the organization Lucha por Amor ("Fight for Love"), known as Lupa, and later they added "Truth and Justice," and they work in conjunction with the United Forces for the Disappeared in Mexico, known as Fundem.

Lety says that one day he's going to return, and that she can't wait to see him come in, awake, and pay the toll of so many missed embraces, so much time without him, without her. "I will dedicate myself to this until I die. If I hear a noise, I do a double take. I wake up. I think 'it's him.' It could come any day. And if not, I'll keep searching."

Neither the time, nor the money, nor her age matters. None of it. They are mere trivialities in front of her hopes. The hands on the clock don't mark a looming death, but rather the ticking of hope. That's how she sees it. That's how she lives it and feels it. That's the beating of that heart of hers that doesn't want to retire, that hopes and searches, that fights and punches. And her hands, less tired and more enthusiastic than her eyes, keep her going: she takes a needle, holds up fabric, and embroiders handwritten letters, without a pen or ink. These letters are written patiently, with drops of blood, the missives of grandmothers and mothers who refuse to give in, who stitch and stitch, who don't want to be Penelopes but rather mothers with children, children who are present, not absent.

"Embroidery is a form of protest, of writing the story of our children. Of keeping ourselves alive . . . on a handkerchief."

"YOUR FAMILY IS WAITING FOR YOU"

On the blog *Our Apparent Surrender*, the family reported: "Roy Rivera Hidalgo. Personal description: He has a mole under his right eye, full eyebrows, a slim build. Height: 1.68 m and curly hair."

And there followed a tender and piercing monologue, enormous and sad, a desperate shout of one lost and alone in the desert, and at the same time an expression of healthy resignation, a missive written by Roy's mother, Lety Hidalgo. In it one can feel the immeasurable pain, the wounded hide, the severed soul.

The heading reads: "Letter to Roy Rivera Hidalgo, student in the School of Philosophy and Letters in the Language Sciences Major, of the Autonomous University of Nuevo León (UANL). Kidnapped and disappeared at eighteen."

I love you so much, my child.

My child: today I have to tell you, my boy, that since you've not been with us, everything has been a disaster.

Why I haven't died, I don't know, nobody knows, and many have asked themselves the same question, with the customary answer: "You are very strong. I would have died already."

When they ripped you out of my life, they left me with only half of my heart. How could someone live with only half a heart? Where are you, my child? When will you return? Why can't I find you?

Let me tell you that I am searching for you and that I know that you know that I'm searching for you, but alas, we're in Mexico and it's a disaster.

Since you've been gone, I always carry a photograph of you, so that for the last year and five months, I can see you, and I can believe that you can see me.

And every morning, afternoon, and night, I feel as if all of this were a dream, a bad dream, and I'm going to wake up and it won't be real. Please someone, wake me up!

Why weren't we rich or from high enough social or political class so that we would have been shielded and this wouldn't have happened?

My child! My child! I explain to everyone who were are, who you were. I tell them how your grandmother adored you and always took care of you [as a baby], and that if she could have prevented it, she wouldn't have even let the outside air touch you. That you were her pride and joy, that she misses you and is consumed with grief. I tell them that Richi is very lonely, that he secretly cries at night, so that no one can see, suffering in silence for your absence and that your father had to go to a psychiatrist in order to go on living.

I see your photographs, your books, your clothes, your room, and I want to believe that I can still smell you in there.

My child Roy, where are you?

I want to tell you as well that I've met many of your friends, boys and girls from school, who since the very first day have been involved in our lives, who haven't given up asking after you, who are still awaiting your return, and who have become your brothers and sisters, and although it sounds paradoxical, have expanded our family. Now I know Gabby, Gera, Elio, who recently admitted that it was your fault he turned back to God, and what's more that he's decided to enter a seminary, and all thanks to you, to your absence, for this tragedy.

We have also many other people who love you, the great majority of them young people, young people like you, who have continued to search, and who have helped me to shout and to ask for justice so that you might return. They help me to live, and their support gives me strength, it gives me hope.

Your friends from the block cry for you along with Richi. They painted a mural on the corner, ordering you: "BE STRONG, ROY!" On your birthday, many showed up there, and they lit candles, sending you the light that you'll need to find the road back home, where you belong.

I dream and dream about that day, they day in which you'll cross the threshold of our house, the day that you'll return for real, that you'll be a little changed, I know, that perhaps you won't be exactly the same. I know that maybe you'll have long hair, or be fatter or skinnier, I don't know what, but that your eyes will be the same, your beautiful eyes . . . and I ask God that he permit me to see them again, that we get to see each other again, that we can embrace and kiss.

I'd kiss your face, your head, your eyes, your soul, your heart, and never, never again would we part.

Oh, God! He's the only one who knows what I dream and whether my dreams will come true and we'll see each other again.

Can I tell you something else, my child?

I've also met God (as Elio says, on your account). Aye, my child! If you could see how different he is, if you could only see how much I wish you could also come to know him.

He's not the same as I had taught you, the one to whom we prayed when you were small. Sure, he looks the same, but he's not the same.

This God, who I know today, in whom I have taken refuge, he speaks to me, he teaches me, he gives me light, and he has taken me in his hands to sustain me and to sustain you.

In reality, he sustains the whole family, your family, your uncles, your aunts, your cousins, your grandparents, and he's brought us together even more in his love. Ah, my child! How much I long to introduce you to him. . . .

I tell him about you, and, you know what? I've told him that he couldn't have chosen a better child than you for me and all of us to turn to him and recognize him, and for us to confide in him, to hope and believe in him.

Thanks to that, I'm sure that you're not here with us because God has a plan for our lives, and as I read once, they ripped you from my side but never from my heart, never from my memory.

See you soon, my child. I'm not saying good-bye, since you're always with me, but simply that I'll see you later, see you soon, see you very soon, the next time I grab the pen to write to you. Maybe when that happens, you'll be here, and the letter will be very different than this one.

I miss you, my child, I miss you a lot: your smile, your voice, your eyes, our serious chats, deep ones, full of smiles, plans, projects, illusions. I love you with all of my heart, my child.

I love you very, very much.

Your Mama,

Lety Hidalgo

CHAPTER 3

In the Assassin's Shoes

A GOOD DAY TO DIE

El G started out a son of a bitch. He had everything he needed at home, and he didn't start out as an errand boy or a lookout, what in other places they call a *halcón* ("falcon"), or selling drugs on the street. He went directly to hit man, to killing people, and from there on up. He was nineteen when a friend of his told him that if he wanted to work for the *narcos*, they would pay him five thousand pesos a week. He answered without thinking about it: it was what he wanted, having weapons, pulling the trigger and feeling the kick, palming the roll of bills, and being a *bato pesado* ("heavy dude"). He wanted to be "heavy" and to carry himself that way.

He received his first training from Sidarta Walkinshaw, commander of the State Ministerial Police (PME) assigned to the municipality of Navolato. Those were the days in which the Sinaloa and Juárez Cartels were part of a common organization. They kept their businesses separate, but they understood that to maintain this relationship, they had to share routes, roads, and backyards.

The first casualty

Apparently, Sidarta was one of the favored sons of Jesús Antonio "Chuytoño" Aguilar Íñiguez, then director of the PME, who had called him in for a meeting. Aguilar Íñiguez had been pursued by the Special Prosecutor for Organized Crime (SIEDO) for his supposed ties to drug trafficking but ultimately exonerated. He returned to the directorship of the PME in 2011, with the arrival of the new government of Mario López Valdez and its mandate for "change."

Through the halls of the department and the criminal underworld it was rumored that Sidarta could become the new chief of the PME command post in Navolato. Even more serious, it was rumored that Rodofo Carrillo, one of the youngest brothers of Amado Carrillo Fuentes, founding boss of the Juárez Cartel, was going to be assassinated. The order had already been given.

But Sidarta was an idealist. He liked to do things well, and he was a career police officer, among the most prepared and best trained within the department. And this cast doubt on whether or not he could handle the new responsibility, and whether he was going to serve the interests of the criminal organization, of those who had power inside and outside of the government, on the margins of acronyms and institutions.

According to unofficial accounts, the Carrillo family had made an offer to Sidarta to work for them. He did not take it. The looming dispute between the two criminal organizations was being forged in the dark rooms and basements of power. The fall of Rodolfo, El Hijo del Oro ("the Golden Son"), marked the schism and the point of no return between the two cartels.

The death of Rodolfo Carrillo Fuentes was planned. On September 11, 2004, armed men waited for him to leave a movie theater, where he was attacked with AK-47s while trying to get into his car with his wife Giovana Quevedo and their two small children. The couple died minutes later, along with a parking attendant. The children survived. Their escorts, directed by the commander and investigations chief of the State Ministerial Police, Pedro Pérez López, tried to repel the attack, engaging in a prolonged firefight, but they were not successful.

In the wake of the September 11 incident, the SIEDO opened an investigation of the director of the PME, Jesús Antonio Aguilar Íñiguez, and eight other police bosses, for providing security to the drug cartels, specifically to the Sinaloa Cartel.

Aguilar Íñiguez was absolved years later, but Pérez López and Guadalupe González Posadas were detained in the prison in Puente Grande, Jalisco.

"What the Carrillo family told Sidarta was, 'You come to work for us or we'll kill you,' but we understand that he did not accept," confided a person close to the investigation.

Sidarta was called to a meeting in the central office of the PME, in Culiacán, located on Zapata Boulevard, only three blocks from the main offices of the state government. But apparently he sniffed them out. He knew that they had been ordered to dismiss him. So he spoke with members of the Carrillo Fuentes family first, in the municipality of Navolato, and he told them that he would accept the offer to work for them. But he didn't go through with it. He couldn't. Immediately after leaving the meeting with Aguilar Íñiguez (where he was dismissed), Sidarta was gunned down.

News reports indicate that five armed persons intercepted the truck in which Sidarta Alfredo Walkinshaw was traveling, and they shot him until he was dead. The triggermen traveled in two luxury trucks. In order to kill this policeman, considered one of the best investigative agents at the national level, they fired at least 116 rounds with AK-47 and AR-15 assault rifles.

The fuse

Almost from the beginning, El G had at least ten gunmen under his command. Almost all of them were older than him, and some of them were ex-cops and ex-soldiers. Before unleashing him in Sinaloa, they sent him to Tamaulipas to continue his training in the mountains. Later he returned to Navolato and to Culiacán.

The confrontations were sculpting his character. It wasn't mallets or hammers or chisels, but rather gray projectiles, lead cylinders with fine points, that were knocking out of his personality whatever could be spared or didn't serve their purposes, until they made of him a faithful young man, a hunting dog, loyal to his people and what they thought, an icon and shadow of whatever they proposed, whatever job was entrusted to him by the bosses.

He was in many battles whose true toll only the bosses know. When the Carrillo family ordered him, he went with various men armed with automatic weapons and grenades and tossed at least two explosive devices at the central offices of the daily paper *El Debate*, located on Francisco I. Madero Boulevard in downtown Culiacán.

News reports indicate that two people threw fragmentation grenades at the newspaper building, which led to the destruction of a glass door, the floor, and some walls. None of the staff were wounded. The bombing took place at about one in the morning, on November 17, 2008. The bombers, dressed in white shirts, fled on foot, toward Riva Palacio Avenue.

The next day, when he read the papers—an activity he carried out every morning, by way of the Internet: *El blog del narco, Línea Directa, Ríodoce,* and others—he saw accounts of the attack. He smiled. He fondled the piece of steel that hung from the thick gold chain around his neck; it was the pin from the grenade that it was his turn to toss. And he sure let them have it.

Clear out!

If something was going down in some part of the city, El G would call his brothers and people close to him who are not involved in crime in order to warn them. "Clear out! Clear out of here, for fuck's sake!" This was his way of saving them.

Among the confrontations and murders that he went ahead with, in which he was a principal protagonist, was the one that began in the Plaza Forum, a shopping mall located in a very wealthy section of the city, known as Tres Ríos, which extended four or five kilometers beyond there. The bullets, the perforated vehicles, and the dead were scattered across several neighborhoods: Las Quintas, La Campiña (in front of La Comercial Mexicana, a popular supermarket), in the center of the city, and in the Villa Universitaria.

The ambush had been prepared by the Carrillo Fuentes family, and the majority of the dead were from the Sinaloa Cartel, despite the arrival of a wave of their own reinforcements. It began about 3:10 P.M. on December 9, 2008. Among the dead was José Alfredo Álvarez Núñez, known as El Gallero ("Cock Fighter"), a native of La Cruz, Elota.

Levantón *I*

The order was to go get him and torture him until he was dead. It came from on high. Where did he come from, the man who was going to be taken? He was the accountant for one of the cells of the Juárez Cartel in Sinaloa. The man had no idea what he was up against—until the last dim light in those brown eyes went out for good.

It happened just how they had told them. The man was found brutally murdered: the lesser wounds were those caused by the bullets. The discovery was made at an uninhabited spot near the community of Villa Juárez, in the municipality of Navolato.

The plunder from the accountant's machinations reached several million dollars.

Ley del Valle

"I know that you're taking a break." It was the voice of Vicente Carrillo Fuentes, the leader of the Juárez Cartel and heir apparent of Amado, Lord of the Skies, his older brother. "There are problems." El G was at his family home in the Sinaloan capital. He had asked for the day off, and they had given it to him. And, now, just as easily, they took it away. "That time, *El Señor* Vicente calls you and tells you, asks you, orders you to protect his mom, and then warns you, 'Too bad for you if anything happens to her, because you won't see your own family again.' And so El G got into his car and went through his ritual of returning to work in Navolato, the same he followed when he returned to Culiacán," recounted a close relative of the gunman.

El G was prudent. So much so that he appeared to be an assassin right out of the movies, James Bond of the *narcos*, a rock-solid private detective, a well-thought-of horse thief from the old West, a movie actor in films full of suspense and bullets. He left a car in the parking lot of a supermarket called Ley del Valle, located at the western edge of the city, right where the highways to Navolato and Eldorado intersect. There he kept a stash of clothes and weapons, disguises for coming and going, weapons for any occasion, a macabre inventory and a ritual nod to the lady in black. And from there, in another car, he left for work.

On this occasion, Vicente Carrillo warned him that a commando sent by the bosses of the Sinaloa Cartel was headed for Navolato. The convoy had been baptized the day before in the mass media as "the caravan of death." Each vehicle that took part in this criminal operation was marked with large white painted X's, so that it would stick out even in darkness or in the middle of a firefight. The toll from this criminal action would be several dead, some of them relatives of Aurora Carrillo Fuentes, Amado and Vicente's mother, whose ranch is located in the community of Guamuchilito, just north of Navolato in the same municipality.

Doña Aurora was evacuated by gunmen under El G's command. She was transferred out of the back of her walled residence in that community, through the surrounding towns, up into the hills to Cofradía.[1] That's why the caravan of death didn't reach her.

The exchange of hostages

On November 10, 2010, an armed group entered the home of El G's parents. A lifelong friend, a man he'd known since they were small children, betrayed him and handed over his father. Well-informed sources claim that in exchange this friend received some drugs and a wad of bills that added up to nearly twenty thousand pesos.

"This was a lot of courage they were showing, because El G had done several similar hits, including killing the family members of people close to El Fantasma, one of the most powerful gunmen in the Sinaloa Cartel, and he had caught them off guard several times, forcefully, with bullets, and thus they must have been looking for it," explained a relative of the *sicario*.

El Fantasma was Jonathan Salas Avilés a triggerman in the service of Joaquín Guzmán Loera, El Chapo, boss of the Sinaloa Cartel. His death was rumored at the beginning of 2012, during a supposed encounter near Quilá, within the municipality of Culiacán, with personnel from the navy, whose helicopter fired upon several trucks, some of them with armored windows. One of them exploded in the middle of the shooting. Apparently Jonathan was in that one, but this has not been confirmed.

El G knew about it: the kidnapping of his father (whose identity is withheld) was a response to the illegal detention of one person and the killing of another, in the Barrancos neighborhood, on the south side of the city, between seven and eight o'clock the evening before.

Two weeks earlier, El G had spoken with one of his cousins, the one he was closest with. He told his cousin that he had to see him, and they met up in the parking lot of Ley del Valle. He gave his cousin a hug and a pistol, because "it could be offered," and El G went on to explain that he had to defend himself, because he didn't know what was going to happen after the fracturing of the Sinaloa Cartel—with the detention of Alfredo Beltrán Leyva, El Mochomo, in February 2008 by the Mexican army. In the state capital the story went around that he had been "handed over," which split the organization and provoked the departure of (and confrontation with) two of its principal operators: the Beltrán Leyva brothers. Moreover, El G told his cousin that as a result he was looking for a safe house, in another place, in which to put his parents and siblings. He also gave his cousin a cell phone, Unefon brand, with a direct line between them (two-way radio).

That day his cousin was at home. He was about to leave for El G's parents' house when he opened a drawer and looked at the weapon. It was a forty-five. He took it out and put it in his back waistband. His wife saw it and questioned him. He answered that he was going to go and get El G's parents, and that he didn't want to know anything else. At that moment the Unefon rang. "*Cabrón*, they went into the house and they took my dad, and now they're coming for you. Clear out and head for Ley del Valle. I'll see you there." When the cousin and his wife got there, El G asked who was with him and he answered that it was his wife. El G ordered him to leave her there and to go alone, because it was very dangerous.

The husband and wife were arguing about this when a white Jetta pulled alongside. One of the occupants, a man with a very young face, had a weapon in his hand. He told them to get out. When the man walked around the car to get in, the lights of a car that had pulled up behind them distracted him, and he turned his head away for a split second.

"They didn't think that I carried a weapon, because I was calm, and they knew that I was not involved. But I couldn't let the opportunity of this distraction slip by, and I took the weapon from the back of my pants and I shot. The guy who was getting into the passenger's seat went down, and the others returned fire, and I kept shooting, until we had gotten out of there. The only thing that occurred to me was to get the children and flee. And that's what I did," he remembered.

Between eleven and twelve o'clock that night, the Unefon rang again. El G asked his cousin how it had turned out, and he answered that it had gone well. El G cut in: "You rolled the dice, *cabrón*." He knew that his cousin had taken out the weapon and fired and perhaps killed one of the gunmen sent after him.

A young army deserter who served as El G's guard dog had informed him. This ex-soldier carried a device that fit into a large military-style backpack, and it scanned all kinds of signals and communications frequencies from the various police departments and the army. That's how El G had learned of his cousin's feat.

"You pulled it off, *carnal* ['buddy']."

He explained to his cousin that the abductors had returned his father. El G had barely had time to respond to those who had taken his father, before he would have been killed, and he turned over three men, one of them a close relative of El Fantasma, in exchange.

The old man had been handcuffed, his neck had been burned with cigarettes, and there were bruises all over his body. El G's cousin remarked on his uncle's courage, saying that he himself wouldn't have been able to withstand the beating.

Free agent

After these clashes, El G declared himself a free agent. I'll go with whomever I want, he explained, those close to him recount, with a smile that portrayed him as he was: a charismatic young man, determined, sure of himself, and handsome to boot, a magnet for women.

Accounts from the underworld claim that the bosses of the Beltrán Leyva and Juárez Cartels fought over him. But El G, of his own accord, decided to do some work in Tamaulipas instead, and he stayed there for nearly three months. In a meeting where his cousin was present, a short time later, he told his family that he was weary of the life and that he'd had enough of it: "I am tired of this scrap of a life [*chira de vida*] that I've got," he used to say in that period in his life. And that was when he was only twenty-something, on his frenetic and sinuous path.

I get out in order to shoot

El G's philosophy: "I get out in order to shoot, to kill, not for them to hit me, because if you get out of the truck with fear, they're going to give you a bullet."

"He believed strongly in the thing about negative energy, about attitude," his cousin explained. "[El G] used to say 'if you go around with slumped shoulders, your life will be a fiasco. If you go around with your head held high, and your chest out, your life will be happiness.' And that's how he lived: happy, unencumbered, with his AK-47 rifle, a Norinco special edition model, with a short stock and a loader, or if it was down or not at the ready, his forty-caliber pistol and a grenade in the fanny pack."

A technical defect

El G was famous for being a whiz and a daredevil. He was bold and audacious. That's why Alfredo Beltrán Leyva, El Barbas ("The Beard"), boss of the Beltrán Leyva Cartel, sought him out. A person close to El G claims that he was there when Beltrán Leyva rented out the entire top floor of a hotel in Mexico City, on that fateful day when the plane carrying Juan Camilo Mouriño, the interior minister, fell out of the sky, in the second half of the administration of President Felipe Calderón.

"A *bato* from the United States came, and he brought a special device. It looked like an antenna, some kind of modern device. And he also brought a rocket launcher . . . in case the other thing failed. All of this about technical failures was true, but it was provoked by El Barbas, because they made the plane crash with that device."

The interior minister died on November 4, 2008, when the Learjet model 2000 in which he was traveling crashed into a neighborhood near Paseo de la Reforma in Mexico City. This official, one of the men closest to President Calderón, was coming back from a working tour where he had announced the signing of the "Agreement for Legality and Justice" in San Luis Potosí. Since the turbines and fuselage were in good condition, it was presumed to be an accident (rather than a bomb). In San Luis Potosí, the airplane was guarded by units of the Estado Mayor Presidencial, a special detachment of the general staff of the armed forces, but mechanical difficulties had shown up earlier.

Failed massacres

The night of November 5, 2008, on the highway from Altata to Navolato, the convoy of public servants advanced toward the city of Navolato, which is the municipal seat. The mayor, Fernando García, was part of the retinue, after having eaten and socialized on the bay in Altata. Suddenly the parade of trucks was blocked by another convoy, one made up of armed men who began to fire indiscriminately using AK-47 and AR-15 assault rifles.

Few survived, among them the mayor, who was injured but not gravely. When the killers went through the trucks and bodies to make sure that they didn't leave any loose ends, they saw the mayor, shot and apparently dead, and thus they left.

Two city councilmen died, César Villaescusa Gastélum and Jesús Andrés Carrillo Ramírez, along with a former mayoral candidate, César Villaescusa Urquiza, and the son of one of the councilmen.

"The people from the Juárez Cartel alleged that the mayor was taking money from Joaquín Guzmán Loera, El Chapo. That's why the order went out to kill him, and El G was mixed up in this, but he was pissed off when the next day he read in the newspapers that he had survived . . . 'that asshole was saved,' he said when he read it. 'And now it's going to be a bitch to kill him, because he's going to have a fuckload of security.' And so it was," reflected El G's cousin. Afterward, the gunmen headed for the esplanade along the riverfront in Navolato. Many young people milled around, but El G and his people were only interested in two or three of them, who were allegedly robbing cars along the coast highway (without permission from them). The triggermen arrived and located the men they were going to kill, but there were many people gathered around. They shouted at the other young people, among them several girls, that they had better clear out. But some of them stayed, declaring that the *sicarios* wouldn't dare do anything to them, right up until the gunmen gave up and opened fire.

The toll that Saturday, August 29, 2009, was eight people killed, among them two women and two minors, and four wounded. The victims lay side by side along Las Palmas Avenue, in the neighborhood of La Primavera. They were identified as Dalia, sixteen years old; Marisol Moreno Verástica, twenty; Rigoberto Niebla Benítez, eighteen; José Manuel, sixteen; Jordan Erick, fifteen; and Óscar Manuel and Cirilo López Obeso, thirty-two and thirty-six, respectively—the two on whom the attack was apparently directed.

Levantón *II*

They brought a man into the truck. They hit him again and again, and he didn't speak. They took him to a closed-off area somewhere, and they continued to torture him there. They got no results. They told him that they didn't want to kill him but that if he didn't talk, they were going to have to get his wife and children. The result was the same.

"He went so far as to put out his hands when they announced that they were going to yank out his fingernails. And they began to do it, and the *bato* insisted that he wasn't going to talk, that they could do whatever they wanted to him. He pissed himself, he cried, he vomited. But he didn't talk. El G finally said, 'Well, whatever. Go get his wife and his children. He doesn't leave us any other option, this *güey*,'" El G's cousin recounted.

A little while later, his wife was in front of him. Then, yes, after so much insistence, he let it all out, "even the name of the guy's dog." They let his wife go, but not him.

Levantón *III*

The order was to get the *bato*, torture him, and then kill him. It was easy to find him, in the streets of a small city that doesn't have many dark corners that aren't safe houses, many of them in the hands of the Carrillo Fuentes Cartel. They found him and loaded him into the truck. They had started to hit him, along the way to where they would keep him captive, when he passed out.

They tried to revive him, but they didn't know what to do. In a matter of two minutes, after several clumsy efforts to assist him, they realized that the man had died, apparently from a heart attack. Annoyed and frustrated, they tossed him on the sidewalk in front of his house.

"El G said: 'Motherfucker, we had a fuckload of plans for that *cabrón*. Whatever.' And they tossed him out," declared El G's cousin.

Hunting

One of their gunmen had been killed in Los Mochis, the municipal seat of Ahome, about two hundred kilometers (124 miles) north of Culiacán. That city gave birth to, raised, multiplied, and strengthened one of the most important cells of the Beltrán Leyva Cartel. When things got ugly there, they guy who intervened was Alfredo, El Mochomo. And then, with the control he had over the cops, the street dealers, the public officials and functionaries, everything returned to normal.

That's why this city, and later Guasave, fifty kilometers from Los Mochis, was theirs and nobody else's. But this iron control started to crack when the Sinaloa Cartel split and the Beltrán guys left and skirmishes started to break out between them and Joaquín Guzmán Loera, El Chapo. The municipal police were with the Beltráns, but not the PME or the army, who operated on behalf of the Chapos, as Guzmán's followers were called.

One of the operations in Los Mochis came out of this. They detained two and killed one. They carried the detained in a caravan toward Culiacán. The Mochomos wanted to negotiate. They spoke by telephone with a commander nicknamed El Lince ("The Lynx"), who was the front man for the organization in the PME: they asked him to hand over the detained men and several wads of cash, or there would be a bunch of fighting and killing. The police official declined. There were already four patrols carrying recently apprehended men, taken from the Beltráns, and he thought that they had enough cops, weapons, and ammunition to put up a good battle. But he didn't count on the fact that they weren't going to get the chance to put up a front: Los Mochomos fell upon them before they ever realized it, hunting them down when they passed by the community of Guayparime, in Guasave. In the attack, six members of the Elite Group, an anti-narcotics SWAT team, were killed, and six more were wounded, along with one civilian, who later died. Some of the agents managed to escape, but they were pursued and riddled with bullets again near an overpass, where another agent lost his life. The ambush took place on Sunday, March 6, 2011.

The names of the dead personnel are José de Jesús Rufino Parra, Carlos Humberto Villegas Favela, Félix Ramírez Osuna, Ernesto Félix Rubio, Óscar de Jesús García, Martín Juvenal Vázquez Gutiérrez, and Raymundo Torres Díaz.

Commander José Luis Ibarra Velázquez—El Lince, the PME investigations coordinator—was shot to death with his brother in February 2012, in a parking lot at the corner of Ángel Flores and Corona Streets in downtown Culiacán.[2]

It's about to get good

Giovanni was detained by the Ministerial Police in May 2011. He was one of the most wanted criminals and the boss of the *plaza* (drug trafficking territory) in the city of Los Mochis, for the so-called Mochomos, who were by that time a mix of people from the Beltrán Leyva and Carrillo Fuentes organizations, even though some accounts of the group include people from the Zetas.

"Hold on, it's about to get good," El G told his cousin. He confided that this detention, which apparently had been the result of a "fingering" (a tip from an informant), meant that *he* would become the main boss of the city. And he was happy about it. He was no longer a killer in front of an army of ten or fifteen *sicarios*. He was going to be the boss, the biggest boss.

But, El G's cousin explains, "the army guys located him [El G], it would appear, because El Chapo's people found him and they went with the soldiers. They were going to kill him, because the head of the Mochomos, El Chapo Isidro (Isidro Meza Flores) was also there. In the firefight, which took place in the community of El Huicho, in the municipality of Guasave, El G's leg was wounded. This had never happened to him before. That's when he told his boss and the other gunmen to get out of there and to leave him to battle with the soldiers. And that's what they did."

He left when he wanted

He was generous, even in his own death and with that of others. Each of his gunmen who was killed was buried "with honors": El G paid for the funeral service and continued to send the widow and children money. And he never stopped doing this.

He said that he would die when he wanted. He would decide. He cited the scene from the movie *Troy* when Achilles says that when he dies, he will be remembered for the battles he fought. He was the same. He wanted to be remembered for the lead he shot and that they shot at him, here and there, in and around Navolato or Guasave or Los Mochis, in Tamaulipas or Culiacán.

After taking a rest, he returned. One of his bosses told him, 'I am sending you some armored trucks so that you'll come back,' and he went. His siblings and close relatives tried to convince him otherwise. He left them as if overcome by a blast of frigid air, when he announced that it was stupid to continue on quietly, that he hadn't killed anyone in two weeks, and "it was unbearable."

He was an idealist. He decided to die upright. *I'm hobbled by this wounded leg*, he thought, *but not overcome, never.* "They're not going to detain me or throw me in jail; nobody's going to torture me, and I'm not going to die tied up," he used to say.

And that afternoon, amid the *carne asada*, the shots of Jack Daniels that he liked so much (even in this he was a contrarian—the Chapos prefer Buchanan's, which is much smoother and more expensive), the hits of marijuana, and the Pacíficos, he told his clique: "What a beautiful day it is, a good day to die."

It was the third time he'd returned to crime—and the last one. But it was because he wanted it that way; he had said it. The .223 caliber bullets picked him out, fired by soldiers who, on that occasion, according to unofficial sources, were accompanied by *sicarios* from the Sinaloa Cartel.

He came to the rescue of his boss, and he succeeded. He arrived on the scene of the bloody confrontation like the star of an action movie, busting through a gate in his level-seven armored truck, and firing everything he had. He brought a .50 caliber Barrett M60, capable of piercing inch-thick steel armor, and fragmentation grenades. He threw at least two of them, but they didn't go off right away. "He [had] played with them . . . and altered them so that they would go off moments later, when the soldiers, confident they were duds, would return to the scene," related a family member who knew about the firefight.

They shouted at him: "Surrender! We're going to put you with some people from Culiacán, who are waiting for you." He answered, "No way, you're not going to kill me while I'm tied up. You're not going to carry me off. To the fucking end, you fucking little soldiers [*pinches sarditos*]."[3] And the assault rifles kicked in.

According to information put out by the military command, which was the published news, several soldiers were wounded and one person killed: him, El G. "Unfortunately, it was our turn today, as well," related General Moisés García Melo, commander of the Ninth Military Zone, on that June 26, 2011, referring to the two wounded soldiers who went sent to area hospitals. But other accounts claim that a larger number of soldiers fell wounded, at least ten of them.

"I'm not going to jail, cousin." And he did not go.

THE APPRENTICE

It looked like they were going to train Julio. That time he went with some others, and they told him that the orders from the boss were to "go get a *bato* and make him pay with his life." That's what his friend told him, the guy with a direct line to the boss, the guy who gets the instructions for the new "hacks" who must be put through the paces. Weeks had passed, and the kid, the one who'd been fingered, didn't want to pay up. He'd put it off until they came looking for him and it was time to settle accounts.

Julio was excited, and he swallowed hard. He was sixteen years old and his palm itched on his right hand. He was anxious to grasp the butt of the Beretta, to slide in the magazine, click off the safety, pull a round in the chamber, and squeeze the trigger. *Pum, pum, pum.* He had good parents, and he wasn't a bad person, it was just that he had some friends, neighbors, influences who stretched out those fateful city nights. All of it at the head of a bullet, peppered with blood.

Behind that always-smiling face, the twinkling of nobility and solidarity, there was a budding killer. A devil was at work inside of him, an assassin dressed as him in order to appear decent. A bad seed that peeked out and smiled with Julio's mouth, full of malice. From then on it wasn't nobility shining through, but rather the devil he carried inside.

"I asked the other killer, 'And what'd this *güey* do?'" Julio remembered. The other gunman explained that part of the cocaine they gave the guy to sell had gone up his nose, and now he'd have to pay for it.

"They told me that the *cabrón* had been around here, going from party to party, with a fuckload of girls, not giving a fuck about anything. That's what this *bato* tells me. And then they said, let's go, and I answered, 'All right already; let's go to the promenade.' We went in the store and located him quickly. There were four of us. We took him by the arms, and, shoving and punching him in the abdomen, we got the *bato* under control. We shoved him into the truck. We laid him face down on the floor in front of the back seat," Julio declared.

"Three of the guys stepped on his body. A kick for each time he opened his mouth to say, 'I'm not him, you've got me confused with someone else.' They'd told him to shut his hole, and every time he moved, he received a rifle butt. They did him in with the third one. They used the butts of the AK-47s they held by their legs."

Julio took the opportunity to enjoy the flow of adrenaline, his power and that of his companions—he had dished out some of those blows to the guy's abdomen and back. He was new in this clique, with its spotters or *halcons*, its *sicarios*. He needed to carry out the *patrón*'s orders. But he had never come across a case like this one.

The unemployed

Upon shifting its operations in the trafficking of drugs, weapons, and money to other regions of the state and the country, the Sinaloa Cartel

generated unemployment and underemployment among the young people of Culiacán. These young pistoleros, trained in the use of weapons,
addicted to death and to drugs, are dangerous to a superlative degree.

With legitimate work paying less than what they received when they were
involved with drug trafficking, despite its irregular paydays, young people
have opted for robbery, assault, and illicit businesses on their own.

The toll continues to be disastrous and bloody. Many of them end
up being sacrificed by the same criminal groups to which they once
belonged, killed or incarcerated. Now these armed and trained young
people, with access to safe houses where they keep *fierros* ("irons")—
firearms—and ammunition, steal vehicles and rent themselves out to the
highest bidder as *sicarios*.

But they don't leave Culiacán, and they don't leave the business. The
narco cell might not come looking for them to do a job all that often, but
they know that if they inch outside of the business ever so slightly, they
could be identified as enemies or snitches, or as loose links, armed and
dangerous, with information about contacts, names, addresses. They're
quarrelsome and undisciplined thanks to the use of drugs and they're
often disgruntled for having been displaced. And thus, they should be
eliminated. They should be killed.

Trimming the personnel

One of these cells, which operates for the Sinaloa Cartel in the western
sector of Culiacán, was made up of twenty young pistoleros. Some of
them, at least half of them, were under eighteen. Changes in the internal
structure of the drug trade meant that only five of them were going to
remain on the payroll, getting a regular cut from the organization. The
rest were incorporated on an ad hoc basis, when they were needed for a
particular operation.

"Those guys rent themselves out as *sicarios*. That is, they no longer
work for anyone in particular, but rather whoever will pay them. And
when there isn't any work, they go around assaulting and robbing,"
explained a person who's part of an organized crime family.

"The war isn't here," he said. The battles with opposing cartels are outside of Culiacán, in Mazatlán, Guasave, Los Mochis or outside of the state

entirely. Other regions in the state require special attention thanks to the presence of other criminal organizations, like the Beltrán Leyvas in the municipalities of El Fuerte and Ahome, to the north of the city. Personnel, operators, and *sicarios* are also sent to other states—Tamaulipas, Coahuila, Nuevo León, and Veracruz. This has meant that the capo or boss has gotten rid of triggermen, because he hasn't needed them.

Others among these groups have reduced payroll—they had nine and now they've only got four, for example, and those are the closest, the most trusted, those who cling closest to the boss, especially when he's in the city.

"The people are addicted to killing, and if they're not killing because someone's paying them or because they've got outstanding contracts, they're capable of inventing any kind of pretext, a dispute in the street, the stupidest little thing, and they go after the guy and kill him. Just like that," an organized crime source reflected.

The guys in "the troop," the lowest rung in the structure of the cell, who act as killers, receive around five hundred dollars every two weeks, but it can be as high as eighteen hundred, depending on the case. Others, of a higher rank, who are closer to the boss, earn two or three thousand every two weeks, which could go as high as ten or twenty thousand if they take on a special job.

The same organized crime source explained, "In general they are disciplined young people, who are waiting to get called for a job, who assume that they're going to have to kill, and that they're going to die soon. They don't last more than two or three years."

The neighborhood police

The same little *narcos* come for the assailants and petty thieves in the neighborhood. "If they learn that other guys are knocking over the store, the pharmacy, or the tortilla shop, or affecting the people in the neighborhood where they live, and which they supposedly control, they come for them," the source explained.

"Their boss, an informant revealed, isn't aware of everything that his pistoleros or ex-*sicarios* do, but if he learns that they've done something, he brings it to their attention or punishes them. In other cases [he] can terminate them, but this depends on the closeness, trust, or power that [he has over his] subordinates."

"These guys don't get involved in *broncas* very easily. They know what they're doing. They carry themselves calmly. But, it's the truth, they are the neighborhood police," declared another informant with years in the business.

Some changes

Among the tasks carried out by the organizations that make up the Sinaloa Cartel, both the groups who operate at the behest of Joaquín Guzmán Loera, El Chapo, and for Ismael Zambada García, El Mayo, are the purchase and transport of gold instead of cash. Using gold is a financial maneuver to evade customs, police checkpoints, domestic banks, or general government surveillance, and, of course, the payoffs each involves (because gold is much more compact than paper money and can be formed into a variety of innocuous items to evade detection). This has yielded lower costs and a reduction in the employment of people who carried out these operations.

Another change is the handover of cash, generally dollars, at "currency exchanges," informal businesses that buy and sell greenbacks, such that they appear, as if by magic, in some other country the next day without any problem or risk.

The mafia doesn't pay

"The mafia isn't paying anything. I don't know if it's because there's no money or because they want to play us for *pendejos*, but for the *plebes* [young people] it's enough if they get a car and an ID badge, the password to get out of any kind of *broncas*, and with that they're happy. . . . Money, they get it when they really need it," indicated a teenager who's intent upon leaving *la maña* ("the criminal life").[4]

His friends, boys between sixteen and seventeen, have committed murders and taken part in kidnappings. They'll often go for two or three weeks without getting paid. They've dedicated themselves to assaults and robberies, and they have confronted the police and the Mexican army.

They run on luck. They're close to powerful people, and they know how to get out of *broncas*, but they could also be handed over to the government or other bosses thanks to a lack of discipline on their part, and it could end with a bullet in the head.

The ones who know, who are in the operations of the drug trade up to the hilt, introduced him to everything: from marijuana to cocaine, everything but heroin, "because it's very rough."

Recently a group of about ten young guys was sent to Tamaulipas, to fight against the Zetas. It was the middle of June. The Culichis each received ten thousand pesos and a car—stolen, like those of all of those who are dedicated to this business—which they could choose. There they clashed with a cell from another organization, and they were subdued after a firefight. One was killed and the rest captured. They managed to escape with their lives, because it wasn't the Zetas, after all, but rather another group affiliated with the Sinaloa Cartel. They were located, and somebody "heavy" from Culiacán vouched for them and ordered them released. They had been tortured savagely, and they'd been lined up, one step, mere centimeters, from being executed.

From *pusher to* sicario

El Zurdo ("Southpaw"), as we'll call the young pistolero, began as a pusher, as a retail drug dealer, and over time, after earning the confidence of the boss, he rose to the rank of pistolero. He made five thousand pesos every two weeks when he sold drugs. Now he gets more, and they give him late-model vehicles to move around in. All of this at just sixteen and a half. And he has been part of "the clique" for barely two years. Now he's the front man for a cell of killers.

El Zurdo has taken part in confrontations with other criminal organizations, auto thefts ordered by the boss, *levantones* of debtors and snitches, and, of course, homicides. He knows about safe houses and everything you need to avoid confronting soldiers and how to negotiate with the authorities when the conditions demand.

Others serve as lookouts, falcons, who are located strategically on street corners and elsewhere in order to monitor the movements of people, who might be enemies or members of the police or the army, and pass the information along. Lookouts work for twenty-four hours at a time and then take a day off to rest. They often go two or three weeks without receiving the ten thousand pesos that they earn each pay period. When too much times goes by without pay, they have to look for other options, "because they can't stand it, and they get involved in some business selling drugs or cars, . . . they don't like hanging out with their friends or chasing *morras* ("girls") without having drugs and money to blow."

A bank robbery

Some young lookouts and killers decided to carry out a robbery. Three weeks without income had them chomping at the bit. They were part of a cell of seven, but only three of them were in on the robbery, the seventy-eighth to take place in Sinaloa from January to the middle of June that year. The take was trifling but sufficient to lighten their load, about twenty-two thousand pesos, according to the report handed over by the State Ministerial Police.

The robbery at the Bancoppel branch, located in the Plaza del Río in the capital city, turned into a hot pursuit and confrontation with officers from the municipal police of Culiacán and the PME. The criminals used two vehicles and traded shots with the uniformed men. The skirmish covered more than twelve blocks, to the Colonia Antonio Rosales, where the three got out and fled on foot. One of them was apprehended, identified as Carlos Eduardo Ochoa Quiroz, thirty-one years old, but it later turned out that this wasn't his real name.

Car thieves

They brought Raúl from the northern border of the country so that he could be incorporated into the workforce of the *narco* in Culiacán. A few weeks later, a commando left him in the entrance to a hospital located on Madero Boulevard. The young man, who was twenty-four, had bullet wounds. Inside he died in surgery.

The victim had had a serious addiction problem. He never backed off the cocaine and ice. The guys in "the clique" would see him and give a crafty smile. Each time he had a different vehicle, and while they weren't necessarily new, they were always in good condition and never very old. When they asked him, he explained that whenever he felt like it or when other criminals asked him, he would head up to Navolato and steal a car.

When they killed him, somebody who knew him asked how it had been possible, since he was in good with them. They answered that all of the stolen cars had created a big mess, and the bosses, who weren't the ones who asked him to steal particular cars, had become aware of it. It was a business on his own account, not theirs, and had "gotten out of hand." That's why they killed him.

From punishment to punishment

In a robbery, a young female student was beaten by criminals, *narcos* from an area near her school. They hadn't been getting any income, and they were getting desperate. They hurt her despite the fact that she was taking off a gold chain in order to give it to them.

Others nearby, who were also part of *la maña* ("the life"), heard about it and thought it was an abuse. That's why they blocked the robbers later on. They were going to take them to "the office," a safe house they had nearby, in Culiacán. And that's where the robbers were when they were rescued. A cell phone call and the assailants' bosses were informed. They were people from Gonzalo Inzunza, El Macho Prieto, one of the principal operators of the Sinaloa Cartel, that's why they let them go. El Macho Prieto—El MP—is known for his exemplary punishment for any lack of discipline. Nothing more is known of those guys, the robbers.

"In this, the punishments go from being 'frozen out,' so that they don't give you work, or 'locked in,' which is worse. Also, they might send you to work on the ranch, which is also very bad, because there's no work, nothing comes your way, unless the bosses send it to you," explained an informant.

"In the case of the stealing of cars carried out by people who don't have permission," he declared, "the sanctions are worse. They can take ten or fifteen thousand pesos, but if you don't have good contacts and you're detained by the police, they call the *narcos* and they merely agree where you'll be handed over, and then they kill you."

Another of the faces of the unemployment and underemployment cre-ated by drug trafficking is the cheapening of the *jales* ("tricks" or "jobs"). One of the sources interviewed for this piece, a young man of barely nine-teen, claimed that the lack of money has reached such a level that *sicarios* will accept five hundred pesos and a little marijuana to kill someone.

"They, for that cash and for a little bit of weed, will hand you over and kill you. And now it's rough, and now you don't know what's what, and it's very dangerous. It's rough: there's no money and many jealousies, and any of them could kill you."

Death, that silence

Julio remembers that he was a young man of eighteen, with a shaved head (because that was the uniform of the *narcos* he rolled with). He could do bad things without losing that sparkle in his eyes, and he had a sneer, off to one side or the other, his mouth never symmetrical.

Julio asked what they were going to do. "I remember that everyone remained quiet. I half-smiled. The truth is that I was very nervous, because I realized that they knew what I was up to, what I had been doing," he said, confessing that he felt like his muscles were fighting among themselves beneath his skin, between the tension of the moment and the relaxation of the diversion.

"I wasn't carrying weapons. They didn't yet let me carry one, even though I liked that chrome Beretta."

The other young man could barely breathe, Julio recalled. What are they going to do to me?" he asked and asked. "Shut up, *pendejo*," Julio replied. The other young man shouted, and they responded with rifle butts. "Let's go, the guy told us," Julio remembered. He and the other young man were face down on the ground at this point. The young man begged them to inform the boss that he was going to pay, to forgive him. "He said, "I swear on my poor little mother, I swear.' The *bato* started to cry," Julio remembers. "In truth, I broke down too. But I never said anything. Motherfucker. I endured." The other young man confessed.

The sound of a large electric door swept over him. "Get him in there," said the guy next to the driver. They tied his hands behind him and covered his face with a dirty white dishtowel. They grabbed the other young man as if he were a sack and took him to the room in the back.

It was a safe house in the middle of a residential area, in the heights of Culiacán. A house with automatic doors and bars on the windows, security cameras, electrified fences, and sensors that activated lights in the front and on the patios in the case of an intruder. The street in front was desolate, the garages and gardens secretive.

The boss said, "You, hold it there." Julio stayed outside, on the bench. There were other young people there, one of them fifteen. They all had weapons with skeletons painted on them, new guns without a nick on them. All except him. Julio heard far-off shouts. "They're cutting him down, they're shocking his balls," someone explained.

A little while later it was understood that they had killed the other young man. They didn't hear any shots, that was what surprised Julio the most.

WRAPPED IN A BLANKET

"What now? For the last time, where is the *cuerno de chivo* (AK-47)? The money isn't worth a damned thing, but the *cuerno de chivo* is," said the triggerman. The boy was shaking and not from cold. One of them pointed a pistol at him. Another pistol-whipped him and then shoved the dark barrel into his mouth: an invader with a bitter metallic taste.

He stammered. "I, I, I. D-d-don't. I don't know. I don't know, b-buddy. I don't know anything." His jaw became unresponsive and twitched rebelliously. The one closest to him responded that he had better drop the bullshit. "We're going to kill you if you keep telling us lies, you fucking *tlacuache* ['opossum']."[5]

They wrapped him in a checkered blanket. His hands were tied with a yellow nylon rope. They bound his feet with brown packing tape. The way they upholstered his body, swaddling him with that thick green-and-black garment, might have reminded his parents of when he was a baby. But no. Death was three words away.

"Who was it, *pendejo*? Say it." The prisoner confessed that it was El Chute who kept the automatic rifle about which those murderers were so concerned. He let out the cry of an abandoned baby.

"Shut your hole, *cabrón*. If you don't, we'll kill you right here." They whacked him with the butt of a pistol and put their feet over him. He was riding on the floor of the backseat of a car. He told them who El Chute was and what he was like. And where he lived. They went after him in Colonia Emiliano Zapata, in the southern part of Culiacán.

El Chute heard the voices. He recognized the ones from the barrio and shot out of the back of the house onto the street.

"There he goes, there he goes!" someone shouted. They got back in the car and chased him through the streets, crashing through wood-and-plastic hovels. The clomp of footsteps, the dust they stirred up, entering noses, mouths, pores, and eyes.

Now shouts, brakes squealing, cars starting, police sirens. *Crac, crac.* One of them cocked his weapon, pulling a bullet into the chamber. "I've got him here, *plebes*." One of them had El Chute on his knees, face down, sniveling at the ground.

— It wasn't me, boss, for real.
— Who was it, then, *cabrón*? Who?

He told them everything. They wrapped him up in a blanket, just like the other guy. They tied him up and threw him on top of the guy who'd given him away. The owner of the automatic rifle and the money lived in that part of town. He was the boss of those killers. His house had been visited by thieves, who took the weapons and wads of cash. The money wasn't a big deal. I was already lost. But the AK-47 was something else. And they went to find it. Someone dear to him had given him that rifle with parts made of gold. He was obsessed with that weapon. He couldn't lose it.

Next they dealt with a third implicated individual. They dragged him into the car, balled him up, and then headed for the southern part of the city, talking about chicks, drugs, messed-up songs, and all of that stuff. They stopped in front of an empty housing development and brought the two blanket-covered ones out of the car onto a wide, empty median on Torres Boulevard, near the Infonavit Barrancos development. There they threw them on the ground.

The two wrapped in blankets heard a *crac, crac,* and they thought it was the end for them. They sniffled and begged. But their captors didn't pull the trigger. "Go fuck your mother, *cabrones.* And too bad for you if you turn your heads," one of them said.

They remained there for a good while, bewildered. Eventually they wriggled around like worms to free themselves from the blankets and the packing tape with which they were bound. They never heard from the third guy again. Police later found him floating in Canal #7, a development nearby, his body showing signs of torture and the bullet wounds that had caused his death.

Those guys had found the AK-47.

THREE HEADS

At Salvador Allende High School he went around telling everyone what he had done in that city, just a week before: "I went to knock off a couple of heads. Two *batos,* they told me, 'Go and kill them,' and I headed out there and onto the trail of those *cabrones.* The truth is I felt like a badass."

In school he looked anxious. He wasn't one of those guys who was addicted to death, who killed for free just to experience the emotion again, the fear, the adrenaline, the pleasant power of disposing of the life of another, finishing with a squeeze of the trigger, a single burst, all of that person's tomorrows.

This school is located between the Guadalupe and Rosales neighborhoods, in central Culiacán. It is part of the Autonomous University of Sinaloa, where organized crime has dipped its hand. Criminals with money whip up the students, seducing them with those luxury cars that they show off while they appear to be waiting for someone outside of the school. The young people show up at school armed. They sell and consume drugs. And it's a great showcase for prostitution, disguised in a school uniform and Ferrari T-shirts.

He wanted to enter *la maña*, as they call those who are part of organized crime. And to know killers and *narcos*, to carry a weapon and walk around like a *cabrón*. He didn't do very well in class, but he didn't lack for things to tell his friends. He was getting in deeper, bit by bit, without realizing it. And one morning they told him, "You're in, but you have to throw yourself into the work."

"What do I have to do? Who has to be killed?" They let him loose, without anything else.

"Look, these are the *batos*. They're petty little shits, but they've caused a lot of harm to the boss. They owe him money, they do whatever they want, and they make a mess." They explained to him where and how. He'd get a thousand pesos a day.

"You kill them, and you come back. I don't want any bullshit. As soon as you're done, you come back." "*Órale*," he answered, "right on," as if he were speaking to some other high school kid. "We are going to give you five thousand. But from there it will only go up, to one hundred thousand with us, straight up and up."

He was confident: "It's good and easy. I'll get to the spot. They're sure to come by there. I'll wait for them, and as soon as I see them, *pum, pum, pum*. And then I'll get the fuck out of there, as fast as possible. Tomorrow, for sure, we'll see each other, and I'll bring you those two heads."

The next day he set off. He got there and didn't have to wait long to spot them. It was exactly as they had explained it. He approached, and while taking three steps he slid back the top of the automatic pistol, pulling a cartridge into the chamber. And when he saw them less than a meter away, he fired at them. He saw how they fell, gasping for air, trying to prolong their lives. Once they were on the ground, he gave each one another bullet to ensure success.

He laughed nervously. While he got out of there and concealed the gun he felt like he couldn't wipe the smile off of his face, trapped there by so many different muscles. It was dead set on his face, even though he didn't want to smile at all. He thought, "It must be nerves." But he continued like that for hours and only forgot his expression once he got back to school.

There, in the classrooms, in the hallways between classes, he told his friends. And they told others. And they, in turn, told others. "One day they told him, the same guys from before, that he shouldn't go around talking about it. . . . 'Quit going around talking about it, already, *güey*,' but he never caught on, because he liked to show off," declared a security guard at the school. "They are going to fuck you up," they warned him.

"He didn't laugh anymore, confident, as if he hadn't heard the advice, and answered, 'They're going to scalp me? Whatever. What could they do here? Nothing!'"

The kid said that he could defend himself. And he let the black barrel of a pistol poke out, a Glock that looked brand-new. "I haven't done anything but tell you how it is, crazy fucker," he was told. "Get ready. *Órale güey.*"

But they didn't give him time. He couldn't even get his hand on the weapon that he carried in the fanny pack. "Don't try any bullshit, *morro*.[6] Let's go."

His body showed up in the woods, thrown from the side of the road. "They had tortured him *gacho*," it was said.[7]

News of the kidnapping ran through the halls of the school. Everyone understood what happened to him, found dead, with signs of having been tortured, in an uninhabited spot at the edge of town.

"Poor *bato*, it was his first job, and all of that for wanting to enter into *la naracda* [the drug trade], to be part of the clique," said a schoolmate. "Those who saw him when they went to take [his body] away said that he wore that same expression, like he was smiling, like he wasn't afraid. They didn't realize that he couldn't keep up the smile any longer, that he trembled within, that he was really saying good-bye."

I'LL BUY HIM FROM YOU

"They took your bro," a friend told him, someone who'd been there when the commando showed up.

"Who? When? Why?" he asked, petrified.

"I don't know. They were some hooded *batos*, armed to the teeth with *cuernos de chivo* and dressed in black. Man! It was pretty ugly, *bato*. For real."

He asked himself, *What should I do? What should I do?* He paced back and forth, then grabbed the phone and started to dial. Somebody told him that he needed to find the ne'er-do-wells who had taken his brother, before they killed him. It was the only way. "It's a bitch, but there is no other way."

He called and called and called. In one of his conversations, a name came up. It was that of the killer who had taken his brother.

"And what's that *bato* like?"

"He's a bastard of a *bato*, really bad dude, a complete son of a bitch."

"Whatever," he responded. He knew that he didn't have many options, and he got the man's phone number. And he called.

A dense, labored voice hammered in his ear. The man asked him who he was and what he wanted. In this business there are no greetings or pleasantries, even less so if you're dealing with a job—a *levantón* or a murder.

The caller explained that they didn't know each other, but that he needed to speak to the man because the boy he had in his possession was his brother. The man told him that the boy had stolen drugs and that they were going to kill him, although first they were going to "heat him up" (torture him) and get some information.

A friend later explained, "My pal told me that his brother had been many things, but never a thief. This *bato* [had gotten] got him into marijuana, cocaine, and I don't know what else, but drugs and more drugs. It had been a few years since he [had] started, and he [had gone] from there. [My pal] accepted that part. But later he asked if they would please return [his brother], and he emphasized the 'please.' He begged, straight up," the man remembered.

The man answered sarcastically that he was very sorry: "We're going to kill him."

But the caller insisted that this was an injustice.

"It was then that the phrase escaped him," his friend said. "'If you want, I'll buy him from you. I'll buy my brother from you.' It was his last attempt to rescue him, to save his bro."

In the phone conversation, a heavy silence followed. The caller could hear heartbeats, an echoing shout that never made a sound. Then the *bato* conceded that the caller had balls to phone and ask for this "favor," and he announced that he was going to send some of his boys for him, "so that we can chat." He picked a corner, near Colonia La Campiña, on the west side of Culiacán, very close to the place from where he was calling.

Four of them arrived, and they stopped in front of him. Two got out, folded him over with punches, and loaded him into the car. They tied his hands and hooded him. He didn't offer any resistance. He'd known that this was going to happen and that he was taking a risk.

When he was in front of the boss, they took the hood off of his head. The man repeated: "You've got a lot of balls." The older brother insisted that he wanted to take his little brother back, that he was sure that his brother hadn't stolen anything, because he wasn't a thief. "A druggie, yes, for real. But the *bato* did not go around robbing people. I'll buy him from you."

He swore on the saints, his children and "on whatever else you want, on my mother, that it wasn't my brother. For seven months he hasn't been mixed up in anything. As I told you, he's an addict, not a thief. The *bato* is trying to remake his life. He's fighting. Give him a chance."

From the other side of the wall, in another room, he could hear sobbing, insults, and begging.

The man answered that they were going to return the brother but just not at that moment, not until the following day. But this wasn't convincing, and the older brother asked again that they hand him over immediately: "If I don't take him with me, I'm not moving."

The same friend referred to above later recalled, "From what I know, that man told him: 'Look, *compa*, I know you think you're pretty ballsy coming in here and talking to me like that. I could have both of you killed right now. I could do that. You'll both stay and nobody's leaving. But the thing is, I like you.' The *bato* made a signal with his right hand and a movement with his head, and they brought his brother in."

His face was swollen, his clothing ripped to shreds and blood-stained.

"Get him out of here, *compa*. Just because I like you. I'm going to continue investigating, and if I discover that it was your *carnal* who robbed me, it'll fall on your head."

They were walking toward the door when another warning stopped them: "And if he goes down that road again, if he returns to the weed or the coke or the crystal, I'm also going to fuck him up. I want your brother to keep himself clean, at least for two years. If before that he goes crazy, then there's no pardon. I'll come for both of you."

Twenty pesos

On June 22, 2012, less than two years later, before the time was up, before everything, death came knocking on the door again, on their street, in their neighborhood. The telephone rang. His sister asked for twenty pesos. They were going to buy cigarettes at Oxxo, a convenience store nearby in Colonia Guadalupe Victoria. It was about three in the morning.

He took his bicycle and headed for the store to meet her. On the corner of Fray Balbuena and Andrés Pérez they were waiting. Unofficial accounts claim that they approached him first, and they chatted, but this wasn't confirmed by the State Ministerial Police, who initiated the investigation, an investigation that didn't lead anywhere or to anyone.

They heard shots. His relatives ran out and found him all shot up, thrown down next to the bicycle but still alive. His sister arrived and embraced him. The wounded man wanted to say something: his breath filled with gurgles of blood. Maybe he wanted to say goodbye, to tell her how much he loved her, to share his last breath. And then he died.

On the scene there were various .57 caliber casings, for weapons known as police-killers, for their ability to penetrate the bulletproof vests used by the local police forces. Accounts from witnesses indicate that there were eight shots. One grazed his head, and several hit his back and chest. Holes pockmarked the wall behind him, and the wounds never cauterized. Nor did the memory. The holes opened in a neat line, one right next to the other.

Unofficial information indicates that a patrol from the municipal police of Culiacán was only a few meters away, but the officers didn't intervene. When they heard about the assault and gunshots over the police radio, they turned around and casually showed up at the crime scene, a few minutes later, on the other side of the street.

The reports indicate that at about three o'clock, authorities received a report from the Calle Fray de Balbuena, on the corner with Andrés Pérez there was a man shot down in the street, and when the police arrived they saw the dead cyclist, on whom there were several wounds.

The police asked for assistance from Red Cross paramedics, who showed up and tried to give the victim first aid, but they soon realized that he was already dead.

"Minutes later, the officer from the homicide squad showed up to do a forensic examination of the crime scene. He found at least eight shell casings that appeared to be from 'police-killer' weapons," recounted a brief item published in the police blotter of *Noroeste*.

And there, a few centimeters away, a twenty-peso bill took flight, blowing in the wind. It bid farewell, faithfully, to the body of that young man of thirty-four, the same man who a year and a half earlier had "bought" his brother back.

TWENTY-ONE YEARS OLD

El Rolls is twenty-one, and he's been using coke since he was eighteen. He started out like many others. First tobacco and beer, then some marijuana, and now cocaine. He admits that he was afraid of it because it's a drug that gets hold of you, and it's difficult to quit, and because he didn't know how he was going to keep up with it.

He's worthy of suspicion. White, with a receding hairline, lots of body hair, and short in stature. But he's a man who checks you out while you can't see him, and when you turn around to get a look at him, to find his eyes, he hides them, lowers his gaze, half-closing his eyes or squinting. You don't realize it, but he's studying you. He does it crouching in the shadows.

He didn't know how he'd react to the coke. "I tried it, and the truth is it bucked me up. And now I can't leave it. . . . I'm not a rebel or anything like that, and I do know how to control it," he recounts, without anyone asking how he's done with that magic white powder that can suddenly open your eyes as if they were two invisible toothpicks and make the neurons in your brain and the blood that flows through your body work at an accelerated pace for hours on end.

That barrio

In that barrio everything was there to be spoiled. The guys on the corners watched over it. They spied. They had late-model cars, sporty trucks, jacked up tall and decked out with all of the equipment. Not long ago these knots of young people surrounded the stands on the corners after playing some football or baseball. They had a coke accompanied by some fresh bread. They told each other jokes, and nobody was waiting for anybody or anything in particular; they were just there, having fun, challenging the wind, fugitives from the grasp of formality. They wore shorts and beat-up tennis shoes and thin T-shirts.

Now they don't just hang out in the store on the corner. They are all around. They watch, they pass along reports. They don't let go of their cell phones, and they don't leave their houses without their denim pants, their blue shirts, and new tennis shoes that they leave untied. As if they're going to use them for actual sports. They watch and watch. And they place a call if the police or soldiers come by, if enemies pass, if it's someone they don't know or find suspicious because they go around asking questions about someone who doesn't live there.

In these spaces, they dole out *los bucanas* (as they call Buchanan's) and cocaine, but not marijuana (because they're not *tacuaches*—"morons"), and, of course, they're surrounded by good-looking *morras*.[8] They never put down their Blackberries or abandon the street: everything belongs to them.

They are *halcones* or lookouts. The boss around there, of the block, of the *colonia*, might pay them about two thousand pesos a week. And they aspire to move up. More than one of them goes around armed and wants to be a *sicario*. He dreams, and one day it will come true, but he's got to accumulate points and add up merits.

They're young people of fifteen or seventeen or twenty years old. They never leave there. They're taking care of the boss, the *patrón*. And they cease to be those diaphanous, chaotic, and shouting kids from high school; they've abandoned school. And they're no longer the healthy, noble children from the barrio. There's a shadow over them. They don't have lips, or faces with spontaneous muscles, but rather forced expressions. And they're always there, day and night, watching. They suspect everything—everything that's not them.

They have control, even over crime. If somebody commits a robbery there and they detect it, they capture and beat him. And after the torture, or "heating up," as they call it, they hand him over to the police. But if the cops arrive of their own accord, "and they want to make a stink about it, wag their dicks around, we send them away to fuck their mothers, just like that, nothing more. And they go because they're going."

The robbery

El Rolls popped some pills; he'd added to his addictions. He carried one of those electrolyte drinks for dehydration because he was hung over, and who knows what other substances course through his veins, between last night's fiesta and noon today. He's in the living room of a house that isn't his. He's uncomfortable. His watch is slow: he's in a hurry, he trembles, he can't string together words well. There are long and dense pauses in his speech. His tongue misfires. The only thing missing is foam about the mouth. An addict.

"They've just got to ask for it, and I've got to do it, to go and beat someone up. . . . I've done it before. That's the least of it." He takes some medicine. A tranquilizer to "help him out": diazepam. And if he doesn't have money, he gets it by robbing. And even when he has it, he urgently needs to have his dose of adrenaline. And anyone who's tried to stop him he's split in half.

"He gets prescriptions from a doctor I know," a friend says. "I used to go and buy them from him and then head to the pharmacy, where they'd fill them for me without a problem. He needs a prescription because they are controlled substances." Seven pills a day, 2.5 milligrams each. And that's how he was, half drugged, when a mugger surprised him, near the *tortillería*. He knew the *bato* and thought that nothing would come of it. He was overconfident. The man took out a knife and ripped his cell phone away from him with great agility. It was a new one, a Nokia.

When he realized what had happened, he went for a friend, and they got into a car. He remembered what *colonia* he'd been in, Rafael Buelna, located three kilometers away. They rode up there in a newish Corolla, and after asking around everywhere, they located the guy.

"The *bato* was in the street, walking. We overcame him, and we took him down hard and made him submit in a flash. I was angry, and I told him, 'That's how you wanted to jump me, *cabrón.*' He resisted, but we didn't give him time, for real. We wanted to stuff him in the car, but he wouldn't let us, until we softened him up with blows, and then he got in."

The patrol

El Rolls recounts that they were looking for a police car and says that he wasn't armed. Nor was his friend. It strains belief. It's difficult to think about him, in the street, in these streets, in that barrio, without an automatic pistol tucked away, but within reach.

They started to ride him. And to beat him. One and then the other. *Pum, pum.* In the belly, in the head, in the face. Also in the back. El Rolls believes that by that time someone had reported them. Some neighbor, somebody who saw them. And so the police were already around. He also claims that in reality they wanted to turn the guy in and that they were looking for a patrol to give the guy to.

In the meantime, the beating and the verbal aggression continued. To be in a strange car with men like them after having robbed one of them, to be subdued, beaten, and terrorized. It's dangerous to dispose of the life of someone who harmed you in a robbery, it can be very costly, but the life of that guy was theirs and it wasn't up for discussion. Not among those three men in that Corolla. Killing him was a privilege, a pleasure, a right, something well deserved.

And he began to cry. They gave him six whacks with the butt of a pistol, and his mouth started to bleed. They told him to shut up. He begged them not to kill him, and they asked why he had he done what he'd done: "Why did you dare? Now you're fucked, you son of a whore."

"Don't kill me, please. Don't kill me. We're friends. Forgive me, I'll never do it again, boss." But El Rolls's mouth was already foaming from so much rage and so many pills, and his blows merely intensified. Until a municipal police patrol turned up. Without getting out, they explained from one car to the next what had happened, and they handed over the young man.

El Rolls says that he felt relieved when he saw the police. Perhaps he didn't know what was going to happen or how far the rage, the drugs, and the affront would take him. He picked up his cell phone. It lit up. He says that he went to department headquarters to file charges that day.

But it doesn't seem believable. At twenty-one years old, with so much cocaine snorted up his nose and diazepam coursing through his blood, nesting in his brain, there are many black clouds hanging over his life. You can see it in his sickly glare. He takes a hit of the apple-flavored electrolyte drink and ducks his head.

—Who do you work for?
—I don't want to talk about that.

And his gaze sharpens. His eyes are like daggers.

I'M AFRAID

El Vampi is scared. And then again he's not. He comes and goes in the conversation: he turned up in Tijuana, on the border, where he worked for drug traffickers from Sinaloa, and then he returned to Culiacán, where many have identified him as an enemy operator.

What's certain is that his boss is dead, along with many of his killers, bodyguards, operatives and people close to him. He's not. But he knows that they're going to kill him, that they're looking for him. The only thing that worries him is the possibility of his being killed in front of his kids. "I want them to take me far away, where nobody sees me, and without tortures that will prolong my suffering, and cut me into fucking pieces," he admits. And then he asks for another Tecate.

He says that he's a man, and that's why he won't try to run away when they come to take him. He'll know the precise moment when they come for him. He keeps an eye on the door, noting everyone who comes and goes in the restaurant. That explains why he's chosen the seat he's in, the one that allows him a view of every diner in there. He sees all of them. And it looks like he's thinking it could be that guy, with the table next to ours, or the guy who's just coming through the door and pretending to look for someone else.

"I'm afraid, but I'm very macho. The truth is I'm not afraid. Others, them, many of them, are afraid of me. They know about me. That it won't be easy. But whenever it happens—well, it'll happen."

Twenty thousand pesos a week. That's what the guy with the beard gave him, just because he liked him, and he did the jobs asked of him, and he was a loyal dog. That was on top of the fee they gave him for each one of those jobs.

"Have you killed anyone?" he's asked. He answers in a garbled voice, stammering, and with the steely expression on his face cracking, that, yes, he had.

Up on the border, he got involved with coke. He consumed it and he sold it. He would buy a pound worth of powder, and from that he'd sell the equivalent of a pound and a half. He killed those who got in the way of his business, and also those that the boss wanted out of the way to keep control of the market. Coke and crack—that's what they were slinging up there, in that city on the border with the United States.

"I killed, and I'm scared, but I'm also not scared. When you go to kill some of them, they cry. Others ask you to give them the chance to say good-bye to their families. The other day, we let one guy call his son on the phone, because the *bato* was on his knees, begging us to let him say good-bye. But instead of calling his kid, he called his clique. '*Plebes*, they're going to kill me. Cut 'em up, all of 'em.'[9] Then we took away his phone," he explained.

"The toughest thing is that they all look at you." He was referring to his victims, during the rite of torturing them and keeping them from fainting or losing consciousness. Even those who close their eyes or cover them with their hands, they all look at you. They do it for the last time.

"They turn their heads and look at you. And they tell you everything. They tell you their hatreds, their hopes, their entire lives in that moment. That's the toughest part, the real bitch. I sleep with that every night, even though I don't have nightmares, nor do I wake up in a sweat, like in the movies."

He looks like he's shooting when he talks. And those words about the dead, who look at him and tell him everything before they go, come like bursts of fire. And suddenly the cadence of his voice allows the words to separate. Shot by shot.

El Vampi is tall, he has bags under his eyes, a sunken head like Cuauhtémoc Blanco, the soccer star, as if he didn't have a neck, and the veins in his eyes stick out. He tears up briefly, but a quick pass of the napkin dries them. "I know that they're going to kill me." And he turns his head again to see who's coming and going. He follows some of them with his gaze, uncomfortable. He keeps it up, and they look down. His trips are bad. His words bleed, they flow, broken and garbled.

"If they'd only just come for me. They know that I killed many. They could pick me out me in the street one day and identify me as a *bato* who worked for the other side. I'm a man, and I'm not going to cry, I'm not afraid. Well, actually I am. If they would only just take me out and not cut me up."

He's treading in the territory of Joaquín Guzmán Loera, El Chapo, and of Ismael Zambada García, El Mayo. Culiacán, this city is still a sanctuary for these capos and their families, a sacred city, their territory. They have a monopoly on crime. "If someone kills, it's because I asked them to do it," they seem to say, those who control everything here. If somebody steals a car or takes a person or carries out a purge in one of the cells that work for them, it's because they authorized it. They give the orders. They're in the police, the state apparatus, and the army. They own everything, even the streets, the benches in the park, and the stoplights.

El Vampi raises his gaze. One sees where his eyes are looking, and it's a blank space on the wall. That sickly, sad gaze. "I've decapitated people, cut off heads. That's the toughest part, the real bitch. They grab the neck and say, 'Here, this is where you cut.' And I assure you: it's not easy, you can't cut them like that in one slash."

"That is the most difficult. People don't let themselves go. It's the tough, bony part. Give me another beer."

AT YOUR SERVICE

She answered the cell phone. They had just snatched her fiancé. They had been walking, hand in hand, very near his house. Suddenly armed men had surrounded them. They'd beat on him and stuffed him into a truck.

She didn't recognize the voice of the guy who called her at that hour. Days later they buried her fiancé. Her swollen eyes, the white and running snot, the flood of pent-up tears continued to flow.

"Look, we know who you are. We know where you live, and what your name is." She still didn't recognize the hollow voice. It seemed to her that it belonged to someone young, maybe twenty-something. The clipped tone, the words piled on top of each other and a few particular curses. The *muchacho* had a difficult time expressing himself.

She asked what had happened with her fiancé. "It's just that . . ." The man got tongue-tied. She asked, she demanded, she shouted wholeheartedly, enraged. Just the day before yesterday they'd buried him. They took what little she had in the world. They were going to get married in December, and now she was left with nothing. Nothing. "What can you tell me about my fiancé? I don't think you've got anything to add. He's already dead," she declared, without loosening the knots in her stomach and throat.

The man didn't have any words for her. He heard her renewed crying. She sobbed and once again shouted. "My Fernando was a good person! I don't know why you've done him harm, since he never disrespected anyone. He had just finished his degree, and he was working here and there. It wasn't going well, but he was hardworking, and he never stopped fighting."

They had taken him and kept him prisoner. And she couldn't make herself stop suspecting him. Even though she knew him, it crept into her internal dialogues, the most remote and timid of them, wondering if her fiancé had gotten involved in something bad. Maybe drugs. Maybe he stole something or didn't pay a debt, or he'd gotten involved with a married woman. She didn't know. But it couldn't be. She couldn't believe it. She went over it and over it in her mind, torturing herself, like a jackhammer going off in her head. Not my Fernando.

"That's why we called. Listen up," the guy told her. "It's just that this *bato*, for real . . . well, how can I tell you? I don't have the words. We kept him for three days. By force [*al chile*], but it doesn't matter. We beat him and beat him and beat him. *Gacho, la neta.* ['It was ugly, for real.']¹⁰ And we questioned him a fuckload of times. We told him to confess, to spill the beans."

"But the *bato* fought it. One day, the second, I think, the *bato* took ill and fainted. He was sleeping like a little baby. I said that I thought he'd left us, but no. The *bato* woke up and you know what the first thing he said was? 'Listen, don't kill me. I'm a good person. I've never done anything bad to anyone.'"

"But we didn't believe him. We just kept going, on and on. We were stuck on the idea that the *bato* was *de la bronca* ['in on it'].¹¹ We continued hitting him. We tortured him so that he'd tell the truth. Listen, we gave him a real bitch of a time. And that's why I'm calling you. After a little while, the *bato* quit responding. That's when we took him to where they found him."

The young doctor, who was doing his residency in pediatrics, was found in his white coat, his uniform, shot to death. There were signs of torture all over his body. The discovery was made near the community of Mojolo, in the northern sector, a few kilometers from the city.

"The things is, what hurts me the most, what hits me right in the balls, is that your fiancé didn't do anything wrong. That's why I'm sending you this crown of roses. We made a mistake. And, well, I'm calling you to put myself at your service. To see if there's anything I can offer you."

She stopped crying. She gasped for air. She shouted: "Is there anything you can offer me?" And without waiting for an answer she said, "The thing you can offer me, the only thing, is to give him back to me."

YOU'RE GOING TO CRY

That predictable life of dull routine led her to give it all up: children, husband, and the dusty home without heat. First she started going to yuppie bars, and then she took a dive down the dark paths of loud night-clubs, with slippery, unstable floors.

She got drunk with people she knew and with men who told her lies about their identities and job titles. She rolled around with them in their sweat and other liquids when she found them handsome or interesting. And she got rid of them without ever recycling. She tried things that she'd always refused: tequila, vodka, whiskey, and the white powders and barbiturates they passed around.

And thus when she met him she went smilingly into the cellars of the nightlife and submerged herself gladly and submissively, open to the city's erogenous zones, its dark orifices and catacombs that only open and allow entry when the hands of the clock lose their numbers.

He was a good-looking man, with rough features. She liked him because he was a bit gruff or because he was powerful or because of those clumsy hands that knew how to grab her but not how to let her go. Pincers trapping her. He took her to his house in a luxurious part of Culiacán, and there she burned her bridges, all of them, including those most dear to her, born in her flesh and nurtured at her breast. He gave her a sports car and told her that all of it was hers, just stay.

Powder and pills were never far off. She had jewelry and luxuries and trips and comfort. And she released the animal, the beast that had been hidden behind the "pretty woman" phase, good-natured and well-behaved. Domestic. One day he arrived with a hot pistol, and, squeezed by the hands of that sensual robot, she got excited. Another night he surprised her with a Kalashnikov rifle hanging from his back, and she threw herself at him with redoubled enthusiasm.

She quit making the rounds at the bars and frequenting darks alleys of the city and held court in that seven-bedroom house, with an industri-al-sized kitchen, salons, and a swimming pool. She ate and drank every-thing while sitting in the Jacuzzi, and everything came from him. From his bloated body. From that fine piece of work as if he were made of gold. One dark day, when the swallows never appeared and their muffled songs couldn't be heard, he returned from a job. He looked like he was stuck halfway in a mutation between a man and a werewolf: there was hair in his fingernails, blood on his arms and abdomen, mud on his boots and the bottom of his pants, bruises and cuts all over him.

"What happened to you?"

"Nothing. Wash this."

"And while she cleaned his boots, the beast inside of her stirred. She overcame him while he was scrubbing off the blood and hair of others, the mud, and all the rest, and she devoured him with kisses and panting.

Dawn broke, and she asked herself what had happened. *Who am I? What am I doing?* And she told him about it. He answered that he was a *bato pesado* ("heavy dude"). A tough *cabrón* within the drug trafficking mafia. He suggested, "Read the newspapers and you'll see." There had been a scrap, she read in the headline.

"You didn't leave," he fumed. He approached her and said: "The day that I leave, you're going to cry. I've never left a woman, and I won't do it with you. If you go, there'll be no problem; just don't take anything with you. That way you'll know that you wanted me, that it wasn't for the money."

She took her car and went back to her old life and her kids, but she didn't want anything to do with her husband, and they divorced within a couple of months. One of her closest friends recounted that one time she was sitting in a chair in the living room of her house, in a working-class housing development in the northern part of Culiacán, in December 2012, when she came across the crime section of a newspaper.

"And she saw him. He was the same *bato*. First she was hypnotized, her eyes glued to the page of the newspaper, his photo, his frozen gaze. She was leaving, already beating a hasty retreat. And then the *morra* started to cry."

CHAPTER 4

Dying for Good, Forgetting

DON'T LEAVE ME HANGING

His passport, a little notebook, the tape recorder, credentials, and a date-book that he used every day—there in his miniscule backpack, he carried his life and also his death. It was everything that he needed if the moment arose and he had to flee: one of his feet, one of his hands and arms, one of his eyes, half of his existence was always on the other side, thinking about saving himself, getting the hell away from the bullets and gun battles, the police blotters, the executions, and the terror.

He was afraid that they'd turn him in, that police or government officials or reporters, even those from the newspaper where he worked, would put him out. And so, surrounded by detractors and immense craters of mistrust and doubt, he decided to leave. He left, and they took him. Now no one knows where he is or whether he's alive or dead.

"Hey, *cabrón*, don't leave me hanging." That was his expression, the one he used the most, when he talked with his friends, the close ones anyway. He didn't do it with everyone. He asked them not to abandon him, not to leave him alone. "Hey, *cabrones*, assholes, don't leave me hanging." He insisted. He repeated it and repeated it. It was almost a plea, an endorsement of friendship and solidarity, in the presence of a death that was always close by, that he could feel. That's why he was always smiling, or half-smiling, like he was making a face.

But it was also an acknowledgment of the sharp and cutting mistrust that always accompanied him. Fear wasn't hard to come by. It was with him always.

Alfredo Jiménez Mota was born in Hermosillo, in the border state of Sonora. He was eighteen years old when he began to study for his degree in Culiacán. He lived on Constitution Street, which for a long time was called Nicaragua Street, about a half a block from Jesús G. Andrade Avenue and the Ángel Flores baseball stadium, in the Miguel Alemán neighborhood, a central section of the Sinaloan capital. He started out at the School of Social Communications in the University of the Occident, because he wanted to be a journalist.

He was tall and overweight. His smile, which came with ease, rose rapidly across the rest of his face, all the way up to his eyes. Hopeful sparkles, tenderness, innocence, goodwill, honesty, and humanity, all were reflected in those eyes, in that smile.

The seal of death

Alfredo was at the daily newspaper *El Debate* in Culiacán. He'd worked in the field, for the newspaper *Noroeste*, cutting his teeth as a reporter on the police beat. He'd soaked up the tricks of the trade from his colleagues in the crime section for covering these things and getting the facts, but he also went much further: the street, the night, the radio frequencies of the police departments and the Red Cross, the law enforcement operations, the code words used by the police, the movements and reactions of their agents. The police reporters appeared to be a lot like cops. It's a type of mimesis. Years earlier, some of them went around armed, and stashes of weapons and drugs were even found in their offices. They had rights as privateers and immunity from prosecution. But not Alfredo, he was a real journalist of the street, of instincts and nosing around with a magnifying glass and eyes in the back of his head, in the slums and in the muck.

His heart walked a tightrope in every story, news brief, or investigation.

That time he asked his friend Gerardo to take him in his car. It was already night, but he worked that way, a vampire with a notebook, a pen, and a tape recorder. "'All right already, let's go,' I answered." They had just left the office, and it was already late for supper, judging by the hands of the clock. Alfredo told him, "Head down here, straight." It was

Obregón Avenue, the main street in this city. They headed south. They ascended up to the "temple on the hill," as the church of Our Lady of Guadalupe is known, at the highest part of the city, behind the stairs on which many people exercise in the mornings and late afternoons. They were in a black Topaz, an old one that belonged to Gerardo.

"Where are we going, *güey*?" he asked, somewhat intrigued, taken by surprise. It was very late, and this *cabrón* is taking me who knows where. We continued down Obregón and entered a new development, a big one full of enormous houses and many vacant lots. And since he didn't say anything, and only laughed, I asked him once again where we were going," Gerardo remembered.

Alfredo looked at him with a celebratory smile, his round face lit up, victorious. And he announced, "I know where El JT, Javier Torres, lives, and we're going to his house to see if the *bato* will give me an interview." His friend hit the brakes hard. He whacked the steering wheel. He could've slapped Alfredo. "I told him, 'You're being stupid, good and stupid. How did it occur to you to go to his house and ask for an interview, *cabrón*?"[1] He spun the wheel around and headed exactly in the opposite direction. He told Alfredo, with a nervous smile, that Javier Torres Félix, El JT, wasn't an artist or a movie star, some guy on a red carpet who you might ask for an interview or autograph. He was a very dangerous man. In terms of power, at the end of the nineties and the first decade of the 2000s, this capo was second only to the bosses of the Sinaloa Cartel, El Chapo and El Mayo.

Gerardo, his close friend, told him off. He knew that Alfredo, this wild, young, chubby, and innocent reporter wanted to drink in the entire world in one gulp, and on his own. "You can't go around sticking your neck out, Alfredo. I told him just like that, no more, no less. 'You don't want to swallow the whole world, *güey*.' It was my turn to calm him down, to pull him back to earth. But there in Sonora, they let him swallow the whole fucking world. And he was fucked."

Alfredo pulled Gerardo into a room at the back of the newspaper office so that they could talk without being overheard. It was the same lack of trust as always. It was his last week in Culiacán, after having worked for *El Debate* for almost two years. He told Gerardo that he'd been offered

A MAN WHO WAS EVERYWHERE

The Sinaloan drug trafficker Javier Torres Félix, JT, returned to Mexico on April 11, 2013. A federal judge in the Central District of California had sentenced him to eight years in prison, which he served in West Virginia.

Torres had been extradited to the United States on November 29, 2006, a couple of hours before Vicente Fox Quesada left office as president of the republic. After his arrest for the murder of soldier Julio César Samayo, the drug trafficker confronted a US extradition case that lasted nearly three years, until the Mexican federal attorney general suspended the criminal case against him in Mexico City and ordered him sent to stand trial in California.

El JT was an omnipresent *narco*. His power and influence was felt and suffered all over. He was one of the principal operators and the boss of all of the *sicarios* of that criminal organization, the Sinaloa Cartel, and a key lieutenant of Ismael Zambada, El Mayo. His life, his capacity to operate and to impose his will upon others, sparked many tall tales: "He's there, we saw him here"—an armed ghost with automatic rifles and grenades, who moved around with thirty pistoleros. He was no mere migrant. But his error was having participated in a supposed confrontation with soldiers on that January 27, 2004, near the San Lorenzo Valley, in the southern part of the municipality of Culiacán. An infantry corporal, Julio César Samayo, assigned to the Ninth Military Zone, headquartered in the city, was killed there. And thus, the next day, very early, the military fell upon his house, located in a luxury housing development.

El JT had been arrested in California back in 1992. He was tried and sentenced—along with four accomplices—for conspiracy to traffic cocaine and possession of earnings from the illicit sale of narcotics, in criminal case #BA 063312 in the Superior Court of Los Angeles County, California.

Javier Torres had pleaded guilty to both charges, and they'd given him a little less than five years in prison, after which he returned to Mexico, where he was once again engaged in into criminal activities. On May 27, 1997, he was arrested by the Federal Judicial Police (PJF) in Quintana Roo, with a shipment of 348.1 kilograms of cocaine. Ramón López Serrano, Raúl Maza Ontiveros, now deceased, and Manuel Meza Zamudio were also arrested. They had just left a warehouse where the drugs were stashed, when they were surprised. Various vehicles, two boats, and weapons of various calibers were seized as well.

two jobs in his home state of Sonora: one in the customs office, where he could earn lots of money, and one at the newspaper *El Imparcial*, in which he was offered a low salary but where he would be able to follow what had always been his passion: reporting and writing.

A week later, he went to work at *El Imparcial*. They bid each other farewell like the best of them, without saying goodbye. Gerardo trained his eyes on another country, another world. His gaze left with the afternoon and the retreating sun. He looked without seeing anything. It was already June, but it hadn't started raining yet in the city, only in his eyes.

"I hoped that they had said no to him."

Throwing stones at the sky

Alfredo Jiménez Mota was twenty-five when he went to Hermosillo to join *El Imparcial*. He had journalism in his veins, and he had specialized, perhaps accidentally or without seeking it out, in high-risk affairs—drug trafficking, above all else. In Culiacán he had published stories about important people in the Sinaloa Cartel, and that had caused him various problems, including some threats.

In Sonora, supported by his contacts in the federal attorney general's office, the local prosecutor's office, and agents of the various police departments, including those affiliated with organized crime, he started to write. The majority of his reporting referred to *sicarios*, bosses, and operators from the Sinaloa Cartel and the links between criminals and politicians at all levels of government.

The journalist was prolific in publishing reports and news briefs about the power of the Beltrán Leyva brothers in the state of Sonora. Their local affiliate group appeared to have been formed in San Bernardo, in the southern extreme of the municipality of Los Alamos, for the transit of drugs and the establishment of a corridor for this purpose. Unofficial accounts indicate that at one time the cell made up of the Beltrán family, who were from Sinaloa, had a branch in the Juárez Cartel, but this ended when they became part of the criminal organization headed by Joaquín Guzmán Loera, El Chapo, from whom they split in 2008, after the Mexican army units arrested Alfredo Beltrán Leyva, El Mochomo.

The Beltráns claimed that the arrest had in reality been a handover by the criminal organization to the government of Felipe Calderón.

This rupture between the Beltrán Leyva group, and the rest of the Sinaloa Cartel, directed by El Chapo and El Mayo, provoked an avalanche of criminal activity that began in Culiacán and extended across most of the country. It was one of the root causes for the wave of violence that rose and spread like a voracious fire, through many areas. Add to this the clumsy operations of the federal government and the existence of newer cartels that had distinguished themselves with especially atrocious executions, like the Zetas, and violence reached unprecedented levels.

In Sonora, the Beltrán Leyva brothers were known as the Three Horsemen. And Jiménez Mota dedicated himself to laying bare their links, transactions, influences, and complicity with the government. Among the other cells that used to operate for Guzmán was the one commanded by Adán Salazar Zamorano, the boss of the Salazar family. His name also appeared in the stories stitched together by Alfredo Jiménez.

"Since 2005, Jiménez Mota [has] published in *El Imparcial* an X-ray of the activities of the brothers from Sinaloa known as the Three Horsemen," read a bulletin published on the website of the Impunity Project (www.impunidad.com) from the Inter American Press Association (SIP), on the case of the Sonoran reporter with experience in Culiacán.

The work of the journalist, the document added, bridged the criminal activities of members of the families of Beltrán Leyva and Raúl Enrique Parra—leader of the cell Los Güeritos y Los Números, "which resulted in more than seventy executions within the state for control of the drug trade."

The US Drug Enforcement Agency (DEA) cites the SIP bulletin, which in turn cites one of the reports by published by Jiménez Mota in *El Imparcial*, claiming that members of Los Números y Los Güeritos "were sought for bringing drugs into the United States by way of light aircraft and *Velocity* planes, according to arrest warrants, at least two of which belong to the Beltrán Leyva clan."

In November 2004, the young reporter published a story about a drug trafficker executed that month whose tortured body was thrown into an abandoned building where police officers were doing an inspection. This might have set the whole thing off. This fact was included in investigations of the case of Alfredo Jiménez Mota. There are credible accounts that elements of the state and federal government participated in the November 2004 killing. Some of the killers, unofficial sources indicate, used to be or are currently members of the security forces in Sonora who were giving information to Jiménez Mota. They were "trusted sources," who might have used him to disseminate this or that news that was convenient to their criminal interests, and later they got rid of him, turning him over to *el hampa* ("the mafia").

That April

Alfredo turned in three news briefs. It was April 2, a Saturday, a day for relaxing, chatting, and amber-colored drinks. They knew that he had left his offices at *El Imparcial* and headed to his apartment, in Hermosillo. He lived there alone. It seemed strange that he was late. Among those who were waiting for him was his friend Shaila Rosagello. Someone told her that before meeting her in the bar, he had gone home to bathe and then left in his pickup to meet with "a contact," a police official, perhaps, likely from the attorney general's office (PGR), assigned to the local delegation.

   She didn't know any more than that. He didn't arrive at the bar that night or the next day for Mass at the Cathedral, something he never missed, as he considered himself a fervent Catholic. He didn't show up for work the following day either. The managers of *El Imparcial* thought that perhaps he'd been drinking on his day off. This theory was positively criminal when applied to a reporter specializing in issues of security and drug trafficking, who held in his hands "heavy" connections, high-level sources, and information of transcendental importance. But that's how it was. His friends called his cell phone. No answer. The *tuuu, tuuu* indicated that the device rang and rang. Later it went to voicemail, one, two, three, twenty, fifty times. The endless ringing skewered them, faithfully and punctually. Alfredo isn't there. He's not there. He never will be again. On Tuesday, the most worried of them went and filed a formal complaint alleging the illegal detention of the young journalist.

Combing through Jiménez's cell phone, which he left behind, it was discovered that beginning at 11:04 the night before he'd had a long conversation with the then-sub-delegate of the federal attorney general's office in Sonora, Raúl Rojas Galván, who first denied it but later contradicted himself in a judicial interrogation to which he was submitted, thanks to the weight of the contrary evidence. But this important suspect was reassigned to a different function in another state and sent packing, which effectively put the brakes on the investigation.

"The confused and contradictory proceedings remain stagnant, despite the reiterated petitions of management at *El Imparcial* and the SIP, to the federal government. No one has been held responsible for the disappearance of Alfredo Jiménez, even though everyone acknowledges that it is linked to his reporting on drug trafficking. The probable responsibility of municipal, state, and federal officials could explain the stagnation and lack of results," notes the document on the website of the Impunity Project, under the subtitle "Crimes against Journalists."

Everywhere

Alfredo went around everywhere. Nobody knows how or when his Matra radio suddenly appeared, one of those used by police agencies in Sinaloa, a device that supposedly prevents conversations from being scanned or overheard. He had one with its own charger, and he listened to everything and everyone. Suddenly, in the wee hours, he'd be seen during operations of the State Ministerial Police or the municipal police of Culiacán, at crossroads or in disputed territory, where someone had been pulled over, at crime scenes, next to the bodies of the murdered. He was there, notebook in hand, with his tape recorder and that little backpack hanging from his shoulder. The backpack was the sign that he was ready to flee, to take a flight or to grab the first bus, and get lost. That's how he got around invariably. It was his fatal destiny.

"[He had it all.] In that little black bag that he wouldn't bring with him. He was an at-risk reporter, a fearless *bato*. But he was a *bato* who seemed gullible in many ways—for example, in the relationships he had with those contacts or with other cops. He didn't doubt that many of them used him for their own interests. But Alfredo was that way, and he generated a lot of trust. He was good at it," Gerardo recounted.

He and Alfredo used to have dinner together on any given weekend evening. He liked the *tacos de ubre*, udder tacos, that they sold in a stall on Obregón Avenue, near Aguilar Barraza. There they tossed back their share of meat and tortillas. One midnight, Gerardo got a call: Alfredo was in the emergency room at the regional Social Security Hospital. He found him, slumped in a chair, pale, with an IV in his arm.

"Imagine that gorilla, because he was tall and corpulent, with a baby face, the face of a good little boy, asleep and sick, that big man, that man-child, a bull of a man, sitting there helpless. Strong, brave, fearless, rash, and here was the same person, lying down, weak and vulnerable. It was an image that made me feel great tenderness. Now it fills me with me a fuckload of sadness," Gerardo related.

The contacts

In Culiacán, Jiménez also had his contacts in security agencies and institutions. Included among them were the offices of federal and state attorneys general (PGR and PGJE). In the PGR, which is charged with fighting organized crime, the Sonoran journalist met an official from the state delegation identified only as Vigueras.

Records from this federal agency identify one Norberto Vigueras Beltrán, who in August 2005 was named regional boss of the Federal Investigations Agency (AFI), now the Federal Ministerial Police, in Durango. This federal functionary had had a nineteen-year career in the PGR, and he had occupied the same post as regional boss of the AFI in the state of Hidalgo.

Also, according to accounts from people close to the situation, a fact that perhaps did not show up in the investigation undertaken by the PGR (which came up empty-handed when it came to locating the disappeared reporter or detaining the persons responsible), Alfredo Jiménez Mota was in communication with a DEA agent, identified as "Ramona." The contact was constant and regular, always by telephone. On occasion the consultations were endless and thorough, depending upon the situation and the interests at stake.

Other clues

In December 2003, Alfredo covered an automobile accident when he was writing for *El Debate*, in Culiacán. The accident took place during the wee hours, on the Almada Bridge, a long elevated section of highway in a northern section of the city, and one of those involved was Iván Archivaldo Guzmán, one of the children of Joaquín Guzmán Loera, El Chapo. The toll was one dead young man. On the scene was Reynaldo Zamora, the deputy police chief in charge of arrests for *detenciones en flagrancia* ("crimes in progress"). What was he doing there? Alfredo asked him why he was there and noted that several people on the scene asked him not to include Zamora's name in his story about the accident. He ignored them.

Zamora was annoyed and showed up at the newspaper office, located on Francisco I. Madero Boulevard downtown, to ask for the journalist and threaten him, according to what Jiménez told his friends and other media people days later. And that's what was published in the weekly *Ríodoce* in 2005, when Alfredo Jiménez Mota was already a disappeared reporter and when the authorities had "intensified" the investigation.

"Reynaldo Zamora was afraid. He was worried," a fellow journalist explained. Not so different from the way Alfredo Jiménez felt days before he was disappeared by unknown subjects: desperate, fearful, mistrustful, and, worse yet, alone.

"*Ríodoce* reported that in January 2004 Reynaldo Zamora threatened Alfredo Jiménez, the journalist for *El Imparcial* in Hermosillo, who remains disappeared. At the time, Zamora was the chief in charge of arrests for crimes in progress for the Ministerial Police, and Alfredo Jiménez was a reporter for *El Debate*. They saw each other in the office of the daily paper," the same journalist detailed.

Zamora's presence at the accident, publicized by Alfredo's story, seemed to identify him as a PME official in the service of the drug traffickers. And for that he snapped. Alfredo recounted that Zamora had warned him what would happen if that drug trafficking group were to learn who Alfredo was.

After Alfredo's disappearance, sitting in Los Portales Café, in Culiacán, Zamora says he felt assaulted by the tape recorder.

— Did you threaten Alfredo Jiménez?
— Wait, wait! I am a civilian now. Let's talk, but without the tape recorder.
— But you had a responsibility when you were a public servant and Alfredo said that you had threatened him.
— I'll chat with you, but without the tape recorder.
— Just answer me, yes or no.
— That is not true . . . It is not true!
— Have you made an appointment at the PGR to testify about this case?
— Absolutely not. The day that they call me, I'll go.
— Why did you leave the police?
— Because the assignment was up. The change was normal.
— You didn't have any conflicts?
— Absolutely not.
— What do you do now?
— Well, I work to live, to take care of my family.
— But on your own? You don't work for any [police] department?
— No.
— I'm going to ask you again, did you threaten Alfredo Jiménez?
— It is not true. I'll chat with you but without the tape recorder.
— Did you have a conflict or a problem with Alfredo?
— No, absolutely not.
— None of any kind?
— None of any kind, we did talk about that affair, and I told him why I went there, nothing more, I didn't even lose my temper, nor was there any real conflict.

Reynaldo Zamora stays at the table, seated on the other side of the window from the motorcyclists who get together in the plaza every Sunday. Then, without the tape recorder on, he explains that the young man who died in the accident, Alejandro Magno Niebla, was the fiancé of one of his daughters, and that's why he was at the scene of the accident.

The publication of the news story by Jiménez was enough for him to be called before the internal review board of the attorney general's office to explain what he was doing at the accident. But, as he relates, he never showed up.

Now he's in a hurry to clarify, but he's also afraid and worried. He says that he's selling clothes along with his wife, to make a living. Moreover, he insists that he'll show up wherever and with whomever to testify, if it is necessary.

A new ingredient entered the mix when José Luis Vasconcelos, an assistant special prosecutor with SIEDO, declared that one of the lines of the investigation into the disappearance of Jiménez led back to Sinaloa. In that jurisdiction, the special prosecutor added, the reporter had been threatened, and this might have been related to drug trafficking.

When questioned about this declaration, Zamora defended his record:

— Does this declaration worry you?
— It doesn't worry me that juridically or criminally something is going to happen, but that doesn't make it any less of a precedent. I know that I'm clean, that I have nothing to do with this. Whatever happens, I'm a [public official]. I don't exercise any public function right now, but it is my field and I'm going to try to return to it and work, because I have to support my family. I'm not going to dedicate myself to any illicit activities. I've never done it. I have twenty-three years in this field and I would like to return. I will return with great pleasure. *Ríodoce* used my name on two occasions. I don't know if *Ríodoce* has some proof in this sense, but it is not true; I never threatened [Alfredo]. I never told him what was going to happen to him or that I was going to say something to the family that he was one way or another; that is also untrue.
— Do you feel like the PGR was referring to you?
— Yes, because you guys drove them to—you published it, that I had threatened him, and I don't know if he simply received a threat from somebody else or what. I tell you that it's not true, that I never threatened him. For that alone I feel like they're referring to me, not because it corresponds to reality, nor for any other thing.
— Are you disposed—?
— For whomever, whenever, I am disposed to show my face, in front of whatever medium, before whomever. I am innocent, and it affects me. I would never bring harm to a young guy like

him, and I have never done harm to anyone, I never abused [my authority]. I strictly carried out my duty.

The witnesses

On April 22, 2004, three reporters from local media were called to testify in the case of Alfredo Jiménez. The attorney general of Sonora had sent an agent from the prosecutor's office and asked his counterpart in Sinaloa to collaborate.

There in the PGJE facility in Tres Ríos, Culiacán, three men testified: Óscar Rivera, who then was a public relations officer for the state government but would be shot to death in September of 2007; Paúl Villegas, who worked at the radio program *Nuestras Noticias*; and Torivio Bueno, a journalist from *El Debate*, all three of them very close to Jiménez Mota.

They were questioned about what Jiménez was like professionally and personally, whether they knew his contacts, what they knew about the reports published there, and whether he had told them anything about carrying out his work in Sonora or about any threats he'd received.

Sources from the state attorney general's office indicate that in the statements at least one of the three mentioned then-commander Reynaldo Zamora as the man who threatened Jiménez in Culiacán. What is certain is that various threats against Alfredo indeed arrived at *El Debate*: unknown subjects insulted him and, worse, threatened him with death. Nobody did anything, and nobody knows to what names these threatening voices responded or who they served.

The last hours

"What do I do?" Alfredo Jiménez asked. What do I do? he asked his interlocutor, from the other side of the receiver. All of the contacts who worked with him were from the government. But he didn't dare go to them for protection: he didn't trust them.

Two weeks before they disappeared him, he sounded tired and he looked lonely, which was worse. He didn't trust anything or anyone.

Unknown subjects had set up in front of his home, and they were patiently waiting for him.

On one occasion, away from home, they overtook him, but he peeled away. On another, they intercepted him on a street in Hermosillo. He managed to make his way into a restaurant and out the back door, not without telling the manager to call the police.

Until the time he didn't elude them any longer. It was the second of April, in the middle of that solitude, the fear and the desperation, that his life fell into the black hole of impunity. And nothing more is known of him.

A newspaper that speaks

An old datebook was about to be thrown in the trash, at one of the papers where Jiménez worked. A faithful friend spotted it in the rubble, like a wounded little creature. A paper bird: wounded and sick. He recovered it, the datebook that Alfredo Jiménez used as a diary and telephone book. His tiny handwriting was there, his scribbles that no one would understand, his appointments and his friends' birthdays. There was nothing revealing, except that it belonged to a reporter who said "Present" when death called him in, because to disappear is a form of dying. So says the guy who'd asked his friend if he was actually going to the appointment offered by Adán Salazar. "Get on a plane that I'm going to send for you, and we'll talk there." He'd consulted his friend and told him, "Don't go, *cabrón*. They are going to kill you." And he didn't go to that one. But he wasn't used to missing appointments, much less with Lady Death herself. With her, he saw her once and didn't return.

Among the telephone numbers listed there are those of newspapers from the US border, like *Crónica* and also *Frontera* of Tijuana. There are also the numbers for human rights offices, the National Migration Institute (INM), the Red Cross, funeral parlors, agencies of the Justice Department, of the police. The datebook is from 2004. On the page corresponding to Saturday, June 24, two names appear: Jorge Valdez Fierro, shot to death on February 7, 2007, in the Sinaloan capital by a commando, and Héctor Ochoa Polanco, ex-director of the Ministerial

Police of Sinaloa and now a high official in that department. On July 5 the name of Paúl Villegas appears: "birthday." And on the third of that month, the inscription: "Homicides in Sinaloa, juvenile delinquents, unemployed professionals . . . culture of crime in Sinaloa."

The page for April 28 reads: "Little shining star . . . I already miss you." And on the 19th of that month, an email address, and under it the name of Ramona F. Sánchez, which perhaps corresponds to the contact the journalist had in the DEA. On February 18, at eleven o'clock, he noted, "Teaching conference: 'The Fourth Estate: Carlos Monsiváis.'" It was a conference organized by *Ríodoce* to celebrate its first anniversary. And on a Wednesday of that year, whichever one it was, he noted "Ash Wednesday."

Dead or alive

On April 2, 2012, during a memorial that turned into a protest, Alfredo Jiménez Hernández, the journalist's father, read a message in front of the plaque carrying his son's name in the Plaza del Empalme: "We asked that the forced disappearance of my son does not go unsolved [*no queda impune*]."[2]

Juan Fernando Healy Loera, the president and director general of *El Imparcial*, lamented the seven years in which we haven't learned anything more about the disappeared journalist and the fact that investigations have gone nowhere.

According to a news story by Ulises Gutiérrez, correspondent for *La Jornada*, Healy declared that since 2005, more and more deeds like that done to Jiménez Mota have shaken Mexican journalism and that the situation appears to be irremediable. Since then the National Commission on Human Rights (CNDH) has documented and opened files on more than 450 complaints of attacks on journalists and media outlets.

"We want to know what happened to the journalist Jiménez Mota, to take his case out of the archives of impunity in which many others have remained," Healy declared.

In April 2009, the journalist Yesicka Ojeda, from *El Imparcial*, interviewed Alfredo's parents, who lamented the utter lack of progress in the investigation and demanded the detention of those responsible and information about their son.

Esperanza Mota Martinez and José Alfredo Jiménez Mota relate that they keep the memory of their son alive in their home, where the journalist was born.

— Have there been any advances in the inquiries undertaken by SIEDO in the case of Alfredo Jiménez Mota?
— Since November 2008 everything remains the same, nothing has changed, and in truth we haven't asked about it because the people in charge of the case [SIEDO] contact the family if there are new developments in the investigation. We don't have any reason to be there if there's nothing that will reveal to us where our son ended up.
— What did you ask of the federal authorities and the Inter-American Commission on Human Rights?
— Just that they continue working so that what happened to Alfredo doesn't remain unsolved and unpunished, because up to this point we don't know what happened. The motive we do know, but no one has told us where he is and under what conditions, and who the masterminds [behind the crime] were.

The plague

A reporter sits down at a bar in Culiacán. He's visiting from Sonora, with other Sinasonorenses: people who come and go between Sinaloa and Sonora, who are originally from one or the other. By chance, he finds himself among other journalists, but he doesn't realize it. He tells them that he knew Alfredo, that in his final days in Hermosillo nobody wanted to go anywhere with him: "It was dangerous. The truth is, nobody wanted to give him a ride or to ride along with him. He was like a *bato* with the plague." He said it with a certain substance and pride. He also showed criminal imprudence. His interlocutor told him that he was also a journalist and that he knew Alfredo, and that he was sad about what had happened to him. The man asked him what outlet he worked for, and he gave him the name of the paper. The Sonoran guy took his beer and said that he had to go to another table where the friends he'd come with were waiting for him, but that he'd be back in a minute.

He didn't come back. He didn't even wave or say goodbye. Alfredo and his friends had the plague. Perhaps they were already dead. Because when a friend dies, they all die too. Something dies. Something goes away. Something never comes back, someone.

That's how Alfredo lived, in solitude, an ascetic. At the same time that his work was bleak, his life was that of a hermit, a madman. Reporters who knew him, but didn't share his methods, out of mediocrity or corruption, lack of interest, or other commitments, saw him from afar. They kept their distance: he's not going to cast a shadow over us, they appeared to say. That tormented soul was for many a dead man walking. And he reeked of death. That guy's the walking wounded; let him go. That's why they left him alone. And that solitude left him more vulnerable. They could find him, and they could cope with him. And many others have been taken with him, reporters in this country who go way beyond reporting official acts of the government and "covering buildings," who drink in the street, the plazas, the night life, the sidewalks, their beat, their flow, and their characters.

Alfredo was like that. He dove into the arms of his cities and towns. He gave himself innocently and passionately to his profession. He wrote; he communicated; he investigated. And that's how he worked, in solitude. And in the middle of a wilderness of devastation, he was lost.

Requiem on the web

An anonymous young man, a former classmate of Alfredo Jiménez, wrote the following on the comments section of web page containing a follow-up news story about the Jiménez disappearance: "El Mota took some classes in my hall, and one time when the teacher asked who was willing to die to defend the pen, the notebook and the tape recorder, he was the only one who raised his hand. RIP el Mota."

The luck of a pachyderm

Alfredo returned to his homeland. He didn't go back to die, like the pachyderms. But, without intending it, he left the last traces of his life there. He was already tired, fed up. In *El Imparcial* he wrote a lot, on things that were beyond thorny: they were downright bloody. For sales, for the spectacle, for demand, the *narco* theme wouldn't let go of Alfredo.

"They asked him for more and more. He was tired. I think that the guys at the newspaper wanted to be important, to position themselves well. They used him, as many others had before," his friend Gerardo remembers.

The Impunity Project report notes: "The violence unleashed since that date (April 2005) in the territory of Sonora has cost the lives of 74 people, 63 of them at the hands of *sicarios* in the service of organized crime, according to the data gathered from federal authorities and statistics."

"The body of Raúl Enriquez Parra appeared on a piece of land in the community of Masiaca, in the municipality of Navojoa, in the last week of November 2005, along with those of three other subjects, wrapped in sheets. So that there was no doubt about his identity, he carried several different credentials—including an IFE [federal elections] ID card and another one from a department store—along with a bank card issued in the United States. The bodies of the four presumed members of a band of drug traffickers were thrown from a small plane, after being subjected to prolonged torture."

Unofficial accounts indicate that this was a sign from the Sinaloa Cartel. The message: the bill for the Jiménez disappearance has been paid, and it stops here. This settling of accounts by that criminal organization included a purge. The city, the state, those Sonoran municipalities had been "hot" thanks to the disappearance of a journalist. Somebody had to pay for it.

Alfredo's disappearance provoked an avalanche of law enforcement operations, and finally the federal government seemed to realize the gravity of the problem that drug trafficking presented in that area. One report reads, "Seven ranches and five residential houses [were seized] from the criminal organization run by the Enríquez Parra brothers in Álamos, Navojoa, and Ciudad Obregón. Also, from the Salazar Zamorano family, four ranches and seven houses were seized in Navojoa and Álamos."

On the Las Tierritas Ranch, located on the highway that runs between Ciudad Obregón and Navojoa, Federal Investigations Agency (AFI) personnel discovered information and facts that were already public knowledge but which no local or federal police had ever bothered to investigate. They found a small zoo with lions and tigers, property of the suspected drug traffickers.

In total, the SIEDO seized property worth 46.2 million pesos from individuals involved in drug trafficking in the state.

Gerardo cries. His eyes are a sea of tears. June rain, a storm that comes on hot and aggressive and feels like it cuts, like it has sharp edges. Alfredo, his friend, disappeared on April 2, and his son was born on April 3. He wanted to name him after Alfredo, but his wife wouldn't let him. Since then, he's talked about the "gorilla," the "man-child," that chubby, innocent, and fearless reporter who distrusted everyone but always neglected himself. His passport and his little black bag didn't do him any good: one foot there on firm ground and the other fleeing, on the other side, wanting to save himself.

"They say that Alfredo was already pretty beat up, that they had him on a ranch, torturing him. That a *bato* showed up, this guy named Rolando, the boss of Los Números, one of the guys that they threw out of the airplane a short while later, because he provoked a schism in the Sinaloa Cartel, between the guys from Sonora and El Chapo, and had to be killed. And he got to where Alfredo was, and he told him, 'You don't know who I am.' And then he shot him in the head."

T-shirts, placards, and rallies

Gerardo says that journalism is shit. And he doesn't want to know anything else. His friend died for it, and they left him alone. Many of those who kicked him around and used him to let out or publish this or that bit of information, for political interests or those of the *narcos*, are now carrying placards and wearing T-shirts demanding justice in the case of his disappearance. They carry out acts of protest. In the photos they look very dignified.

"They kicked him with the toes of their boots. They gave it to him hard in the rear end. The truth is that we're not going to achieve anything in these demonstrations. It's pure circus, like that Phoenix Project—journalists from various media who were going to investigate the

Jiménez case and publish it together, which wasn't successful—pure idiocy."

He smiles, but he doesn't manage to burst out laughing. He describes Alfredo in his car, that black Topaz. He would put on the song "The Little Yaqui Girl" on the stereo: "I had a little Yaqui girl / who wanted a lot in Sonora / and when she danced the *cumbia* / this guy *se enamora* [fell in love]." Alfredo barely fit in the car, he would bounce and almost hit his head on the ceiling. He would take his right hand, and with his palm, that thick and heavy thing at the end of his arm, like a mallet, he would beat and beat on the dashboard, and hard. "Hey, *cabrón*, you're going to dent me." And he would smile. And he would answer, "Hey, *güey*, *cabrón*, don't leave me hanging."

"For me, since that day, since they left him alone . . . journalism can go fuck its mother." And once again the sea and the rain are in his eyes. He doesn't need April 2. He remembers. He misses him. "The truth is, I sometimes think that it's just nostalgia. That the *bato's* going to come through that glass door and say ¿*qué onda, güey?* ['what's up, dude?'] Don't leave me hanging, asshole. I had to hide. I was in danger. Now I'm back."

STORIES FROM TAMAULIPAS

A reporter from Tamaulipas writes this, but it's not published. She asks for information that nobody will give. Her notebook, pen, and digital recorder encounter sealed lips, eyes that don't see anything, hearts that only feel discreetly. She asks for details that go beyond the murders, the *levantones*, the massacres, the government operations. And the fear gets lodged in there, in the editing of the paper for which she works, on the corners, the daily routines, the plazas, and the parks. It wins out over everyone, establishing a reign of silence. Nobody talks, not even on the condition of anonymity. She offers to cut the news, to eliminate anything that might compromise them or put them at risk. Not even like this. An empire of blank pages. Silence and death reign on without so much as the clicking of a keyboard.

Eyes full of terror. Tears filling lakes. Souls ripped away from the lives that they once were, ruined. They no longer pulse with life. Blood in the air. Fire within. A slow death. That's what this reporter recounts. It's what she has to report but that she can't publish. It's what she writes.

I. Happy in the other world

Doña Mary is waiting by the window, her eyes half filled with tears, her heart in her throat. She listens to each boom as if it were a blow to the head. She can barely breathe. I don't know why she thinks that if she holds her breath the booming will stop.

Her husband warns her: "Woman, get out of there—what are you doing?"

But Doña Mary can't even hear him. The booms occupy all of her attention.

It's three o'clock in the morning, and the "fiesta" began two hours ago. Among the invited guests is her son, and she knows it, as does her husband, although he'd rather forget about it. She can't. Nor does she try.

On the TV, some guy swears that he lost forty-four pounds in one week just by drinking tea in the morning. Without going on a diet or exercising. Doña Mary continues to wait in the window with her heart in her throat. *Pum.* Dry. Suddenly, she hears the far-off screeching of tires. A crash and then an interminable horn.

Her heart stops. She feels like crying and crying. Her husband approaches and takes her away from the window: "They're going to hit you with a bullet, woman, understand?"

Her shoulders slump while her companion of almost thirty years leads her off to a chair. Doña Mary stares at the floor, with her heart tied in a knot.

"That was my boy," she almost says, as the guy on the TV shows a huge pair of pants that no longer fit him.

"You're crazy, woman," is the answer she receives. "Let's go get some sleep."

Doña Mary keeps looking at the floor while the booms drown out the sound of the horn. Two hours later, and the noise continues, and the sound of the horn dies out.

In the morning there's no news on the "party." The news outlets assure that in Reynosa, one eats well, that the show of gastronomy was a great success, and that Moreira's exit will not affect the PRI.

While she's drinking her coffee, Doña Mary receives news of her boy. They say that he crashed during a chase and that he was pinned under the wheel of his truck for hours, until they could rescue him.

She keeps slowly stirring her coffee without taking her eyes off of the floor. In her head, she can still hear that interminable car horn. Her heart is numb.

II. A rough patch

Over the last few months I've seen armed men show up at Oxxo to buy cans of tuna and saltines. I've seen army and navy convoys passing through the city. I've seen mere children carrying weapons almost as big as they are. I've seen, in truth, things that make my belly hurt.

But today, on the way to work, I witnessed a scene that crushed me, that crushed whatever it is that feels crushed in your chest when you see something that brings you to tears.

There was an old man sitting against a light pole, stranded, just to the side of the road. He had a long, dirty beard. His clothes were dirty and in tatters.

He was sitting with his back to the road and facing a wall. His face was buried in his hands. He rubbed his eyes and then sat quiet. Then the rubbed his nose and plunged his face back into his filthy and calloused fingers.

He put his hand on his forehead and shook his head. He breathed heavily and repeated the rubbing of his eyes.

We were putting a hundred pesos worth of gasoline in the truck, the one we were going to sell because we couldn't afford to keep two of them on what we make. Grumbling that it cost a hundred pesos, complaining to a machine.

The man had a plastic bag at his side, a stick and a blue towel. Next to him, tied to another post with a yellow rope, was a skinny black dog with white splotches. He was lying down, spent, without moving a hair. Waiting for the bad times to pass.

What an ass I am to think that buying a hundred pesos' worth of gasoline and having one truck less is a rough patch!

III. The power of custom

It's a lie that you get used to it. Some may say so, but no way. It's not true. The violence that engulfs the city is common and quotidian. It's the topic of conversation everywhere, it's even a natural topic among small children. This generation of children has grown up seeing soldiers and hearing bullets. They talk about it like it was a television program. But it's still not true that you get used to it.

Because when you get used to something, it's like it ceases to be important. You deal with it automatically and it doesn't bother you at all. You don't get used to hearing gunshots. Every time it happens, you feel your stomach tighten. Every time, a chill passes over your body. And you try to carry on like nothing's wrong. You try to get on with whatever you're doing. But inside you're shitting yourself, macho man. You're afraid. You pity yourself and those around you for living like this. You feel impotent. You feel rage and a strong desire to cry.

And you see those who don't hide their fear, those who throw themselves on the ground or put their backs up against a wall. You make fun of them, saying: "Enough already, it's not worth it. They're just bullets." But deep inside you're saying to yourself: "Fuck it; I'm just as afraid as you are, but I'm not going to give in. I'm not going to give the fear an opening." And then you say that you're used to it.

But when the windows shake or explode from the sound of a bazooka, or when you hear the dull thud of a car crashing and then the *pum, pum, pum*, hard, short, without an echo—it's a frozen embrace.

So the next time you ask me if I've gotten used to being in this city and I say yes, and I assure you that it's not so bad, that they're only bullets, you'll know what's up.

IV. An uproar over nothing

His son informed him that he was heading for the other side. Joaquín felt like a ferocious ray had penetrated his body. From the big toe on his right foot it cut through him all the way to the left side of his chest. The young man, José, twenty years old, told him that he wasn't the only one, that several others were going together to look for work, opportunities, and a little bit of money—"just enough to survive, Pop."

The father took out a cigarette. His left land stayed in the back pocket of his jeans. He left the cigarette dangling from his lips and remained deep in thought, pondering, distracted. His son approached and lit his dad's cigarette with a blue lighter, which he put back in the front pocket of his wrinkled shirt.

"Everybody's going, Pop. We're going in a group. Nothing's going to go wrong," he said, trying to gain ground on his father's despair, which had set in among the furrows of his brow. The father watched his son and later turned his head, trying to penetrate the door with his eyes and travel along with his son and take care of him.

He remained like that, suspended in a far-off gaze, his eyes penetrating the unwashed shirt that his son wore that day, while he disappeared in the always uncertain and far-off firmament of those afternoons in Matamoros, Tamaulipas. They're from San Luis Potosí, a neighboring state in the grip of the violence generated by criminal groups in the hands of the Zetas, Golfo, and Sinaloa, above all others. Every plaza, city, and region has its owner, and all of them fight over the market for drugs, but also the lucrative businesses of extortion, kidnapping, and robbery.

Not wanting to find out

Joaquín hadn't heard anything more about him in a long time. The year 2010 was beginning, and his heart was dried out, lean with sadness, shrouded with nostalgia. He didn't know it, but his son, who had made it a long way in his path to the border and the United States, had been taken by armed men. There were many of them, and they all had assault rifles, goat horns—AK-47s.

Joaquín made it to the border town with three other men from his pueblo. They learned that there were many dead bodies there. Bodies had been found in mass graves. The majority had not been identified. In his pueblo they called for a "roundup" (*una vaquita*) in the region where they said that many people had disappeared, about halfway to the city, in the border region of Tamaulipas.

In his backpack, he carried photos and papers from sons, brothers, fathers, and uncles of all those who'd left in the group with José. And three others from his pueblo accompanied Joaquín, all of them relatives, who joined him on this macabre journey to find his son. That time, among so many mutilated cadavers, with bullet holes and dried blood everywhere, unnerved by the signs of torture, they hoped not to find anything or anyone they recognized.

Hopefully, they'll just kill me

José's heart beats fast. A freezing sensation ascends from his feet to his throat. His hands go numb. It's difficult to breathe. It's as if a wet towel was pushing on his nose and mouth, suffocating him. They had been advised that the path would be dangerous. That it didn't matter that there were many of them if the others were armed. Well-armed. The truck in which they're traveling stops near a gap in the road. Necks strain from the seat backs. José knows they are coming for them. He is paralyzed with fear.

Three of them get out of a white SUV with tinted windows. They aren't even men. They are barely older than children. They have pistols on their belts and rifles in their hands. They are dressed like soldiers. They get on the bus and shout something that José doesn't understand. He is just concentrating on breathing. The imaginary towel over his nose tightens. His chest caves in, his throat closes, his heart is about to explode. Suddenly he feels a strong pulling. One pull is enough; he doesn't resist. There is no point to it. They all get out and line up next to the truck. Then their hands are placed behind their necks, and they are made to kneel in the dirt, to keep their heads down. The attackers keep shouting, giving orders that all of them follow in silence, despite the fact that there is much in this scene that none of them understand.

One of the guys grabs José by the hair and ties a rag over his eyes. The rag smells of gasoline and the guy smells of smoke. The knot is tight, but not as tight as the one he feels in his throat.

"I hope they kill me fast. I hope that they just kill me," José thinks over and over again.

Watery eyes

Joaquín is stopped along the line that divides Mexico from the United States. That's where he and the others looking for the disappeared ended up. An army of the deported walks crestfallen in their direction across the international bridge. Soldiers dragging their feet and their illusions. He strains his body to take it all in, and he squints to focus his myopic eyes. His heart rushes. He wants to see his boy in the crowd. One and then another pass by. None of them familiar.

Zombies who come from desolation, on the way to further desolation. A fatal destiny. A desert without an oasis separates them. Joaquín's eyes fill with tears as it starts to get dark, and they still haven't seen their people. Watery eyes, they seem to melt along with his hopes.

Now I'm going to charge you

Thrown on the cold floor of the pickup, José starts to feel that the blood isn't getting to his hands. That's the first thing that goes numb, even though in reality his entire existence has become rheumatic. He has tape wrapped around both of his wrists, pinning them to his back. He feels like oil, like dirt, like blood. His body is jolted as the truck makes its way along a winding road that is full of holes. Dusty. He is shaken back and forth, banging his elbows, his ribs, and his back.

Finally they stop. *I hope they kill me fast, I hope they just kill me* continues running through his mind. A strong shove and José tumbles to the ground. It's dirt, rocks and dirt, with a little bit of grass. He feels a kick in the gut and then hears an order: "On your feet, *cabrón!* On your feet!"

With effort, José gets up, and he can barely walk. He is blindfolded. Shoves, laughing, voices, music in the background, like his life and his turbulent breathing. Moans. More beatings. A hard throw against the cold wall of a colder room. He hears crying, hard breathing. He smells sulfur, gasoline, sweat, and roasted meat. Or something burned, anyway.

He can barely feel the rag over his eyes. *I hope that they just kill me*, he repeats in his mind, while he opens and closes his hands to fight the numbness.

He gropes around, trying to get comfortable. He hears shouts, threats, and laughing. Then he feels the hot, foul breath of the guy who threw him out of the truck: "Now I'm going to charge the fuck out of you."

José gulps and thinks: *I hope they bump me off soon.*

The pueblo of the dead

After several days, Don Joaquín and his traveling companions arrive in the town where it is said more than two hundred dead bodies were found. It's called San Fernando. Hopefully this name, the name of that saint, of that pueblo, will never be forgotten. They carry in their backpacks a fraying treasure of photographs and papers of their disappeared people, looking for anyone who can tell them something worthwhile about what happened to them. They ask one and then another, but it's like they're invisible.

Sitting on a bench in the office of the migration authorities, they see a truck arriving from a distance, with the letters SEMEFO painted on it. Officials from the Forensic Medical Service get out. Dressed in white, they start to unload large bundles wrapped in black trash bags. The smell makes Don Joaquín sneeze. He tries to prevent it, but exhaustion overcomes him, and he stumbles to the floor, surrounded by the ghastly smell. The smell of death, of dried blood, stiff muscle tissue, like a branch office of hell.

As they pass by, he asks if they'll let him take a look at the bodies. He offers a quick summary of his journey in vain to find an answer, some kind of understanding or pity. He's trying to awaken in those men in white a little humanity, to make them recognize the tears that he's wasted so far, to awaken their sensibility, to remind them that they are carrying the bodies of young people, sons and daughters who have someone waiting for them.

Nothing happens. The men ignore Joaquín as if he were another corpse. There are other bundles, other bodies to dig out or rescue from unmarked graves in order to take them to other graves and to a common grave, the grave of oblivion and forgetting. A group of policemen explain to him that nobody is going to let him see those pieces of death wrapped in black plastic.

SAN FERNANDO

In San Fernando Tamaulipas, the first bodies were found on April 1, 2011, by personnel of the state attorney general's office. Five days later, the media reported fifty-nine dead in eight common graves.

Officials from the federal government, who declined to reveal their names, explained that the victims had apparently been traveling on a bus headed toward the US border when they were intercepted by presumed members of the Zetas Cartel, whose reign and criminal presence in the region is beyond any discussion.

This *levantón* and others like it took place in March of that year, and it was managers of the company Omnibus of Mexico who formally denounced the crimes on March 24, and thus investigations began. It was business as usual, however, and nothing happened.

The news media reported that a woman from Matamoros, very near the US border, with a husband who had never arrived in San Luis Potosí, where he was headed, had witnessed the kidnapping of a passenger bus. There had been other reports since then.

Authorities believe that the criminals had chosen some victims they'd intended to forcibly press into duty as killers or lookouts, others for purposes of ransom, and still others from whom they'd planned to extort a passage fee. None of this has been confirmed. The only witnesses are dead. If there *were* others, they wouldn't speak: no one trusts the government.

On April 8, two more mass graves were found, with twenty-three bodies in them, all men. On April 10, the secretary of national defense reported that Armando César Morales Uscanga had been arrested, had confessed to having participated in the massacres, and had provided details about four more gravesites, in which there were sixteen bodies. Afterward, the federal attorney general said that the number of bodies totaled 116, that seventeen people had been detained in connection with the murders, among them Johnny Torres Andrade, and that they might be part of the Zetas. The federal government had also arrested sixteen members of the municipal police of San Fernando, where the number of bodies kept rising.

The toll rose to 193, according to data from the attorney general. But unofficial sources claim that the number of dead could be higher, as many as five hundred. The official reports claim that 122 of the victims correspond to passengers from the hijacked passenger buses.

Martín Omar Estrada Luna, known as El Kilo, eventually was arrested by the Ministry of the Navy as the supposed mastermind behind massacres linked to the mass graves. Federal authorities issued arrest warrants against eighty-five more individuals.

Silence and cold

The noises have diminished. José assumes that it is nighttime, because the music that roared at the beginning has died down to a murmur, intermixed with the chirping of crickets and the yowling of some coyotes. The night screams in silence and nobody hears it.

His legs begin to get cold, and he doesn't hear any more voices. He knows nothing of the fate of those who came with him. Nor does he know if he should pray that they're still alive or that they've been killed quickly.

It's very cold now, and he can't tell whether it's just him or truly cold outside. He can't feel his legs. Even the animal sounds diminish to almost nothing. He's alone in silence, cold, and darkness. A roar of nothingness. *I wish they had just killed me,* José thinks.

Nobody knows if they let him go, or if he managed to escape. If he's alive. Alive in Matamoros and San Luis or in some place nearby. Here in this region where nobody talks, not the government, not the journalists. Fear stuffed the same damp stinking rag in their mouths that José felt when they captured him and tortured him. Death keeps close watch over everyone. Silence reigns. That's why José doesn't say any more.

THE PRICE OF CHARISMA

He wanted to get started in the drug business. And he made it. And with the same speed that he got in, he got out. A fateful withdrawal from crime in Culiacán. Julio lived with a woman who had two children. One of them, who was almost twenty-one, Julio loved as if he were his own, and he led him by the hand until he joined the ranks of the Sinaloa Cartel, in one of its cells composed mostly of kids of that age or perhaps a little older.

"The boy liked to dress well. A good boy, a good person. Women liked him, and he could chat anybody up, and so the other boys felt cast aside, because he soaked up the spotlight with friends and women," explained a family member who knew him well.

"They didn't like it," he added, "that he wanted to dress well, and they even complained about how he dressed, with a certain elegance. Wherever we went, people treated him as if he were the boss."

Envy and rancor. Those two words describe the feelings of Julio's relatives, who came to know the fate of that young *culichi*, up close and personal. But none of them would have foreseen the violent consequences of his decisions, the threats from the top echelons of the Sinaloa Cartel and its well-oiled criminal machinery.

The hunt

It was early February 2011. The young man was with a woman. He'd come in his car and hadn't parked it at his house but rather a little ways off. Perhaps he hadn't wanted them to see him, or he wanted to avoid being seen with the woman. But at least two men had him in their sights and watched him arrive at the apartment where he lived, in a private development called Valle Alto. Those who know about the case later claimed that he'd gone there to pick up some money he had stashed.

They were there, parked. Hunting. They opened the doors, got out, and moved stealthily toward the apartment. From the right-hand side of their clothes two firearms emerged and then were raised.

He didn't see them until they were very close. The minimum distance between life and death. Nothing separated him from death except perhaps a brief dialogue, a dozen heartbeats in those tense movements of the second hand of the *sicario*'s racing clock. Perhaps nothing.

An ephemeral exchange of words. Monosyllables that barely reached his eardrums. Demands, insults. Words that don't hurt any more than the bullets. The weapons pointed. "You've hit the end of the road." *Pum, pum.* They used 5.7 caliber "police-killer" weapons, capable of piercing armor. On the scene, authorities later found eleven shell casings, according to preliminary reports from the State Ministerial Police and the Intentional Homicides unit from the State Prosecutor's Office.

The young woman watched the whole thing from the car nearby, but the murderers didn't realize it. She shouted, on instinct, then covered her strawberry mouth with her hands, holding back a sea of shouts and pain and fright. Her eyes were open. She saw the flashes from the guns. She saw them shooting. Him on the ground. A body in the throes of death, that didn't stop moving, even down on the pavement. They turned, went back to their car, opened the doors, and everything froze.

And she was there. Covering her mouth. Swallowing her shouts. Containing howls. Emotion overflowing from her eyes, the eyes of the woman who saw. Who had watched him fall. Who saw their faces, their hands, and their weapons. The victorious smoke of their barrels. Who saw their faces. She knew. It was them: they killed him.

She trembles and can't manage to press the right buttons on her cell phone. Then she can't speak. Her hand is at her mouth again. The words pile up within her. Finally she manages to emit syllables, to construct words. She speaks, she warns.

They killed him. *Click.*

Vengeance is a double-edged sword

His mother is knocked over by the news. Her pain overflows, beginning with her eyes, from which come resounding, tumultuous tears. She speaks with Julio, her partner, the man with whom she's had two of her four children. Even though they boy didn't belong to him, Julio loved him as if he had.

She comes up to him, makes a fist, and wipes the tears from her eyes with the back of it. "I want vengeance."

The man loves her, and he embraces her. He wants nothing more than to console her, to be there for her. He knows that the murderers are from the same cartel for whom he worked. That it's a tangle. That once you wade into it, it will be difficult to get out. That it's dangerous, very dangerous. He decides to stand by her, but he doesn't want to get involved in settling the score with the murderers. She insists. Julio tries to calm her down.

A few days pass and she remains firm. He backs away. She starts to move on her own. She has contacts, money, and a thirst for vengeance.

"Without her partner realizing it, because he wasn't convinced that taking vengeance was the right thing to do, and he didn't want to get in trouble, because he knew the kind of people who killed the boy, her son, she sought out and managed to hire seven pistoleros. Their job was to deal with the two who killed her son."

Two taken

Two men were taken by a commando. They didn't appear in the police blotter. Everything was calm in the city. The daily toll in Sinaloa is five to seven murders, a number that occasionally reaches ten. But these guys didn't make the count. Nor would they make the pages of the daily newspapers.

The commandos captured the two men who killed that boy. Then, out of nowhere, the imprudent idea came to them of demanding a ransom. They contacted the families of the two and asked for 500,000 pesos for their release. The relatives, all of whom were involved in organized crime, responded rapidly, and without verification they handed over the money.

For the commandos, it was easy—too easy—and quick. And they felt confident, in the face of a good business deal. Not only did they refuse to release their captives, they now asked for more money in exchange for their lives: 500,000 in US dollars.

For those from the cartel—in whose ranks the belief seemed to predominate that there were no kidnappings in Sinaloa, but, if ever one were to occur, the kidnappers should be eliminated immediately—they appeared suspicious. The captors hadn't carried out their end of the bargain and now they were asking for more money. "They've developed a taste for it."

The *narcos* started investigating, and they found them, the kidnappers and captives, in a safe house. They surprised the seven captors and discovered that one of the young men for whom they had paid a ransom was already dead. Then the torture and mutilations began. Confessions.

The seven *sicarios* started to fall. The blood smelled like a backed-up drain. Pieces of life going here and there, pieces of men who used to give orders and who'd always had a finger on the trigger. A bullet in the head. Among the confessions: one of them said that he had overheard a conversation between the woman who hired them and her husband. The *narcos* knew this guy, the husband, was the father-in-law of the young man killed in the private housing development. They looked at each other and questioned each other without saying a word. Then they killed all of kidnappers and went looking for the father-in-law—and the mother.

They found that the mother, the woman who had hired those seven *sicarios*, was no longer in the city. She had vanished. She had known that someone would come after her, and so she'd taken off with her children.

They didn't find the father-in-law either. When he heard about the trail of mutilations, the bodies plugged full of holes, and the pools of blood, he went to see them.

A week of safe conduct

It was early 2012. The year had begun, suspended in front of the dark barrels of AK-47 automatic rifles, in front of a buzzing electric saw, under a hammer, under a long, sharp, bloodstained butcher knife, a wide-handled knife narrowing about halfway down the cheerful blade.

"She called before she left. She said something that sounded like 'they took the boys from me.'" He understood perfectly well what she was talking about. She knew, and he did too. At that moment, nothing else meant anything. He knew that they were looking for him. Before they got moving and their rabid mouths foamed in his face, with their fingers on triggers, he went looking for them.

He didn't plan to hand himself over, but rather to negotiate. He spoke with someone close to them. A guy who had some authority to give orders, but at about the fourth or fifth level in the structure of the Sinaloa Cartel, outside of the area, from Culiacán but operating in Baja California.

A commando found her house, in the Lomas del Sol development, and unloaded their weapons on it. But the house, now shot full of holes, with the front door kicked in, was empty.

Hooded

They don't give special treatment. The argument that Julio and his companion had come "to clarify, to resolve the matter" didn't matter to them. They hooded the two and took them to a safe house. Here there were several bodies and body parts strewn about, likely the same seven that they had recently killed.

The person Julio had brought with him turned out to have no influence. The captors set the conditions, and they demanded that the husband promise to turn over his wife. He said nothing.

A woman who knew they were in trouble, a relative of the Julio's, went looking for one of the principle *sicarios* of Ismael Zambada García, El Mayo. She couldn't find him but did find her brother, who had some sway. She knew that Julio was innocent, that he'd had nothing to do with what had happened, and she asked that they leave him alone.

One of the guys who had taken Julio answered a call on his cell. He and his minions were warned: "Don't get mixed up in this. That *bato* that you have there is my brother's compadre, and if anything happens to him, it's going to bother him, and there will be trouble, serious *broncas*. People will get fucked up—you know the drill."

There had been death threats in that cold and foul room. One of the murderers had hit him in the knee with a rifle butt. But after they received that call everything changed. That's why they let him go. But they also told him, as a warning, that he should hand over the mother of the young man they had shot dead. Find her and turn her in. He didn't agree to this and left with his heart and his stomach tied in knots. And a heavy, incessant *what do I do, now?* thumping in his head.

Are you going to turn over your wife?

When Julio got home, he found his siblings, friends, and his father well informed. All of them had experience and weight in the Sinaloa Cartel. With words that bored into his brain like a drill, his father told him, "How are you going to turn over your wife, the mother of your children? It would be like if I decided, on the spur of the moment, to turn over your mama. Do you believe that I would turn her over?" The old man simultaneously berated and questioned him, as did everyone else in his family, recounted a person close to them.

The husband remained stone-faced. His eyes cracked as if they were stained glass windows. His cheeks puffed out. Finally, at the end of that conversation in which they dressed him down and called him out, he decided that he had to take measures into his own hands, to get out of there and prepare for the worst. He left his house and headed to another he had in Culiacán, and there he put on a bulletproof vest. He "chested up" as they say in the argot of the *narcos*, referring to vests that carry loaders, cartridges, and grenades. He took a goat's horn and stocked up on bullets.

They didn't let him go it alone. Two or three of his friends and relatives joined him and entrenched themselves in that house. They thought, *If they come, we'll be waiting for them. We're not afraid of them.*

Meeting at the summit

The head of *sicarios* for El Mayo returned to the city. His brother filled him in on everything, and he immediately went looking for his compadre—Julio, the husband, the father-in-law of the kid who had been killed. He found the man holed up in his house, located in a populous sector that used to be at the edge of the city but had been devoured by the hungry urban growth, to the west, near the Tamazula River.

He endorsed what everyone there had been saying: Don't turn over your wife or your kids or anyone else. "If they want her, let them look for her, and if they find her, we'll see what happens."

A person close to the family explains, "That guy, who was one of the real bosses, on the third level, more or less, said that they were together on this one and that he would support them. They had all of his backing for whatever happened. He was very angry that the person who accompanied Julio [the husband] to resolve the issue, when they were hooded and taken away, [hadn't known] how to pull rank. Known as El Seis, 'He didn't know how to react; he must have been wringing his hands, because he's a damned nervous type' . . . but regardless, he didn't make them respect him."

The boss spoke with those who had kept his compadre captive. Apparently the matter was cleared up, and that was it. One of Julio's wife's relatives went to the Dominican Republic, after everything had calmed down, and he was detained there. US and Mexican authorities accused him of having transported drugs, but other sources identify him as a participant in an encounter at the summit between a former president of that country and Joaquín Guzmán Loera, El Chapo, head of the Sinaloa Cartel. After his arrest, the young *culichi*, an airplane pilot, was taken to New York, where he remains a prisoner.

The Ministerial Police and dirty work

Early in June, Julio was driving a late-model pickup down Universitarios Boulevard, near the University City, in Culiacán. Julio was confident. He wasn't carrying drugs or guns, and he wasn't driving drunk. That's why he didn't even frown when he saw the turrets and the black patrol cars without plates or any kinds of numbers on them, cars that bore the seal of the Ministerial Police that seemed to be waiting for him.

The officers, about twenty of them, were on both sides and in front of four patrol cars from the PME. They signaled for him to stop. They wore masks and carried G3 military-style assault rifles. On their belts hung new pistols that appeared to be 9mm Glocks. They asked him where he was going, what he was doing, and what his name was. They asked for identification, and they went over the vehicle, a 2010 Jeep Cherokee, meticulously. They took out cell phones and communicated his name. The boss talked privately with the guy who called in his name.

It would appear, according to unofficial accounts, that the police were members of a cell of the Sinaloa Cartel known as Los Anthrax, who were influential in the southern sector of the city. They were infamous, known for being dangerous.

Julio was still confident, even after they told him that he had to go with them. That he should advise his family that he was being detained. His relatives went to police headquarters, on Zapata Boulevard. "We don't have him detained here," an employee answered. And, in effect, they didn't. The police took him, and he found himself among armed men. They handed him over. They put him in a vehicle and he was taken to a safe house. Then he frowned. Now he felt himself at a disadvantage, lost. He had no idea what was going to happen.

He didn't know either that another commando, whose members were identified as Ministerial Police, had arrived at the house of one of his nephews, who was between seventeen and eighteen years old, in a sector near where he himself had been taken, and carried him off. Nobody knew where they were. Both were in the hands of the same criminal group.

Zambada's operator and the compadre of the captive husband went once again to meet with his family. He had details on the two *levantones*. He talked and talked. Three long phone calls.

Then he called a higher up in the Ministerial Police: "The police explained over the phone that one of the officers informed headquarters that the two had been handed over, that they no longer had them in custody. Then the boss got mad. He shouted at them, 'I want you to let them go immediately [otherwise] I'm coming down there, and I'm going to send all of them to fuck their mothers, and you too!' And then he hung up."

A little while later, armed men who worked for the boss released Julio and his nephew. They left them at a remote crossroads, on lands that were part of commercial development, in an area under the influence of *los narco juniors*, the spoiled children of prominent drug traffickers, a place called Isla Musala.

The police and the armed group to which they had handed over the two men returned two trucks they had taken from the nephew's house and the Cherokee Julio was driving when he was intercepted by the Ministerial Police.

"When they arrived," a relative said, "the boss told them, 'We've gotten to the point at which you must decide what you want to do. If we fight with them, how're you going to feel about it? If you want to fight, we'll fight. I've already had it up to here with those *cabrones* . . . or strike me down right here.' He was very angry. I've rarely seen him this angry, this pissed off."

The same source claims that his compadre remained calm. That he answered that fighting should be the last resort: "I just want them to stop bothering me." The boss spoke with the captors again: "These people are with me, and you have to respect them, and this is the last time that you're going to pick [up] anybody of mine, anybody from here. And if there's something else you want, let me know. And those who want a piece of me, you know how and where to find me."

A chink in the armor

Julio was outside of his house. A close relative arrived and was surprised to find him there. He responded that they hadn't come for him yet, that he was still waiting. The relative asked him why he didn't go out in his Cherokee anymore, and he shrugged his shoulders. He twisted his mouth and closed his eyes. "I don't know," he replied.

— Are you afraid?
— Yes. I don't trust them.
— Yes, you're right. There are still quarrels, wounds left behind.

And yes, there were quarrels, wounds, cracks, interstices. Some went away or healed but others remained. Nobody knew when or how this would all end, and it was already June 2012. Those cracks, aching wounds, and hatreds clogged up the works, left scores unsettled. They could grab him and his family at a traffic light, take them, and disappear them forever. Even though the big shots, those at the summit, assured him that nothing would happen: they feared Gonzalo, better known as El MP or Macho Prieto, and they weren't going to lift a finger against him.

Many knew about this conflict in which two strong bands within the Sinaloa Cartel confronted each other. Those who needed to know, knew. From Guzmán Loera, El Chapo, to Manuel Torres, alias El Ondeado. Up to this point, it added up to nine homicides, and the media had only taken notice of one of them, the very first, the murder of Julio's son-in-law in the Valle Alto housing development.

"It seems like a fantasy, as if none of it ever happened. Where are all of the dead? Who knows. One asks who's looking for them, where are their friends and family, the complaints, the police investigations. There are a lot of dead, and nothing happens. It seems unreal. You get to the point where you doubt that it happened, that it's true," affirmed a person who knew about the unfolding of this case firsthand.

What's certain is that it did happen, that it included the death of at least nine people, the participation of fifteen Ministerial Police officers, three *levantones*, seven disappeared who have yet to be identified, and one woman and her children, fugitives, all within seven or eight months. And it is not over. This happened, and it continues happening.

I DO HAVE HOPE

José Luis Zavala has all of the names in his head. He remembers everything, and that's why he's got sixteen years fighting the good fight, and
he will not wait twenty-four more as hope prescribes. That's why he asks
for justice, and he wants it already. He says that he's waiting for a courageous governor to appear, "somebody with balls."

He's wearing a white, long-sleeved shirt despite an oppressive heat,
and the hands of the clock indicate that it's already seven o'clock in
the evening. The shirt has capricious pen marks all over it. And there,
behind that seemingly fierce expression and that large round face, a
righteous man comes to the surface.

He was the second special prosecutor in the case of the three young
people disappeared from Las Quintas. A disappearance forgotten by
many, a ghost case, a vague remembrance, dyed gray and sepia, a wrinkled sheet of newsprint covered in dust and soot, diffuse, vast, and
blurry.

But the three young people had names. They lived and celebrated,
justifiably, their beating hearts: at a fiesta in the Las Quintas development, among friends, fiancées, relatives, and neighbors, with some
drinks swimming through their veins and the throbbing of disco music
in their chests and their feet moving to the rhythm of their dreams.

They were the cousins Jorge Cabada Hernández, nineteen, Juan Emerio Hernández, eighteen, and Abraham Hernández Picos, seventeen.
Since July 30, 1996, nothing has been known about them. This is, perhaps, the case that swayed Sinaloan society, the one with the greatest
national coverage, the case that provided clear evidence of the sewer of
corruption and complicity between state and federal authorities and an
entrepreneur with a fortune of questionable origins.

And this man in the ink-stained shirt, the ex-prosecutor who is now
unemployed, who gives classes without charging for them and who
attends to the cases that fall to him now and again, pokes his nose in
and takes a shot when he can, in his quest to clarify the disappearance of
those three young men. In pursuing this case, he crossed a governor and

an attorney general and lost his job. He got guns pointed at him and a price put on his head.

The night that never ended

It was dawn on Saturday, June 30. The three cousins, Jorge Cabada Hernández, Juan Emerio Hernández, and Abraham Hernández Picos, left a crowded party in Las Quintas after quarreling with the host, Rommel Andrade, who had apparently interceded in defense of his sister Helga and was the loser in a scuffle with one of the guests.

The security detail for the Andrade family participated in the row, and the three cousins had interceded to separate the men who were fighting and had taken a couple of blows in the process. Rommel, the son of the powerful and influential businessman Rolando Andrade Mendoza, threatened everyone involved: "You're going to pay for this, *cabrones*. I'm going to fuck you up. Because nobody touches my family."

The young men got into their 1995, sea-blue Grand Marquis, Sinaloa plates VFP-2576. They went to a home nearby to drop off one of their friends. They stayed there for about forty minutes. They left, and shortly thereafter they were intercepted by four municipal police officers. And from that point forward . . .

"We wanted to go where they were, we'd thought we'd find them in the places [where it was] said that they'd been, we chatted with them . . . just a few blocks from the house, and since then we've heard nothing more from them," reads a notice by their parents, published in *Noroeste* on Friday, July 19, that year.

The ledger of death

Zavala can't stop shredding a napkin. He rips it into tiny strips. He does it with fury, with passion and anger against oblivion. He's got it all written down on twenty sheets that he keeps like his most personal memories, but which represent, in reality, putrid pieces of the life of a city, a state, a country. The pestilent life of corruption, impunity, and collusion among the powerful, a brotherhood of evil, those who are among the elite in

government, business, and organized crime, whatever their particular
modality.

He wears a yellow tie. He keeps most of it in his head, under his
proper haircut. And on those sheets he's never stopped updating. He
has a photographic memory and sees the past with numbers, names,
dates, and everything. He's a fly on the wall. He looks up, to the side,
and he appears to step back and look into himself, his insides. He says
that he doesn't forget, that he's got it all there, and he presses his finger
against his temple dramatically, as if he were going to push it in by force.
It leaves a mark on his skin, and he resumes shredding the napkin. But
he doesn't surrender his blue Bic pen.

"I want to get the splinter out of me, to bring this mother to light,
to see justice done," he says, almost shouting. Nobody turns around,
because the restaurant is half empty, and he doesn't care if the waiter
hears him or the manager at the other end of the room or the cashier.

"It's symptomatic," he repeats, a chatterbox of facts, dancing with an
unedited memory or making a long oration, like a *novenario* (a nine-day
funeral ceremony), enumerating the precise number of patrols and the
date and time of each. And his memory, which doesn't tell him lies, puts
on the table the name of Karina Polanco Núñez, who was the cashier on
the dawn shift at the tollbooth in front of the community of El Limón de
los Ramos, in Culiacán. It's her job to keep track of the patrol cars that
pass by without having pay to toll, and thus she noted patrol number 023
from the municipal police. In that car were the officers Juan Luis Quiroz
Ávila and Héctor Manuel Medina. They passed from north to south,
headed in the direction of Culiacán. A blue and white Suburban did the
same, accompanied by a gray pick-up, with the label PC 1002 from the
Intermunicipal Police (now defunct), about 4:52 the same morning. But
they were headed from south to north, from Culiacán toward Mocorito.
On the way back from the north, the patrol car didn't pass the tollbooth,
as it apparently traveled on the road that runs through the community of
Mojoso and thus avoids the Mexico City–Nogales Highway 15. It wasn't
recorded by the tollbooth cashier.

Later, at about seven o'clock that morning the three vehicles returned
together northbound. The trucks with the numbers PC1002 and PC1003
were assigned by the Ministry of Citizen Protection (now defunct as well),

of which the Intermunicipal Police formed part, to the security detail of the businessman Rolando Andrade.

According to the investigations carried out by Zavala, when he was the lead investigator for the prosecutor's office—the second one, after the family of the disappeared young men had serious differences with Carlos Gilberto Morán Morales, the first man assigned to lead the investigation—the victims were in one of these trucks. They had apparently been intercepted by the police at about four that morning.

Zavala, who carried out investigations without precedent in the city and perhaps in many regions of the country, who labored in the basements of power, in the dark, polluted, and foul-smelling interstices, discovered many facts that should have led to the detention of those responsible "without anyone else getting hurt," he says. And then he interrupts himself.

"And why am I so stubborn?" And he responds: "Because [of] Governor Renato Vega Alvarado, the attorney general Amado Zambada, and the entire state apparatus, all of it." They protected him. They protected Rolando Andrade.

He continues:

> In the building that Rolando Andrade owns on Revolution Avenue, in the Colonia Aurora, located in the eastern part of the city, several vehicles were seen that dawn. The building is but a shell. It looked like it was going to be a commercial establishment or maybe offices. What's certain is that it barely had walls, in a wilderness, with a large parking lot inside. There was a Blue Grand Marquis that they, the three cousins, had been using, halfway in the door, next to the patrol car 023 from the municipal police, which was just behind it, and next to it, the pickup with the 1002 plate, and also the blue Suburban, and a black Ram truck, which belonged to the businessman.
>
> The patrol car left with the boys, the cousins, down Antonio Caso Street, and then turned around on Gabino Barrera, and then took Xicoténcatl, headed north . . . they carried off the boys, but then a counterorder arrived, and the Suburban overtook them, and the copilot of the one talked with the driver of the patrol car. Witnesses told me this, people who saw it with their own eyes. . . . Then the car started moving again, and [again] the Suburban crossed their path. They got the three out and put them in the

back seat; they weren't wearing shirts or undershirts, and they were
barefoot, hands tied behind their backs. That was on Xicoténcatl,
before they got to the embarcadero.

One witness said that he recognized the copilot of the Suburban "because he was part of the municipal police when I was an
officer, and I identified him clearly." Furthermore, an agent of the
Intermunicipal Police was on duty in the tollbooth and identified
them when they left and returned. And it was the same copilot . . .
as I told you, it's symptomatic, it's not just a coincidence. All of this
has plain evidentiary value. We're talking about the testimony.

The lawyer and professor at the Escuela Libre de Derecho (a private
law school), of which he is the founder and thus received no salary,
affirmed the need to prove that this silhouette, this person, was the same
who appears on the video from the tollbooth. Zavala and his staff followed him, they took pictures of him. Again and again. The same pose,
the arm bedecked with tattoos, the same watch and the same bracelet.
"We followed him and took pictures without him realizing it."

"I have all of the names in my head," he says. He repeats them. It
seems like he's going to explode. An explosion of names, dates, times,
and details. So much information that it's going to spill out. If his overflowing memory doesn't provoke that explosion, his passion for finding,
catching, and punishing will. He still wants justice. The crime still hasn't
expired. But he knows and knows it well—it pains him to know this: There's
no body. There are no bodies. They aren't here. Nor is there death, not
legally anyway. But there certainly are in his memory. Death by memory.

The value of a good drinking session

A young man was drinking with some friends. Two people presumed to
be involved in the cousins' disappearance were there. One said that in
high school he'd met a person who had been there when it went down
and that another guy was implicated as well. This account made it all the
way to the prosecutor's office, and he put people to work on it.

On Zavala's order, the police picked up one person. And this guy gave
them another name. "One of them said at the same drinking session
that he had talked to his family, his kids, his mother-in-law and his wife

about what had happened. That they had dug a hole into which they had thrown Juan Emerio, and another for Jorge and Abraham. 'But I didn't shoot them. They put a bullet in each guy's chest and another in the head."

They kept the detained guy in the barracks of the Ninth Military Zone, in Culiacán. General Guillermo Martínez Nolasco was the local commander. He was also Zavala's unflappable supporter, his accomplice, protector, and friend.

"We trusted each other and we made a pact. We had him in the barracks with everything, and a bedroom, food, and everything set up so that they could guard him. He asked us for protection because he feared Andrade more than the state government, and he asked us to hide him, and the general agreed. But they pulled some strings and complained that we had the guy incommunicado, that we had tortured him. And this wasn't true. But we didn't handle it well," Zavala says.

Jaime Palacios, an old leftist fighter, a founder of the Sinaloa branch of the Party of the Democratic Revolution (PRD) and former professor at the Autonomous University of Sinaloa, a family friend who knew Zavala, was up to speed on the case. He put his own face out there in front of the media to claim that there had been no such torture and that they guy had been taken to the military barracks for his own protection.

The detained man described an uninhabited area behind some motels in the northern part of the city. There they investigated, dug, and searched. Nothing. The ex-prosecutor says that the bodies were exhumed and carried off to some other location.

The weight of millions

Rolando Andrade was powerful, very powerful. He bought and marketed agricultural crops, he owned many properties in the city, and he rented some of them. During the nineties he had nearly ten thousand employees. His fortune was also a suspicious one. In a state marked by drug trafficking, it was said that he laundered money for organized crime. It was a pronouncement, a brand that few doubted.

Unofficial accounts indicate that he handed over $25 million to Renato Vega Alvarado, candidate for the Institutional Revolutionary Party (PRI),

during his campaign for governor. And the case of the three young people from Las Quintas remains open.

"He sold himself," Zavala says. "Renato Vega sold himself. That's
why they didn't punish him [Andrade]. On the contrary, they protected him."

Zavala was the deputy attorney general in the state, and the attorney
general, Zambada Sentíes, named him prosecutor in the case when the
clouds of suspicion and disagreements with Morán Cortés reached the
point that they were insufferable. Zavala likewise butted heads with his
boss. In 1997 Zambada asked him to draw up a document that exonerated Andrade and all of his family. Zavala responded that he couldn't
do it. "It's impossible, I told him. It can't be done. It's impossible." The
prosecutor got angry, foaming at the mouth. They shouted, cursed, and
gesticulated. Staff at the office affirmed that the prosecutor suffered a
fainting spell after this argument and that his health was "delicate" afterward. But the prosecutor remained steadfast.

That same day, Zavala received a call. It was the governor. He called
him to his office. "The governor told me 'Listen, you *pendejo*, son of a
bitch . . . you picked a fight with an honorable man.' I answered that
if he was referring to the honorability of the attorney general, that guy
was a dishonest, corrupt old man. He cursed me. He said, 'You're a son
of your bitch of a mother. What do you think? What are you made of?
You're going to die of hunger, you *pendejo*. You scorned five million dollars.' I told him to fuck his mother, corrupt old man. And I warned him:
I'm carrying a Saturday night special [Colt .38 Super]. Better for you if
you don't cross me."

The ex-prosecutor remembers that he adjusted the bulge made by
the pistol on his waist to the right. The governor moved carefully, like
a surgeon in an operating room. Zavala left the office and immediately
called a press conference to announce that the governor and the attorney general were corrupt.

A lawsuit to get the case file

For a month they'd been asking for the file, which contained records of
the investigations that had been carried out, but Zavala always managed

to slip away, to escape or to hide. The governor called him to a meeting with the person who was then a representative of the federal attorney general's office. The victims' families were at the meeting as well. The federal official wanted the local and federal prosecutors to collaborate on the investigation. But he didn't succeed.

Zavala was also taken to Mexico City, to a meeting of various police chiefs, the governor, and Jorge Madrazo Cuellar, the federal attorney general. "The governor wanted to find a way to execute the arrest warrants drawn from the file, but in such a way that the detained would be released more or less immediately. My plan was to arrest eleven people for illegal deprivation of liberty and see what would happen. I went in front of the Second District Court, which is headquartered in the Sinaloan capital. But the federal judge found that it wasn't a federal matter and handed the file back to me."

In that meeting in Mexico City, Zavala recalled, Madrazo addressed Renato Vega and told him, "My governor, where are the arrest warrants?" and then he turned to the prosecutor Zavala and asked him the same question. Also present were Lt. Col. Édgar Armando Acata Paniagua, minister of citizen security in Sinaloa (later promoted to colonel while he was still in that position) along with the director of the Federal Judicial Police and the family of the disappeared. "'I don't have them with me' is how I answered, and they jumped all over me. Madrazo went first, and he was the toughest. He said, 'Governor, when are you going to get this man under control?' I answered that he was violating the sovereignty of the state of Sinaloa, and, directing my words to the governor, said, 'And you are allowing him to do so. There's corruption here.'" Madrazo banged his fist on the table and stomped off to his office with the governor in tow.

The prosecutor didn't know how to deal with the tense environment. He was afraid he would be arrested, then and there. He thought about using the emergency stairs instead of the elevator. He felt alone. So did the family members, who had supported Zavala throughout.

He kept up the attempt to keep the file away from the governor and the attorney general. Zavala claimed that he had it in his truck. That if they wanted to go and get it, 'Well, be my guest.' But the vehicle was guarded by soldiers, courtesy of General Martínez. Unofficial information indicates that the federal attorney general's office had also sent its own investigators but they didn't find anything. According to a publication from September 4, 1996, one of the federal investigators, José Manuel Everardo Gordillo, in charge of investigating the whereabouts of the disappeared, met in private with Rolando Andrade, in room 114 of a hotel located in the Tres Rios section of town, for about two hours on Thursday, August 22. During the interview, the bodyguard of the businessman Salvador Ponce Rivera went up the stairs with a suitcase. Later they left. The next morning, Everardo Gordillo boarded a plane for Mexico City, without providing any update on the case, and he never came back. The father of Jorge Cabada Hernández, Jorge Cabada Orduño, questioned the behavior of the investigator. Unofficial information indicates that Andrade had dispersed nearly three million dollars among various federal officials.

Weeks later, there was a meeting in the Ninth Military Zone. Zavala approached General Martínez Nolasco in order to advise him that he, the general, was about to be reassigned. Up till then, Martínez had backed the lawyer to the fullest and assigned a military detail of six soldiers to him.

"General, it occurs to me that they're going to switch you to another zone," he said. But Martínez discounted it and made a gesture of confidence.

That night his superiors announced by telephone that the general was being sent to Tenosique, Tabasco (hundreds of miles to the southeast).

Diabolical

"Acata Paniagua was in on all of the governor's secrets, and he continued, of course, to play the game. But he was also a soldier. [A lieutenant colonel then], now he's a general . . . a diabolical general," Zavala recalls. "On one occasion," he says, "the soldier asked for the minutes of the case, arguing that the general commander of the Ninth Military Zone had asked for it." He thought it strange that the general hadn't asked for it personally, though. "I gave him the paper and followed him. He didn't go to the barracks, but rather to the House of Government, located in

POWER AND IMPUNITY

According to a document sent on November 16, 1997, with the seal of the PGR, Rolando Andrade was detained by soldiers at the Hotel Intercontinental Plaza, in Guadalajara, Jalisco, and the military informed the Special Unit for Organized Crime (UEDO, which was later replaced by SIEDO).

On the Sinaloan businessman they found a Smith & Wesson .45 caliber pistol, seven cartridges, a small portion of cocaine, and various credit and identity cards, among them one issued by the state attorney general's office (PGJE), which identified him as a "legal advisor" to the prosecutor, "with an effective date of 1995."

The document was addressed to Samuel González Ruiz, the man in charge of the UEDO, directing him to come for the detainee and put him at the disposition of the corresponding authorities in Guadalajara. At the bottom of the page were the signatures of federal agents Arturo Negrete, Juan de Dios Almaraz García, first subcommander Víctor Hugo Estrada, and Juan Carlos Ventura Moussong, first subcommander of the PJF in Jalisco.

In another file, also in the hands of the PGR, with the institution's seals and part of the open investigation of the three disappeared young people from Culiacán, a member of the Andrade family relates how they supported the campaign of Renato Vega, then PRI candidate for governor, with $500,000—in a first payment—and ten vehicles, including Suburbans, Ram Chargers, and Nissan pickups.

"The undersigned contributed both economically and materially to the electoral campaign for the post of governor, the part in cash being a sum of approximately five hundred thousand North American dollars in various denominations and without taking any kind of receipt, such that the campaign treasurer, Marco Antonio Fox was left to return that sum to him," the document recites.

Fox was the financial operator of Vega's campaign, and he later served as the treasurer in his administration. Currently he is the superior auditor of the state of Sinaloa.

The document also mentions the ceding of four hundred hectares of urban land to Mariano Calderón, at the request of Renato Vega, who offered to pay him with public works that would be carried out during his administration.

"It's important to clarify that the last occasion in which he entered into a personal communication with Renato Vega Alvarado was at the end of November 1996, in his office at the Palace of Government, and when payment on the aforementioned debt came up, Renato Vega answered that the matter would be fixed as soon as the problem of the disappeared young people was fixed."

the Colonia Guadalupe." Zavala, who knew who he was, denounced him to General Martínez Nolasco, who in turn ordered the general staff to go get Acata.

They went on for about twenty minutes in the general's office, Martínez and Acata. When the latter came out, he muttered a complaint. "What did you tell him?," he asked Zavala. "The truth," he responded. He insisted, "And what is the truth?" and the former prosecutor didn't hesitate: "That you are a traitor because you serve a corrupt governor, and you have betrayed the army." Acata had a threat halfway out of his mouth when General Martínez stepped out of his office and faced him. "This cabrón is threatening me," Zavala said. The old army chief took Acata back into his office. Later it was known that the general had prohibited the lieutenant colonel from returning to that military zone.

"I support you, Zavala. I'm a man of noble causes. I don't give a damn if they transfer me." That's how he said good-bye.

Without detainees

José Luis Zavala Beltrán asked for eleven arrest warrants shortly after having assumed the leadership of the investigations into the disappearance of the cousins Jorge Cabada Hernández, Juan Emerio Hernández, and Abraham Hernández Picos. And of these, only five were authorized.

Sixteen years later, no one is behind bars for this crime. The principle suspect, Rolando Andrade, who initially fled to the United States with his family and belongings, returned to Mexico and was arrested in 1997. He was subsequently moved to Mexico City where he remained under house arrest thanks to his presumed connections to drug trafficking and his possible implication in the disappearances of the cousins, and here he died of natural causes. His son Rommel, according to unofficial accounts, lives in the United States and returns whenever he wants to Culiacán, without being bothered.

"Initially, eleven arrest warrants were requested from the third criminal court, but judge Alejandro Zazueta Castaños denied them for lack of evidence. The PGJE appealed and on September 18, 1998, the 3rd Circuit of the State Supreme Court authorized only five of them, in an order numbered TSFA/001/1998."

"The judicial orders that were issued were against Rommel Andrade Almada and his security guards, Arcadio Solís Pacheco, Rosario Gutiérrez Orfila and the brothers David and Jaziel Villareal Toca, the latter two captured on January 28, 1999 in Roma, Texas."

"On August 25, 1999, Francisco Martínez Hernández, the first district judge, granted an *amparo* [a form of judicial protection, akin to a writ of habeas corpus] against the arrest warrant until the judicial authorities could fully support the accusations. Once again, there was flurry of contradictory orders."

Gutiérrez Orfila was arrested on December 6, 2000 in Hermosillo. The three arrested men denied having worked for the Andrade family and any relationship with what had happened with the disappeared cousins. "On January 31, 2001, the Villareal Toca [brothers] received an *amparo* that vacated their formal arrest warrant, and they were set free immediately. That same day, the rest of the judicial orders were vacated. Ten years after the disappearance, the investigation was located in the agency within the public ministry specializing in forced disappearances, along with more than forty other files," says the news story published in June 2006 by the journalist Daniel Gaxiola, published in the daily *Noroeste.*

The case resurfaced in January 2016, when rumors circulated that Rolando Andrade's daughter, Yolanda Andrade, had introduced El Chapo to fellow television star Kate del Castillo (with whom he had become infatuated). Del Castillo, in turn, connected the actor Sean Penn with El Chapo, leading to their secret meeting in Cosalá, Sinaloa, on October 3, 2015, and a widely criticized interview published in *Rolling Stone* magazine. The interview helped authorities to zero in on El

Chapo's whereabouts, and he was arrested in Los Mochis, Sinaloa, on January 8, 2016. Andrade denies the connection to El Chapo asserted by federal investigators, but the ensuing scandal exposed a new audience to the allegations against her brother Rommel and her father and allowed the family members of the three disappeared cousins to tell their stories to a new audience, to keep them alive.

Pursuing the pursuer

His superiors continued settling the score with Zavala. "You're going to end up in the street," the then-governor told him. (Renato Vega Alvarado died of pulmonary complications in 2009.) But it didn't matter to Zavala. They weren't going to give him any work in the government: "nothing was going to happen." He continued teaching two law classes in a school located downtown, facing the building where he used to work, where the Municipal Archives are now located, in what used to be the local prosecutor's office, on Calle Rosales, between Rubí and Morelos. That's where you'll find him in the afternoon, or in the courtrooms, or in the Plazuela Obregón, when he gets his black shoes polished.

Zavala was a prisoner. He'll never forget it. When he encountered the prosecutor Zambada Sentíes in the offices of the Second District Court long after the arrested suspects had been set free, the man tried to greet him. "'I'm your friend,' the old guy told me. 'And I responded, *Go fuck your mother,*' and I left him standing there with his hand extended. Afterward he went around saying that I wanted to kill him. Nothing could be more false."

In 1998, while driving, he ran into a motorcyclist, was taken into custody, and left after posting bail. His innocence was proved, and the state decided not to press criminal charges, but when Zambada found out that they were going to let him go, he issued an arrest warrant against him. Staffers explained that Zavala had already been notified of the resolution of the case, and it couldn't be reversed at that point. Thus, they let him go.

They had also put together a file that accused him of participating in torture. It fell apart when the witnesses discredited it. That same year, Zavala was arrested again, this time because armed men were pursuing him and an army sergeant who was still escorting him, surprised the supposed triggermen and pointed an AR-15 rifle at them. He got them to lay down their arms, but various officers showed up, and after that they tried to charge him with attempted murder. He spent a year in the Culiacán jail and was then released for lack of evidence.

The hopes

José Luis Zavala Beltrán adds it all up. It's been twenty-four years of waiting for justice. The families of the young men are tired, lacking in hope. They don't want to talk about it. They fear for the worst: that the investigations will reveal the death of their children. Not Zavala. He keeps looking for them, he insists. He invites the family to go to Mexico City, to reopen the investigations. He keeps talking with them, staying in contact, despite the death of Jorge Cabada, considered "the soul of the movement against impunity," according to a text published by Arturo Cano in the supplement *Masiosare*, from the national daily *La Jornada* in May 1998.

He adjusts his hair, but not his tie. There seems to be no remedy, as the knot is already loose, a symptom that he needs rest. He leans back to take some air. He feels around for the back support. He looks outside, through the large window that looks out onto the plaza. He's not looking for anything in particular. And he lets loose his conclusion to the case: "The conclusion is that the corruption, the complicity, and the impunity of the government of Renato Vega fixed it so that there would be no justice in this case. And if there hadn't been corruption, the business would have gone off without hurting anyone, without falsehoods. Justice would have been done on behalf of the *muchachos*, the family."

He adds it up. So many names, numbers, and facts overflow with such passion and such an obsessive spirit of justice. He takes another napkin. The previous one is balled up.

That crime took place back in 1996, and now it's 2012. It adds up to sixteen years, but the statute of limitations doesn't expire for twenty-four more. There's still time to do something, for justice, perhaps. Perhaps.

"What we lack is a governor who wants it to be so. For somebody to come in with balls, to get into it. I do have hope, of course."

COMMUNITY AND THE SEARCH FOR THE TRUTH

When the cousins met up to go out and party, they communicated with their parents at 2:00 A.M. in order to inform them what they were doing and where they were headed next, but on this occasion, relates Juan Emerio Hernández, he and his wife went to find their son and his cousins in person.

"We wanted to go where they were, and we found them in the place where they said they'd be. We chatted with them . . . a few blocks from the house, and since then we haven't heard anything more of them," reads a article in *Noroeste* from Friday, July 19, 1996.

According to newspaper archives and stories based on the testimony of the families of the disappeared, the three Hernández cousins drove through El Paseo Malecón, where they were intercepted by seven officers from the municipal police, and from that moment they disappeared. Later this accusation would be confirmed by Gilberto Morán Cortés, the special prosecutor assigned by the government.

The investigator revealed that the cops had been instructed from on high, following the order given by the businessman Rolando Andrade Mendoza, who supported the former governor Renato Vega Alvarado in his electoral campaign. The state executive was known for offering protection to his benefactors.

On Thursday, July 4, 1996, at approximately 8:40 A.M., officers from the security directorate of the municipal police found the car in which the young men had been traveling. The car was located in the garage of a house in the Colonia Infonavit Diamantes, in the northern part of the city. During the search, experts from the State Prosecutor's Office found the shirt that Juan Emerio had been wearing, which had tear on the left shoulder.

After the disappearance, the family began an exhaustive search using two private planes offered by friends. They covered the communities of Sanalona, Altata, El Tambor, Costa Rica, Dique los Cascabeles, Villa Juárez, the city of Navolato, and Mazatlán without success. Out of desperation, the family called a press conference in front of their home, in which they begged the kidnappers to respect the lives of their loved ones and to permit them to come home. They even offered economic compensation to their captors.

"We begged desperately that they not harm them; the only thing that we wanted was for them to return our children. We were willing to make an arrangement under whatever conditions they wanted."

Indignation, urgency, and pressure grew. By way of various announcements placed in local and national newspapers, civic organizations and families demanded the reappearance of the students, the clarification of events, and the imparting of justice. They also exposed the ineptitude of the government of Renato Vega Alvarado. These announcements continued for an entire year. For example, one of them, published in *El Debate* on August 16, 1996, was signed by 115 families and thirty-eight businesses (all of them national).

Protests and marches were organized by relatives and friends who came together with ever greater strength, crisscrossing the main streets of Culiacán.

The family members went to Mazatlán, hoping to meet with then-president Ernesto Zedillos during a working tour. They handed him a letter explaining the case and the fruitless investigation undertaken by the authorities. He was approached about the case again on February 11, 1997, when the mother of Abraham Hernández Picos, Norma, drowning in tears, begged Zedillo to investigate the whereabouts of the young men. His only answer was: "There's nothing to be done other than what the prosecutor is doing."

In search of alternatives, the Hernández family sent a letter to the then-director of the Party of the Democratic Revolution (RPD), Cuauhtémoc Cárdenas Solórzano. In the document, dated September 11, 1996, they asked for his support and that the case be taken up in the Chamber of Deputies. They also petitioned Cárdenas when he visited the Sinaloan capital that year.

Carlos Gilberto Morán Cortés, the first investigator in the case, affirmed, "We were missing only the link that covered the connection between the municipal police and the people who handed over the young men; it was already known that the municipal police participated [in the crime], and there were well-founded suspicions of who handed them over. Among the people highly suspected in the investigation were officers and commanders in the municipal police, the Andrade family, starting with Rommel and his personal bodyguards, the security guards at the party, as well as the security guards of Gustavo Andrade, the brother of the businessman Rolando Andrade."

During the investigation, they searched the Andrade family's buildings, warehouses, and properties, and submitted thirty people to polygraph tests. Later investigators carried out an intensive search with specially trained dogs in the heights above Culiacán, without getting any favorable results. They also carried out excavations in some areas near the city, again without finding any good clues. It was rumored that the remains had been burned.

CHAPTER 5

I Am Here, Sister

I'M GOING TO FIND YOU

Rosario has the voice of a woman of twenty-five, even though she's fifty. And she's got exemplary and enviable energy—many men and women, relatives of the disappeared, gather their fears and bring them to her so that she can push them aside and allow them to keep fighting.

Some give in. Others turn to drugs or prostitution. Some just don't want to know anything, and they look for an oblivion that corrodes their arteries and thickens their blood. Their blood flow slackens; they become deliberate and slow. But Rosario Villanueva, a native of Culiacán who lives in Tijuana, with a life that takes her across a good portion of the country, has chosen to fight until the soles of her shoes melt from under her: trekking, confronting ex–police officers in prisons, and clogging the desks of various government functionaries with complaints and demands, all in search of her son, to find him.

"He's divine," she says, quickly and surely. She's asked what her son is like. She doesn't delay in firing back responses. They're the answers of an upright mother, who flies her flags of hope on Calvary and looks with lantern eyes, trying to see through the dark walls of impunity that exist across this entire country, so that justice will someday be done.

Her son, Óscar Germán Herrera Rocha, is thirty-six. He was disappeared by officers of the municipal police in Francisco I. Madero, Coahuila, on June 15, 2009, very close to the city of Torreón, the state capital. It's about twenty minutes away by car. Very close to terror; about two blocks from hell, to be precise.

Auto theft

Óscar Germán went with his boss, a businessman who owns a chain of pawnshops in Culiacán and other parts of Sinaloa. The businessman seemed to be a good person, and he didn't have anything other than the normal problems, and certainly nothing to do with organized crime or the settling of scores. There were four people in the car.

They were headed to Piedras Negras to buy some household electronics and appliances that they then hoped to resell. Óscar Germán was an electrical technician, and he was going to fix the things so that they could be resold retail. It wasn't the first time that they had made the trip, and it appeared to be going fine, no different from previous occasions.

But police officers stopped them along the federal highway, in front of a business called Establos Tres Nenas ("The Three Sweethearts' Stable") and a station of the Torreón municipal police, at the junction with Caballo Blanco Road. In the car were Óscar Germán, Ezequiel Castro Torrecillas, Sergio Arredondo Sicairos, and Octavio Villar Piña. The pretext alleged by police was that they were traveling in a stolen car, according to the investigations carried out later by the same police department, investigations into which other departments and authorities from Coahuila had been dragged kicking and screaming.

At the moment, nine police officers have been detained for these disappearances, even though many more could have been involved, Rosario assures, and in many other cases. Five of the arrested cops are in the state prison at San Pedro de las Colonias, in Torreón, and four more, who are officers, are in the federal penitentiary in Tepic, Nayarit.

Among the detained are the officers Sergio Ríos Solís, Edgar Iván Hernández Astorga, Ascención Salinas de los Santos, Abel Gaytán Calderón, and Óscar Gerardo López Guerrero. An unofficial account alleges that the investigation revealed that the uniformed police officers turned the four Sinaloans over to members of organized crime. This is the strongest lead that the authorities have found, but it hasn't taken them anywhere yet. It's a different story for Rosario and other relatives of the disappeared.

Roads crossed

If you keep counting and counting, things eventually add up. Family members of Rosario Villanueva, and another person who knows her, spoke of the painful struggle she embarked upon to find her son. She spread the word so widely that she found willing ears and hearts, similar experiences, and an influx of information from across the region. The magic and witchcraft of a bloody and dramatic search, at the various crossroads of which she found smooth flower petals between of the spiny shoulders of the road.

In this journey, she found cases that were just as sad as her own or worse: striking, terrible, and bloody. She heard about nine workers who installed cell phone towers, who were sent to Tamaulipas on a job for Nextel. They were all from Sinaloa, and they left from Guasave, about 150 kilometers (ninety-three miles) from Culiacán, heading to the job site. Perhaps because they were from Sinaloa, they were confused with *sicarios*, for being organized crime or members of the Sinaloa Cartel, and disappeared. Not a trace of them has been found.

Articles in local newspapers, like *Vanguardia*, relate that officials from the area recommended to their families that they not try to look for the missing men, because the same thing could happen to them. "Don't come; you too could be taken," an officer from the State Ministerial Police told them.

The Nextel case, is it is known, was one of the first forced disappearances to provoke a national scandal. The victims were last seen on June 20, 2009 in Nuevo Laredo, Tamaulipas. They were subsequently identified as Marcelino Moreno Leal, Ricardo y Carlos Peña Mejía, José Hugo Camacho Fierro, Víctor Romero, Julio César Ochoa Romo, Constantino García Jiménez, Roberto Gutiérrez Medina, and Eduardo Toyota Espinoza, whose ages range from early twenties to forty-six. And nobody knows anything.

Joaquín Camacho Fierro, the brother of José Hugo, claims that there were some indications that they might have been taken by a commando from the federal government: "We think that the Federal Police kidnapped them. The drug traffickers have everything, but they don't have technicians or professionals easily on hand to create their communication networks, and thus we're convinced that they're alive and they have them working somewhere."

Other accounts indicate that it was members of the Zetas or the Gulf Cartel, the two dominant organized crime groups in the region.

This case coincided with that of a group of miners, among them a retired general from the Mexican army, who were disappeared while transporting a load of gold and silver from the municipality of Concordia through the state of Durango, on the highways of the western Sierra Madre in the middle of June 2009.

The load of nearly twelve tons was the property of the mining company Real de Cosalá. Ten days after the disappearance, the company filed a complaint with the state prosecutor in Durango for the loss of the precious metals. Sinaloan authorities announced the disappeared as Alejandro Camacho Patiño, Ramón Antonio Quiñones Silva, Salvador Plascencia Santiago, and the Mexican army general José Lamberto Ponce Lara. Their destination was Torreón, Coahuila, but apparently they were intercepted by an armed group on a Durango highway.

Company executives point out that the load was made up of dirt and rocks that contain gold and silver, but that they had yet to go through a process of separation. The material was valued at $100,000 dollars.

The attorney general's office in Sinaloa reported that family members of Quiñónez Silva filed a criminal complaint regarding the disappearance of their relative. Angélica, the sister of Ramón Quiñónez Silva, remembered that her brother had worked for the company for twenty years and that he and his colleagues transported the loads in two vehicles, a Kenworth box truck (like a moving van rather than a tractor trailer), and a Nissan SUV, with Sinaloa plates TW-71795, property of the Real de Cosalá (the mine operator).

"The units were being monitored via satellite by the company, but suddenly in the municipality of Concordia they veered off the route, near the border between Sinaloa and Durango, and since then we haven't known anything. It's as if the land swallowed them up," the complaint says.

Another case with a more direct Coahuila connection involved the forced disappearance of three people on May 11, 2009. The victims lived in Tijuana, the border city in Baja California. It appears that some of them had relatives in Coahuila who got information casually from

Rosario Villanueva, details that she had rustled up in search of her son. Something unusual appeared: a nephew of hers and nephews of one of the three disappeared men worked together at a company in Mexicali, Baja California. They recounted each other's sagas, and they connected the dots. And those dots, at least in the painful struggle of the family's demand for justice, bore some fruit.

"I dragged myself around like a worm. I'd never been to Coahuila, and I was afraid, very afraid. I learned of these people, and they rekindled my hopes, because in the conversations and meetings we had, we found out that they disappeared in exactly the same spot that they intercepted my son and the three others that were with him," Villanueva declared.

It appears that one of them was involved in exporting vehicles. He bought them cheaply and exported them, and one day he found a truck on offer. The idea was to take it to Durango and visit family in the community of Santo Niño, in Coahuila, located very near the municipality of Francisco I. Madero. And there, passing by the Establo de las Tres Nenas, the municipal police station, and that road called Caballo Blanco, they were intercepted and stopped, just like Rosario's son.

"It was the same corner, and they were the same cops," she claims. Now they're getting the evidence together to bring to justice at least two of the police officers detained in the case of Óscar Germán, for their participation in the disappearance of these three other people.

"In this case, on May 11, the scoundrels [were] more than just scoundrels, [they were] complete idiots, because they used the victims' cell phones. One of them stupidly made calls to his wife, and we have approached the authorities from the prosecutor's office with this [information] so that they [might] pick up the woman and find out whether she's involved or not, and charge one of the other police officers detained in the federal penitentiary in Tepic for this other case of three disappeared."

The mud of despair

Due to the struggle and ever-growing despair of victims' families, their vitality often crumbles. Many women, Rosario assures, stay in the street looking for their husbands. Others end up alone and desolate. Searching, rummaging through the dark corners of the criminal underworld, holing up in waiting rooms of government offices, and asking here and there and everywhere. And through all of that, in the journey and with the tremendous economic and emotional wear and tear, they look around, forward and backward, and there's nothing, nobody. Just the street. The mud.

One of the young women who participates in this winding journey now sells herself as a prostitute. After her husband was disappeared and after she'd run out of money, she decided to rent her body, her hands and caresses, for cash. It doesn't revive her flaccid spirit but it does fill her children's' bellies.

Another young mother sells drugs in order to have money and nourish her son, in order to keep struggling and hanging on and wearing herself out.

For Rosario, the scoundrels she describes, the corrupt cops, are like rats that have been exposed to gas or poison and will soon die. They feel trapped and so act criminally and desperately. Even though the authorities seldom stop them, sometimes they feel the heat, the collar around them tightening, and they react. Such criminals attacked a family of migrants who presumably live in Chiapas. Corrupt cops looked for a way to pressure the parents to stop demanding justice for their disappeared son and the authorities to give up looking into his fate. They cut the tongues out of two girls, thirteen and fourteen years old, relatives of the victim.

"This reality, these cases, multiply them by a thousand: that's what's happening in this country," Rosario lamented.

A letter to the president

"I have looked desperately for my son Óscar Germán. I spoke with Margarita Zavala, the wife of President Felipe Calderón Hinojosa, and I sent a letter explaining in detail the state in which my son's case remains. How they would have laughed at me, that I dreamed that President Calderón was going to read my letter. And not just that, they made me believe that they were going to help me. 'Go to hell!' I say."

Let's see how they like it when at the national level all of us families come together to seek justice for the disappearance of our beloved family members. If they thought that we were going to tire out, then they were mistaken, that crowd of incompetents who do little more than complicate the families' plain hope that they'll do what must be done.

There's no doubt that the ineptitude of our authorities has no limit . . . [and it seems they will never] come to understand they can't assault us or run roughshod over us. They've taken a piece of our souls!

We keep at it, only because we realize that no one is going to take charge of finding our disappeared loved ones, much less seek justice for them, if that was ever the real proposition they made in seeking their positions and calling themselves authorities in the first place.

They're going to receive news of the organization that we are making of all of the families in the country, and above all else, I'm convinced of the error (horror) I committed in placing my trust in you and in having voted for Acción Nacional.

And know that the war wasn't declared by organized crime (unlike the authorities, they are organized), it has been declared by the pain of thousands of desperate families who feel tricked for having believed that change was possible.

I'm not directing this letter to Señor Llera Blanco [Juan Manuel Llera Blanco, head of the Federal Network of Citizen Services, in the office of the presidency] or to his lackey, Señor Montaño [Israel José Montaño Camarena, chief of the Department of Evaluation in the same office] because I'm going to make sure it gets to the most media possible, and this is just the beginning.

The letter was published on December 17, 2010, in the newspaper *El Mexicano*, in Tijuana.

Melted soles

Rosario Villanueva walked "in a beautiful way," ethereal and uncomplaining, that road that they call Caballo Blanco. She searched the pavement, the roots along the shoulder, the plants that bloom and multiply despite her anguish, the parched earth, and the cracks that the cruel sun bakes into the ground.

LETTER TO THE DISAPPEARED

Hello, good afternoon. My son Marco Antonio disappeared on June 19, 2007, and I'd like to write this letter to him:

> My son, you were always my pride and joy, and you continue to be. I don't understand why this tragedy happened. You were the pillar of our family, and without you we are unprotected and forsaken. The questions, the *why?* and *for what?* are hanging like a whip over my head and heart. You absence hurts; it hurts! Above all else [it hurts] your children. They miss you a lot, as you must know, growing up without your advice, without your care, without your presence. Everything has changed. We're not the same. My life is ruined without you. The authorities don't help us learn your fate, and they don't search for you. I imagine that they know something about you but won't say anything. You were important, and something tells me that someone betrayed you, that they turned you over to the criminals as an innocent, but how to demonstrate it, my son? My heart cries out every second, with each beat . . . , and life goes out of me, [but] I'll continue to suffer your absence as long as it persists. God permitting, I hope that there will be some way for you to understand the great anguish and desperation of not knowing what happened to you, and that God will give me the opportunity to see how he punished those criminals. God has pardoned you so that you are in his glory. You have my life in your hands.
>
> I thank you for this space, and God bless you for your understanding.

Published in the blog *Nuestra Aparente Rendición*, June 20, 2012.

She looked for clues, remains, traces. A newspaper from Coahuila reported that the police arrested for the disappearance of her son testified in front of the Ministerio Público that they had murdered and then buried him. She knows, but she prefers to ignore it. She searches for her son, and she will neither rest nor will she stop. Without respite.

Rosario organized the United Foundation for the Disappeared of Coahuila (Fundec), which is now a national organization, Fundem, because they didn't want to limit themselves to Coahuila cases, of which there are many. So far they have tallied eighty-three cases involving about four hundred disappeared persons. In one of those cases there were twenty-one people taken against their will.

The Federación Latinoamericana de Asociaciones de Familiares de Detenidos-Desaparecidos (Fedafam) calculates that during the Calderón government, until 2011, more than three thousand people disappeared—four hundred for political reasons, five hundred women and children in cases related to human trafficking, and twenty-one hundred related to drug trafficking.

Rosario went from the intensely personal case of seeking her own son, knocking on and knocking down doors, leaving tears and complaints on desks outside the closed office doors of indolent and corrupt public servants, to embracing the causes of other women and men, other children and siblings and cousins of people who have disappeared, people who wish to see them return.

She opens her generous arms to all of the disappeared and their families, their hopes and dreams, their nostalgia and memories. She fights for them. Even though hope fades, she is determined to have justice, and she retains a dignity that many have lost. Even though others opt for resignation and silence, her voice resounds.

"Covering that Caballo Blanco Road, I have devoted *un tiempo hermoso* ["a beautiful time"]. I have swept over it again and again . . . you have no idea. . . . I recall that one time it was so hot that the soles of my shoes actually melted. But that's nothing. I've left a lot of tears and snot in the offices and on the desks of corrupt functionaries. I've left my heart. Now I'm getting stronger, but after getting psychological treatment I've managed to stop seeing myself as a victim and feeling sorry for myself. I think that I was at the point of dying. And while they, the corrupt authorities, appear to be busier than ever blocking investigations and going around looking for dead bodies and clandestine graves, we have proof that there are concentration camps and *conejeras* [rabbit warrens], as they call the subterranean laboratories where drugs are processed."

"In the investigations carried out by the families, we have discovered that there are concentration camps that the authorities never want to enter. We understand the authorities, because there they'd be killed just the same. We've been able to prove that some of them [the disappeared held there] are used as *sicarios*. We have a case from Coahuila where there's a boy they've been using as a *sicario*."

Rosario is afraid, and she says it. Many of those who go around with her and her family members suffer from mental anguish, depression. At the outset, she confesses, she didn't know how to manage her emotions, the evidence, the case itself. They ran a lot of risks on those trips, including the ones to government offices and police stations.

"We were very afraid, and we still are. But now I've stopped letting the fear push me around so that I can move forward," she declares.

On May 9, 2011, she and other family members of the disappeared were received by Marisela Morales, the federal attorney general. On May 10, Mother's Day, she participated in a march in Mexico City called "One More Day: Mothers Searching for their Children and Demanding Justice." They were very well received, and the people of the capital were clearly sensitive to the cause of the victims' families, Rosario recalled.

On February 23, 2012, five deaf-mutes who sold religious trinkets in the streets were taken against their will in the municipality of Piedras Negras, Coahuila. Their families immediately filed a criminal complaint with the Attorney General of the Republic, but so far, they've said nothing about the progress of the investigation.

The story published in the newspaper *La Jornada* reported that Rosario Morales, the sister of one of the victims, was part of the Caravan of Mothers in Search of the Children, which left the capital of Chihuahua and arrived in Mexico City, with the demand that the Government pledge to look for them.

The group of deaf-mutes, made up of José Martín Morales Galván, José Antonio Ángeles Flores, José Luis Vallejo Rodríguez, and Jorge Espinoza Salgado—all natives ofMexico City—arrived in Piedras Negras on February 17, with the intention of selling various items in the street, apparently by invitation of Manuel Adrián González Mancera, a native of that community.

Despite the fact that they didn't obtain permission from local authorities, they began to work with the goal of getting enough money together to return to the capital. But then on February 23, at a about 6pm, they

IMPUNITY AND COMMUNITY

On February 23, 2012, four deaf-mutes who sold religious trinkets in the streets were taken against their will in the municipality of Piedras Negras, Coahuila. Their families immediately filed a criminal complaint with the federal attorney general, but so far the PGR has said nothing about the progress of the investigation.

A story published in the newspaper *La Jornada* reported that Rosario Morales, the sister of one of the victims, was part of the Caravan of Mothers in Search of the Children, which left the capital of Chihuahua and arrived in Mexico City, demanding that the government promise to look for them.

The group of deaf-mutes, made up of José Martín Morales Galván, José Antonio Ángeles Flores, José Luis Vallejo Rodríguez, and Jorge Espinoza Salgado—all natives of Mexico City—arrived in Piedras Negras on February 17, with the intention of selling various items in the street, apparently by invitation of Manuel Adrián González Mancera, a native of that community.

Despite the fact that they didn't obtain permission from local authorities, they began to work, with the goal of getting enough money together to return to the capital. But then on February 23, at about 6:00 P.M., they were grabbed by a group of armed and masked men, who traveled in a black SUV with no license plates, according to an eyewitness account.

Two days later, facing the impossibility of traveling to Coahuila, their families filed a complaint via telephone with the PGR delegation in that jurisdiction, which opened a file labeled AC/PGR/COAH TN-2/022012.

Even though they were assured that with this procedural formality alone they could begin the search, since then they haven't received a single call to apprise them of the state of the investigation, nor have they gotten any support from any other government agency.

"At the PGR they told us that they were looking for them, but we haven't received any further notification. If they're doing something, they're not telling us about it, and they already have all of the information that we could give them. We also contacted Províctima, but they tell us the same thing, that they're waiting to be informed," Morales lamented in an interview with *La Jornada*.

According to unofficial accounts, in Coahuila there are more than 1,800 disappeared people. "Our family members are not the only ones, and I think that this is happening here because of so much corruption, which begins at the top, with the authorities. The governor [Rubén Moreira] promised to study the case, but we know from [cases of] people who have been disappeared for eight years that they'll never be found," Morales said.

were grabbed by a group of armed and masked men, who travelled in a black SUV with no license plates, according to an eyewitness account.

Two days later, facing the impossibility of travelling to Coahuila, their families filed a complaint via telephone to the PGR delegation in that jurisdiction, which opened a file marked AC/PGR/COAH TN-2/022012.

Even though they were assured that with this procedural formality alone they could begin the search, since then they haven't received a single call to apprise them on the state of the investigation, nor have they gotten any support from any other government agency.

"At the PGR they told us that they were looking for them but we haven't received and further notification. If they're doing something, they're not telling us about it, and they already have all of the information that we could give them. We also contacted Províctima, but they tell us the same thing, that they're waiting to be informed," Morales lamented in an interview with *La Jornada*.

According to unofficial accounts, in Coahuila there are more than 1,800 disappeared people. "Our family members are not the only ones and I think that this is happening here, because of so much corruption, which begins at the top, with the authorities. The Governor (Rubén Moreira) promised to study the case, but we know from people who have been disappeared for eight years that they'll never be found," he said.

Divine

"Your son, what's he like?" she is asked. "Divine, divine," she answers. She doesn't hesitate. The syllables are poised on the tip of her tongue, waiting to be shot out, carried by the wind, and considered so that someone will take note of them and pass the message along.

Óscar Germán is divine. Present tense. And this fact never leaves the discourse: the presence of a living memory, latent, current among us. He's been disappeared for three years. He was born in 1975 and has reached thirty-seven years old. He adores the women in his life: his wife (a *culichi* who lives with her parents in the Sinaloan capital) and a nine-year-old daughter.

"He's divine. My son is divine. A marvelous human being, hardworking and responsible. I'm not going to tell you that he's some kind of genius, a scientist or anything like that, with electronics, but he was sought after for this kind of work. Now and again the Panama restaurant chain would call him in to fix their industrial microwave ovens, for example. He's an honest worker, a good person. He lived a quiet life and was just looking at the possibility of studying for a formal degree, because he got married before starting one, in 1998."

Seeing this woman in front of the policemen accused of disappearing her son is unimaginable. But she faced them down, at the point of collapsing. At the federal penitentiary in Tepic they subjected her to searches that left her practically naked before allowing her to see the prisoners. Manuel Castañeda is one of them. She asked him: "Do you know why you are in prison?" He answered: "I don't know, but whatever it is, I am innocent." And he began to cry.

"'You must be a real *pendejo* if you think that I'm going to believe you.' . . . I said that because I was about to start believing in his tears. It was striking to be face to face, to be there, in the prison, where they almost leave you naked with so many searches. I had to run to the bathroom to throw up. I was about to faint. But it's horrible to be face to face with the people who dared to disappear my boy," she maintains.

It took her more than two years, she recalls, to get over many of these things, to get her strength back, to breathe deeply and continue fighting. To maintain her rhythm, to see the firmament above her, to consider the future. To move forward.

She explains that she'd attended a meeting of the recently created Províctima, an institution set up by the federal government to attend to the victims of crime. But she quickly adds that they, the families of the disappeared, don't want psychologists or papers or food vouchers, but rather the return of their children, their men, their women, their brothers and sisters.

"We want our children back. We want justice. It doesn't matter to me that they throw the wife of one of the cops involved in my son's case in jail. All I want is to find him, and I'm willing to give my life to do so, so that things don't remain as they are."

TWICE A WIDOW

To disappear in Mexico is to die, to die over and over again, to be always dying. The family members who have suffered the disappearance or the taking of a relative explain it plainly: it's a living hell that never ends, the worst thing ever. It was like that for her. Laura and her four children have traded Christmas mornings and Sundays going out with the family for trips to the cemetery. And for a flood of tears, some faded flowers, and an emotional rollercoaster.

Her husband was taken against his will by a commando. Some men that he knew tricked him into leaving his house. They told him that another man had been detained and was asking for his help. But then they were intercepted by another group—although some accounts suggest that the first group turned him over along with a young man who had accompanied them. According to eyewitnesses, the men were heavily armed and forced him into an automobile. It was August 27, 2011.

Laura and her four children, especially the youngest ones, felt his death over and over again during forty-five ignominious days that followed. They suffered in the wilderness of anxious waiting, searching, and helpless abandonment. She thought about running through the streets asking everyone if they had seen her husband. She wanted to go house to house, ask everyone on every park bench, on the road, throughout town, everywhere. But she put her trust in the state government and gave up her personal search. Her hope of finding her husband never completely faltered, but her faith in the authorities quickly vanished.

"They have technology. They are going to go over video surveillance records, the calls to his cell phone, track his GPS. They are going to find him. That's what I thought—that they were going to investigate, to review everything, and that they were going to find him. With so many investigators and all of the devices and resources they have. . . . But I was wrong. They didn't move finger. They didn't do anything," she explained.

Impunity and complicity: The United Nations

The United Nations Working Group on Enforced or Involuntary Disappearances reported on March 31, 2011, that it knew of 412 cases in Mexico, of which 239 continued to be unresolved. The Working Group also acknowledged that its methodology was one of sampling, and thus "this data is not representative of the scale of enforced disappearances." Still, the report validated many of the patterns and practices alleged by victims' family members, and it sparked more systematic inquiries by local, national, and international organizations, ultimately forcing the Mexican government to create a national registry of the disappeared (RNPED) in 2012, which includes more than 27,000 cases as of 2016. As they did at the time of the original Working Group report, federal authorities continue to allege that much of the responsibility for the prevention, investigation, and prosecution of these cases lies with state governments, but state governments in turn accuse federal officials of not taking responsibility for the related actions of groups within the army and Federal Police.

According to the Working Group:

> Enforced disappearance has been an autonomous offence in the Federal Criminal Code since 2001 and in the criminal legislation of the following eight states: Aguascalientes, Chiapas, Chihuahua, Durango, Federal District, Guerrero, Nayarit and Oaxaca. The Federal Criminal Code and the legislation of the states which have classified enforced disappearance as an offence do not use the same definition, or the definition set out in the Declaration. The majority refer merely to acts committed by public officials and exclude the possibility that enforced disappearances may be perpetrated by organized groups or individuals acting on behalf of the Government or with its direct or indirect support, authorization or acquiescence.
>
> The inconsistencies between the definition of the offence of enforced disappearance used in the Declaration and that of other international instruments, as well as the fact that the majority of the states have not classified it as an autonomous offence, contribute to impunity.

The Working Group received testimony in multiple cases in which the deprivation of liberty was classified as kidnapping or abuse of authority, despite the fact that they included details that could classify them as forced disappearances. In many other cases, they are classified euphemistically as *levantones.*

Additionally, in many cases "persons were simply considered 'missing' or 'lost' (particularly groups such as women, children and migrants)."

The report also recognizes that civil society groups and NGOs have recorded more than three thousand persons disappeared in Mexico from 2006 to 2010. The National Human Rights Commission (CNDH) registered a marked increase in the number of complaints in this area: the number of complaints grew from four in 2006 to seventy in 2010.

"A potential enforced disappearance may only be ruled out after a complete, independent and impartial investigation. Therefore, the number of cases of enforced disappearance cannot be fully established without proper investigation . . . [however,] the Working Group condemns all acts of disappearance regardless of the perpetrator of the offence."

The Working Group also observed that after the federal government decided to dispatch military forces throughout the country to combat drug traffickers in 2006, complaints against the military have increased considerably. The number of such complaints received by the CNDH rose from 182 in 2006 to 1,415 in 2010. During this period, the commission issued sixty recommendations against the army.

Lamentably, in its report on Mexico, the Working Group found that the country lacks a "comprehensive policy" to confront the phenomenon of forced disappearances, "which includes searching for the victims, identifying remains and exhuming bodies. Furthermore, it lacks a centralized database on disappeared persons and access to information on cases of enforced disappearance. There is no requirement to issue a comprehensive information sheet with the physical description needed to search for, locate and identify the disappeared person. When an information sheet on a disappeared person is available, it is not usually distributed in hospitals, detention centers or highways or to the authorities responsible for locating missing persons in other federal entities."

The Working Group also warned that the migrant population has been particularly vulnerable to forced disappearance (along with women, human rights defenders, and journalists): "In 2009, the CNDH reported 9,578 cases of abduction of migrants over a period of six months, and at least 11,333 migrants were allegedly abducted between April and September 2010, primarily by criminal organizations." In a subsequent report, the CNDH estimated in 2011 that 20,000 migrants were kidnapped every year in Mexico, and their families were charged an average ransom of $2,000.

The CNDH found evidence that government personnel from federal, state, and municipal police departments and the National Migration Institute collaborated with organized crime in a significant portion of these forced disappearances. The commission documented that over a six-month period in 2010, government personnel participated in 8.9 percent of the abductions of migrants included in its data set. Federal officials in Mexico have consistently downplayed government complicity in forced disappearances, claiming official involvement in as little as 1 percent of disappearances. A 2013 report by Human Rights Watch, published after the Working Group had concluded its mission to Mexico, found that law enforcement and military personnel were involved in 60 percent (149 out of 249) of the cases they investigated. Rather than working with large national databases, Human Rights Watch conducted in-depth investigations of a more limited number of cases in the eleven states with the highest incidences of forced disappearance (according to sources like the CNDH). Their researchers note that in most cases they were only able to identify and verify government complicity through painstaking investigative work and multiple interviews, and that most of these cases had not been previously identified (by the CNDH and others) as involving official complicity. So, whether or not the rate is as high as 60 percent, the report suggests that it is likely much higher than the government has acknowledged. In 2015, the UN Working Group issued a follow-up report condemning Mexico's "inconsistent" response to the problem of forced disappearances, the continuing lack of an appropriate diagnostic tool for measuring the phenomenon, and the horrific revelations of government complicity and stonewalling in the Ayotzinapa case and other apparent massacres revealed by mass graves across the country.

Six states

In 2011, the Calderón administration launched the Special Prosecutor for Attention to Victims of Crime (Províctima) to attend to family members and victims of high-impact crimes, like murder, kidnapping, and extortion, free of charge. In its first four months of operation, Províctima reported 646 disappearances in the country. Six states topped the list: Coahuila (113), Tamaulipas (99), Nuevo León (69), Veracruz (61), Chihuahua (33), and the Federal District (28). Of the 646 disappeared persons, only 19 had been located, 3 of them alive, according to Províctima.

Of the total disappeared, 479 were men and 167 were women; 64 were minors. The agency wasn't able to identify the profession of more than half of the victims, and the remainder included a broad mix of students, employees of various types, merchants, taxi and truck drivers, and other assorted professions. Províctima was unable to determine the ages of more than one-third of the victims, but the largest age group of those for whom they were able to determine an approximate age was young people—180 of the victims were between the ages of 18 and 29. In Sinaloa, there had been about 350 victims of forced, politically motivated disappearances as of 2012, according to data from the Commission for the Defense of Human Rights in Sinaloa (CDDHS). Of these, fifty-two cases correspond to the period from 1994 to 2003, and eleven are from 2004 to 2012.

"We question the [following] actions and omissions of the authorities which serve as a multiplier effect for violence: the abandonment of its constitutional obligations in more than eighty percent of the cases reported, the sickening practice of violating the human rights [of the accused and victims' family members] in almost every investigation, and the unforgivable abandonment of and discrimination against crime victims," reads a letter from the CDDHS. This document was sent to Sinaloa Governor Mario López Valdez and Attorney General Marco Antonio Higuera Gomez, on February 12, 2012, when the commission and the Movement for Peace with Justice and Dignity initiated a campaign called "Put Yourself in Another's Shoes." The text includes the names of the missing from 1975 to 2012, "[in order] to ensure that the victims of crime remain present, so that time is not a veil that covers them over, and that the authorities cannot use the passage of time as an excuse for failing to procure justice."

A crime that does not exist

The "worst thing about it," Leonel Aguirre Meza, president of the CDDHS, reflects, is that we're talking about a crime that does not exist in state law; forced disappearances are not classified as such but rather handled as unlawful imprisonment or kidnapping.

"At the federal level it does exist, but with deficiencies. For example, [the wording of the statute] does not [consider] the complicity of government authorities [in organized crime]," he said. The United Nations and the Inter-American Commission on Human Rights have repeatedly pointed out to Mexican officials the need for legal reforms to criminalize this offense, and they have also urged Mexico to carry out comprehensive public policies in this area, including research, prevention, and punishment.

Other sources (relayed through Aguirre Meza of the CDDHS), whose identities cannot be revealed for fear of government or criminal reprisals, note that alliances between criminal groups and senior public servants hinder these legal reforms. "When a *levantón* or a disappearance goes down, the army and the police just disappear. There is total impunity, and [they are all complicit in] covering it up. It is disastrous . . . above all else because this crime is . . . growing and multiplying, without [any kind of] punishment."

Another source, who'd had a family member taken by an armed group, claimed that after the disappearance, there were neither operations to figure out who was responsible nor any meaningful investigations into what happened. The victim in one of these cases showed up dead, shot to death, very near the spot where he was taken. "The government," he explained, "will look for the dead, but never the disappeared: that is not justice."

"What operations did they undertake when this case was reported? None." On many occasions, Aguirre Meza adds, "the relatives look to drug traffickers to find the whereabouts of their loved ones." On this point, he argues that the government, the police, and the military act on the assumption that the victim will show up dead somewhere. "And thus," he laments, "they investigate the case like a homicide and not a forced disappearance linked to organized crime. Either way it doesn't really change anything: nobody investigates and there's no punishment."

The survivor

Right there, in Laura's neighborhood. A new neighbor approaches and tells her that right there, in that sector, all is quiet. "Where I lived before," he explains, "the worst happened." And now he can say he's alive.

And he tells his story.

They came to his house for him. They dragged him out, kicking, and put him in a van. One of them grabbed him by the hair and pulled a hood over his head. Another grabbed his legs and tied them and then did the same with his hands. Seven words: "Better keep your nose out of it."

He began to sob and babble. One of them kicked him in the back. "What did I tell you, *pendejo?*" "I didn't do anything, boss. I don't know what this is about. Please don't hurt me." They pushed their sneakers down on his head, smashed him down. He stopped talking but not crying.

Within ten minutes the car stopped. He heard the motor of a garage door opener. He heard the squeal of tires.

They hauled him out like a sack of cement and left him on the cold ground. Someone else joined the group. He distinguished a fourth voice. "Put him there and heat him up. I want him to talk, to tell all. You know what to do. Keep me posted."

The man withdrew. His hard-heel steps echoed in the empty space. No other noise, not even that incessant babbling and those pounding heartbeats, could compete.

"*Órale, cabrón,*" said one of them. "All right, bastard." Two others joined in, and they moved him like the sack he was. Someone dragged a chair over to him. They sat him there: his neck tied to the back of the chair, his face covered, and his hands tied behind his back.

"Come on, tell us, *cabrón.*" They gave him a slap. That was a softy, the caress of woman's face compared to what was coming. They punched him in the face and stomach. Then he heard a sound like a dentist's drill buzzing behind him, and next he felt a shock.

"Give him the next one in the balls," said one of them. He jumped and trembled through the jolts. Then they took a table and grabbed him by his feet. They were stooping over him when he lost consciousness. And this was just the first round. They took a bucket of water and dumped it over his head. He jumped again as he woke up, and he let out a heartbreaking "not again."

And again blows rained down on his head. Punches landed on his abdomen. The prod attacked his genitals. They asked for money belonging to a man nicknamed El Chilo, for cocaine that had gone missing.[1] "You stole it, *bato*. Who has it, asshole? Talk, motherfucker!"

He said: "Boss, I swear on my dear mother, I'm not the guy. I don't know what they're talking about. I'm just a plumber. Ask around here, ask the neighbors. Call the engineer, right now. I'm supposed to be doing a job with him at a construction site. You've got me confused with somebody else, man. Please believe me. You've got me confused with somebody else."

One of them pulled out a gun. The cold of the barrel traversed his forehead, making him shudder. He fell back and they lifted him up. Three days passed like this.

"Nothing, boss."

"Let him go," the leader ordered.

"And that's how I survived. Hey, I thought I was dead. So I came to live here, to this city."

Laura smiled, sad and ironic, and she told him that he had chosen poorly. "Look, some *narcos* live right over there, on the next block. Now and then there are shootouts, and everybody has to buy new windows."

She did not tell him her story. She was twice a widow. She'd loved her man, a dedicated father to her daughters, who were not his. Affectionate, hardworking, and intelligent. He was hers, even after a failed kidnapping attempt left him with nightmares. And then they took him again.

He seemed so far away

His family last saw him on August 27, 2011. Two women and two acquaintances of theirs had come looking for him early in the morning, on the pretext that one of their sons had been arrested for a traffic violation and needed his help. It was Saturday. The next afternoon, at about two, one of the women came to tell the relatives that he had been taken. It seems her son had been taken as well.

When Laura went to the state attorney general's office (PGJE) to lodge a complaint, a feeling of relief overcame her, and her load was immediately lightened. The staff who received her said that they would review videos and phone calls made to and from his cell phone, and footage from the video cameras installed at the gas station where he had last been seen.

Some acquaintances of his, who apparently are involved in organized crime, told his wife not to worry, that he would surely have some "pull," hinting that he was going to work with the drug traffickers. Others who had such contacts told him that he would be released soon. A few others, however, knew that his body lying was near the community of El Bata-lión, in the town of Navolato, on the road to Culiacán. When she went to report to the Ministerio Público what she'd been told, they told her not to worry, that a helicopter was "combing the area" and if there was something, they would notice.

"The truth is that those people never searched or did anything. It's as if he were a criminal. They didn't even send investigators. I always thought if this happened to me I would search every house, every-where, to find him. He had GPS on his cell phone. Calls were made and received that day. I thought the attorney general was going to find him, using investigators, technology, videos, and everything else. I was wrong."

On October 12, 2011, he was found. His body was clean. There weren't any injuries caused by torture, and he did not appear dehydrated or starved. Unkempt and bearded, for sure, but otherwise normal. His body was with two others, those of a former police officer and Laura's young son, the boy he had gone to help get out of jail.

Laura and her family had spent forty-five days waiting. Their collective life was a wasteland, without a tomorrow or a sunrise in sight. There had been a coup de grace. A bullet had entered his neck and exited near the mouth, a clean hole. That was it.

A story published in the "Justice and Security" section of the newspa-per *Noroeste*, on October 13, 2011, reads:

Three individuals were found shot dead and wrapped in plastic bags, including a former agent of the Municipal Police in the town of Navolato. Information from police agencies indicates that one of the victims was identified as Edilberto Perez Mendoza, 45, a resident of Colonia Cinco de Febrero. Two years ago, this person belonged to the Municipal Public Security Bureau of Navolato.

The other two bodies have not been identified. The bodies were found about 1:30 P.M. yesterday at the junction of the Culiacán-Navolato road with the road leading to the town of San Pedro la Laguna. According to an anonymous caller, three bundles were found lying by the side of the road, in the town of El Batalión. Police officers rushed to the site and confirmed that there were three bodies.

The bodies were wrapped in bags and tied with masking tape in several places. Forensic experts from the state attorney general's office located 7.62 x 39 caliber casing from a 10mm AK-47.

It took two days before they could hold a funeral in the town, due to the lack of investigative resources. Someone told the family, and his father and some of his brothers went to identify him. On their own, they managed to get the body handed over to them.

Where Laura lives, the *narco* reality surrounds them. Shooting in front, to the back, and to the sides of them, daily. Her and her four children. But still, the possibility of this happening to them had seemed so remote. He had worked in a chain grocery store close to the house, and there, in the corner, they tossed back their beers with friends and relatives who visited.

"This is something that has no solution, that is irreversible. Now it is pure pain. Instead of Christmas, New Year's or a family outing, now we go to the cemetery. The same thing happens every twelfth day. Each month."

"The four-year-old girl cries a lot. We all miss him. They were not his children, but he got along well with them." Their father, who had himself married young and was obviously involved in drug trafficking, was killed in December of that year. Relatives told her that he had been going through a crisis of drug addiction. That was the last she knew. His body showed signs of torture when it was found near Limón del Ramos, twenty kilometers north of Culiacán.

At thirty, she thought she was never going to find someone to spend the rest of her life with. Then, for a while, it seemed like she'd been wrong—she had found him, but then he was snatched away. Now, single again, she lives off what family and friends give her, and with help from the Oportunidades program.[2]

"He was a good boy, serious. I remember that he got along with the girls. He read to them. They trusted him, and he took care of one of them when she had health problems, bathing her and everything. The government did nothing, because we are not important people or politicians. Nor do we have a much money."

Behind those bifocals, her eyes mist over with clouds that seem to grow as the light hits the lens. Her head says no. She doesn't believe it. She knows that they didn't deserve it. That he didn't deserve it. Not him. Not them. And so she has rage, against everything and everyone, thinking of what she might have done—and what she hadn't done—against *them*, those who killed him. Laura's life was reduced to that death, the death of her husband. And then it was quadrupled. Many deaths were made from one, a death that never ends, painful, angry, and eternal.

COMMON GRAVE

This embrace was also a farewell. Their mutual affection was such that when they saw each other they wept with joy. They didn't know if it would be the last time they were intertwined, looking into each other's eyes. Meeting and parting tenderly, rapturously.

She, the sister named Alma Rosa, wanted to talk about him in the present tense. To bring him to life with the verb, with the use of words, so that he would breathe again. At least in memory. His name is Miguel Ángel Rojo Medina. He is forty-seven. He was last seen on July 4, 2009.

The harvest was over. And Miguel Ángel, who ran a business transporting agricultural workers, organized a party. A get-together with carne asada to celebrate the end of the planting season in Estación Obispo, a community located south of the municipality of Culiacán. That's where the siblings last met and embraced. And then he vanished.

Since there were going to be elections the next day and nobody would sell beer—due to the "dry law" prohibiting the sale of alcoholic beverages during the elections—he rushed to buy some family-sized bottles. He told his sister that he was also going to see a woman in the community of Obispo, near Estación Obispo, where he was. And that he also wanted to buy shrimp to prepare and eat them on Sunday after the election.

What they learned about him after that came from a phone call. Miguel Ángel called a niece of his named Loreto. He asked her where she was. She was surprised, because her uncle rarely phoned. So she let out a shaky "What's going on? How are you?" He said that he was fine, but she insisted on asking what was wrong. "Nothing, nothing," he continued. "I just called to tell you that I'm going to Culiacán." She replied: "At this hour? With whom?" And then he hung up.

One woman, many roads

She found out about him, but only after a few days. The woman he had been with never told anyone, but his sister, following the trail, asked here and there and figured it out. "I don't know what happened," the woman answered, when questioned about that night. The van was outside in the yard. She said that Miguel Ángel had left evidence of his presence: he took a jug of water, left the keys in the ignition and the driver's door window halfway down, and an open bottle of beer from which he'd barely taken a drink.

"Since then, the days and nights have been eternal," said Alma Rosa, who has starred in this ordeal, with no schedule or end in sight, this drama about a missing brother.

When she went to the prosecutor's office to lodge a complaint, the staff replied that she should wait at least seventy-two hours for it to be considered a case of "disappearance" and trigger an investigation. She wondered what would change in seventy-two hours.

She recalled that the commander initially assigned to the case, once the complaint was accepted, had indeed started investigating, but that he was soon transferred to the port of Mazatlán, located a few hundred kilometers from Culiacán. That commander, Valderrama, was killed while returning to Culiacán, in September 2009, a week after having been appointed chief of the State Ministerial Police in Concordia.

Sources indicate that Valderrama was intercepted by armed men when he was at the tollbooth of the Culiacán–Mazatlán Maxipista road, about twenty kilometers from the state capital.

The discovery was made on Wednesday, September 30. The deceased was bound hand and foot with cables used in electrical installations and wrapped in a blanket. Less than a month earlier, his predecessor, Major Sabino Hernández García, and PME agent Gregorio Camacho Avilez were riddled with bullets along the same road as they returned from a commanders' meeting held in the city of Culiacán. Information from the state attorney general notes that Hernández García's two predecessors were also killed under similar conditions.

Another officer took the case but did nothing. So Alma Rosa decided to look on her own, in Obispo, Estación Obispo, Estación Quilá, and nearby communities. One, two, three, four times, she walked through the woods for about seven hours. Someone told her he had seen the body of her brother way out there, far in that direction. She searched drainage channels, paths, and corn and bean fields. One day she was told that he was in a funeral home in El Salado, but this was just one more false lead.

A person involved in drug trafficking said he would help. Accompanied by a dozen gunmen, she searched and searched. They reached Quilá and several surrounding villages. You are on a treadmill, they warned. This will never end. She didn't find anything.

They're going to kill you

Her brothers were afraid. "They'll kill you," they repeated. "But, not me. I wasn't even afraid. I knew the risk that I ran, but I also knew that my brother wasn't a *narco*. He had some flaws, that's for sure. He liked the ladies a lot, but nothing more than that."

She knows whose turf she's crossing. And she knows who's in charge in the city. You don't need to be a criminal or to have family members involved or to be a journalist or a police officer, none of that. You just have to live here, in a community near the capital, and everyone, absolutely everyone knows who the boss is and with whom you shouldn't mess. Like many in this kind of situation, she turned to drug traffickers to help find her brother. She did this without knowing if they might have been involved in his disappearance. She didn't know for certain, and she really didn't want to know. What she wanted was to find was a missing piece of her heart, torn away at their last embrace. Her destiny, her best friend, her brother.

The best investigator

"I heard that Florentino López Beltrán, of the State Ministerial Police, was the best investigator I could get for this kind of case," Alma Rosa says. He is also is also a relative.

She sought him out, and he agreed. But, she asserts, "He never helped me. What he did was ask me to stay away from public acts of protest, because otherwise he would not help."

The famous investigator also lied. He said a "Oaxaquita"—a term used disparagingly in Sinaloa to refer to people originating in the Southeast, usually employed as laborers in the fields—had her brother's cell phone, and they were going to find him. Pyrotechnics.

On August 5, 2009, ministerial officers found a corpse in Higueras located near Abuja Hill (south of Mazatlán and hours away from the towns she has searched). The body was dry, eaten by birds of prey, on the ground. "For me it was him," says Alma Rosa. She then spent seven months waiting in loving patience, only to find out that they had not even sent in samples to determine the DNA of the deceased and to compare it with that of her family. After lodging a complaint at the state attorney general's office and protesting outside of the office of Governor Jesús Aguilar Padilla, Leonel Aguirre Meza Ochoa and Oscar Loza from the Committee for the Defense of Human Rights came to her aid. "I finally managed to get the DNA testing. The result was negative, but I did not leave satisfied, and I do not trust the truth of it. And then I found out that the samples had been contaminated."

Meanwhile, authorities had sent the body to a mass grave. While the attorney general knew who had sent the body to the mass grave, when asked in April 2011 he would not tell where it was. Alma Rosa began to investigate and found out that they had left the body at the cemetery where the mass grave was located on March 21, 2011. The body was exhumed, and Alma Rosa asked the attorney general to do another DNA test. Officials reported that the Model Police Investigation Unit (PICU), according to their investigations, had decided to conduct the exhumation. She said it was a lie, that they had done nothing. She knew that if she had not moved, nothing would have happened.

The exhumation took place on November 4, 2011. When removed, the body looked shattered, and she said, "This is not him." They had taken another body that was nearby, in the same grave. They insisted, however, that this body was that of her brother. She disagreed and felt devastated, flooded with anxiety and hopelessness.

She told herself to breathe and sat on the grave marker to mourn. José Luis Leyva Rochín, then director of preliminary investigations for the prosecutor's office, came up to her with papers and told the workers that this was not actually the corpse they were looking for. The cemetery manager came over and told them that on April 8, officials had arrived with several bodies. Two of them had been left in one tomb and three more in another. They asked her if she could endure another exhumation. It was ten in the morning and they had started at six. "Yes, I can stand it," she replied.

Alma Rosa watched them take out more bodies. An official from the Medical Examiner's Office arrived, and she told them that none of those was the body of her brother. The official recalled that he had made a cut on a femur in order to take a DNA sample. And he also mentioned teeth.

They took out another body. They had said that the man had been burned after being hanged from a tree. They argued that it had become so skinny because of the time it had spent out in the sun.

In despair, Alma Rosa asked a senior deputy of the attorney general to let her take her own DNA samples to Mexicali or Mexico City or wherever. She was told that this was not possible. An expert from the Medical

Examiner's Office asked if she had explained what the other samples indicated, and she said no. "He said, 'look, I can almost be sure that the body is that of your brother. There is a minimum of error.' And I honestly believed him. All the time I've said that's my brother."

This time she and her surviving brothers took tests. Leyva Rochín informed her that the samples had been sent on December 15. Later they asked about the results. He said, "Not quite yet, perhaps tomorrow," but nothing ever showed up. He said that results would come January 15. In March 2012 there were still no results or developments in the case. And the office has yet to prove that the samples were even shipped.

"This is like another hell," Alma Rosa says. "He lives and no longer lives. Do I stop looking for my brother? No, I cannot. Last year I said, 'This year and that's it.' But I could not [stop looking]. I cannot. I have a no place to send flowers, light a candle, visit him," she said.

People close to Miguel Ángel speak on the condition that they are not mentioned. They live there, they fear for their lives. They say that in this region of Culiacán nothing happens without the *narcos* knowing. Or doing something about it. They claim that the family had to resort to drug traffickers to locate him, because police and forensic investigators do not really work to solve cases but rather to gum up the works when there's a chance of a break in the case.

That's how nearly thirty months have passed. A corpse wandering, like Alma Rosa's faith, misplaced and barely animated. DNA samples that never seem to get to the lab and a sister who will never be able to rest or to live in peace.

"It's all very cruel. Very. I have suffered so many lies and delays. I've been to Mexico City, to state government functions, here in Culiacán, to protest. And nothing happens. There are many, many people involved in this cruelty. And all I want is to know that it's him, to find him. And rest."

A DESERT ARCHIPELAGO

"Before, people in Juárez used to say, 'I wish you well,' when they said goodbye. Not anymore. They've even changed our language." He is

Rubén Villalpando, correspondent for the Mexico City paper *La Jornada* in Ciudad Juárez, Chihuahua, considered the most violent city in the country and the world.

He lives and works in this border city in northern Mexico, in which 10,500 murders took place from 2007 to 2012, in a state with about 15,000 murders over the same period. But 2010 was the most violent, a year after the Sinaloa Cartel, led by Joaquín "El Chapo" Guzmán Loera and Ismael "El Mayo" Zambada García, split with the Beltrán Leyva brothers. That year alone, organized crime was responsible for 3,500 killings in Ciudad Juárez. In the most intense periods, the daily number of homicides averaged more than thirty. The city is but a shell of its former self. Due to war and to growing extortion rackets, also called "the charging of *piso*" ("floor tax"), about three thousand businesses closed their doors, mostly small shops of various kinds.[3] "Organized crime shakes down big businesses, but when it comes to the small shops like these that closed, the guys who make them pay to respect their lives and to allow them to continue operating are the very same criminals who stopped selling drugs out of fear and went into this kind of extortion and kidnapping," said the reporter, who also has a radio news program in the region.

The region: that hollow shell in the desert, rusty and decrepit, synonymous with desolation, plows ahead with impunity, just like the murders and disappearances of women. There are completely uninhabited housing developments, eaten away by vandalism and the theft of doors, windows and bars, copper pipes, bathroom fixtures, electrical wiring, and more. Local media estimates suggest that the human exodus from the city is increasing and attracting attention. A study by the Autonomous University of Ciudad Juárez revealed that there were about 100,000 abandoned houses in the population center in 2012: a city without citizens, ghostly houses that are not homes. It's a shell of apocalyptic abandonment driven by crime, drug trafficking, corruption, and impunity, in which, from the bottom to the top, any government contract is a trophy and complicity with the mafia seems to concentrate everything into a single power.

An example of this disease that spreads through concrete and bricks is the Infonavit public housing development, Riveras del Bravo. All that's left of it are hundreds of hollow and looted homes.

Disappearances

From 1993 to 2012, 132 women have gone missing from Ciudad Juárez, according to data from the state government. But unofficial figures indicate that the number of female victims of disappearances could be more than double that, about three hundred. Here the blanket of impunity covers everything and everyone. The same impunity shelters brothel owners, gangs involved in sex trafficking, drug dealers and murderers, and the thirsty lunatics of the underworld who sever limbs and commit sexual abuse. That's why there are dead women or women who have not been found. The only things that grow are violence and drug abuse, and the only things that trickle down are poverty and hunger.

A report published in July 2012 in *El Diario de Juárez*, by journalist Sandra Rodríguez Nieto, identifies specific routes along which many of the disappeared women traveled. Their memories remain there like ghosts, fuzzy silhouettes on the sidewalks, phantoms looking for work, peering in shop windows, nervously rubbing sweaty hands together, timid and fearful. And everyone, especially the authorities, seems to ask if these disappeared women ever really existed. "The last known path of María Guadalupe Pérez Montes, 17, was passing by the Modatelas shop, on Francisco Javier Mina Street, a few meters from where the 3B bus route stops on its way from downtown to her home in the Guadalajara Izquierda neighborhood."

"It was about six in the evening on January 31, 2009. It was just beginning to get dark; businesses were pulling down their metal shutters, and the only things open on the street where María Guadalupe walked were those of bars and brothels."

"I said, 'Lupita, wait,' but she did not stop. She said, 'I'm leaving because it's very late,'" remembered the last known family member who saw the young woman alive. "Lupita, however, never returned home, according to the analysis in *El Diario de Juárez*, [and] of eleven cases of women reported missing, at least seven other victims passed through that part of Mina Street on the last steps that they ever took or were supposed to have taken before they disappeared." At least five of them, like Lupita, even used the same public transport route, 3B, that connects downtown Juárez with the *colonias* to the west in which they all lived.

"Another case whose last clue lies on Mina Street is Cinthia Jocabeth Castañeda, 13, who was last seen on October 24, 2008 getting off a bus on Route 3B at the corner of Mina and Rafael Velarde, on her way to buy notebooks and shoes from two downtown businesses, where the next day they told her mother she had never come." On Mina the 3B bus also stopped on March 31, 2011, for Perla Marisol Moreno, 16, who left her home in the Plutarco Elias Calles neighborhood to look for work at the Cuauhtémoc and Reforma markets, located on La Paz Street, a block north of Mina where there are bars and brothels."

"A month after her, on April 26, 2011, along the same street, María de la Luz Hernandez, 18, stepped off the bus on the same route—3B, which, like Perla, she took to go to the Reforma market and an adjoining jewelry shop, in which she planned to look for work."

"And, then after those four, on July 7, 2011, Jessica Ivonne Padilla, then 16, passed down Mina, like the others, taking the 3B route to get from her home in the west to downtown Juárez, where she was also looking for work."

"Just five days later, also on Mina down route 2B this time, Nancy Ivette Navarro Muñoz, then 18, who was going to find work in the Modatelas store, disappeared."

"They all passed through this part of Mina Street—between Francisco Villa and Ignacio Mariscal, two blocks south of the Plaza de Armas— because there, among bars and brothels that operate in broad daylight, is where the only public transit for journeys between their homes and the center of Ciudad Juárez stop."

"None of the girls mentioned above has been seen alive by her family again, and only Lupita Pérez has been located. On April 22, her mother Susana Montes received the news that one of the 12 skeletons found in clearing the Juárez Valley—known as Navajo Creek, south of the town of Praxedis G. Guerrero—matched the genetic profile of her daughter."

"The woman, 42, says she has no idea what happened to her daughter—a student at the Guerreros Preparatory school who went downtown buy a pair of sneakers—after she was seen on Mina Street, or how or why she ended up murdered and her remains dumped in the Valle de Juárez."

Fear, care, terror

In Ciudad Juárez, crime dropped in the first half of 2012. The government rushes to point it out: It was us, with our law enforcement operations. We reduced criminality. It's the effectiveness of our actions. We are winning the battle against the criminals. We've rescued the city, given it back to the citizens. It's the rule of law.

Speeches. But down in the street, in their homes, while eating and preparing their children to go to school, parents and citizens in their workplaces and schools, say otherwise. They know it: the *narcos*, the drug cartels, agreed and made a deal, and the city was divided up, so there are fewer crimes, especially homicides. "They divided up the city like a cake. El Chapo Guzmán's people, the Sinaloa Cartel, were left with the El Valle region, and the other territory, downtown, the old city, is with La Línea ["The Line"], a local division of the Juárez Cartel," declared a *juarense* citizen who is a specialized observer of this overwhelming daily reality, this anteroom of hell.

Other reports indicate that El Chapo controls the entire city and has managed, after many bullets and many dead, with government complicity, to subdue his enemies and now has it all.

In her book *La fábrica del crimen*, Sandra Rodríguez speaks of these islands, the complex of real estate developments and maquiladoras distributed in random spots, like islands in the desert. Geography, the distribution of space, urban growth, large tracts of idle land, dense dark sections, they're all conducive to crime, abuse, murder and abduction, disappearance:

> [The residential areas] were constructed around maquiladoras, and over the years they were mixed in with commercial plazas. Other old and barely urbanized neighborhoods—like Solidaridad, Los Alcaldes, Zaragoza or Salvácar—and hundreds of empty spaces of various sizes were left behind in the midst of urban growth. The result was dozens of fragmented neighborhoods, like islands divided by a sea of sand dunes and garbage. The insecurity made walking paths lethal and eliminated public spaces or anything that might create or strengthen a cohesive identity. The beauty of the desert was reduced to an increasingly dispersed and dirty setting, incapable of provoking any feelings of affection.

For that reason and because there is no government but only *nar-cos*, and they're the ones in charge, people stopped going to malls, bars or pubs, nightclubs, dancing and entertainment centers, restaurants, et cetera. "We take care to know what's going on around us, because of the increase in the violent carjacking, and we take care when the cops get too close. We're stressed, it's the truth. That's how we live. We all know people who have been killed, who have suffered kidnapping and extortion. And, of course, we do not trust the government. And now, in 2012, people are just starting to leave. Just barely."

That's why, adds that old *juarense* desert wolf named Villalpando, people went from saying "I wish you well" to saying 'Take care. Take care of yourself.' And that's how they say good-bye. Do you get it? They even changed our language."

HE FOUND US

He was first in everything since childhood. He was the first boy after his mother gave birth to four girls, the first in school and in basketball, and the first to go to work—at six years old, selling chewing gum. And again when she disappeared, he was first. He said: "Here I am, come and get me." But no one listened.

Before he even entered primary school, he sold gum in gas stations and at dances. Although he was thin and small and they trampled and pushed him around at parties, he was determined to work and try to raise some money for his family. They had come down from a mountain community in the municipality of Sinaloa, near the Chihuahua border, to settle in poverty conditions, in a village near the city, in the municipality of Guasave.

And it was sad, his cheeks swollen with tears of helplessness, because when he switched the gum for popsicles, the men who operated the gas pumps depleted his supply. They ate his popsicles right in front of him, mocking and arrogant. But they never paid him. Sometimes, despite his best efforts, those skinny legs got nothing for all their hard work. And sometimes he had to pay the business owner back, when he came up short. "He studied and worked until he got a job in the countryside, one of those tough jobs. A deposit hung over his head, and he set to work with a hose and an applicator, putting chemicals on plants and crops. He grabbed the work because they gave him the opportunity, and it was only on the weekends," said a close relative.

Emilio is not his name. But his family and people close to him asked that a pseudonym be used before relating details about his life. Emilio was good in school: he wrote poems and read them aloud in class; he participated in academic competitions and won prizes, and he worked hard and was an excellent basketball player. He was a tall, strong boy.

These days, in 2012, his teacher Cristina, who taught his primary school lessons, remembers him well and visits his family in Guasave, about 150 kilometers (ninety-three miles) from Culiacán. When she talks about him, the tears well up but don't fall. Aged but lucid, she describes him: "He was a complete student. Intelligent, studious, creative. A reader and even a writer because he wrote poems. He was good at everything, in sports and in all of his school subjects." He had barely finished high school on the Emiliano Zapata campus in Culiacán when he began to study law at the Autonomous University of Sinaloa. By then he was a voracious reader. He had his own collection of books, those he had already read and remained his favorites, and those that waited for him on the shelf where arranged them with religious devotion.

He decided to continue working. Money was scarce and became even more so because he lived an hour and a half from home, things were more expensive, and he insisted on sending some cash to his mother. He signed on as a security guard for a clothing chain called Milano, located on Miguel Hidalgo Street, downtown, next to the Garmendia market. He was surprised to discover customers hiding merchandise in their clothes. It was hard on him, especially when they were women or old ladies. He had to intercept them, recover the products, and sometimes report them to management. He preferred not to do it. He preferred to perform searches and confiscate the goods only when it involved men. But they were not his rules to make, and this was his work.

Emilio was about twenty when he received an offer from his neighbors, with whom he had grown up and who had an impressive history of drug trafficking. They invited him to go to the United States, do a "little job," and make some good money. There and then he lost the first round: that daily struggle of his for years, with him and his family stuck in poverty, faced off against those powerful little bosses who were already masters of the town and various surrounding communities in the area, and of the very city of Guasave. They placed him in a desperate situation without a horizon in sight and then offered to make the sun shine on him and his family. And so he accepted.

The operation was crude. He was to transport marijuana from one city to another, in a stake-bed truck, almost out in the open. Having been a great student, a poet and reader, a graduate with excellent grades, and a good son, an example inside and outside of his home to his nephews and nieces and his girlfriend, he jumped to it. And then he got stuck in the mud.

Unofficial versions close to the case claim that Emilio received instructions from another young man he knew very well since they had grown up in the same town, in Guasave. "If the police arrive, the orders are that you will take the blame, that I know nothing." And so it was. It seemed like a betrayal, a trap. The agents saw and stopped them. They didn't delay at all in finding the drugs. His fall to the muddy floor cost him three years in jail in that country. Three lost years of confinement, accumulating grievances, and hatred, knowing that he had been used by those who hired him, that the drug removal operation had been a distraction to allow the movement of illicit goods in another truck. Three years of waiting and frustration, of his girlfriend, patient and faithful, weaving warm dreams and hopes, in a corner by herself. When he returned they were married. But that couldn't mollify the bitterness that had accumulated in that twentysomething young man. So much work and studying for so little. For three years locked up. For nothing.

Looks as sharp as knives

In 2009, Emilio ran into some of the guys who had led him to the United States to pull that job. He now had children. One of them saw him and said, "Are those yours?" He nodded. They greeted this information with suspicious looks, measured rigor in their words, and studious gestures. They sharpened their knives with the flash of anger and pent-up resentment showing on his face. "We'll see you later."

There were unspoken words between them. Apparently there were different versions of the story of the seizure, arrest, and incarceration. Afterward, Emilio talked with one of his family members, observing that these were bad people, dangerous, which was tough, "because they can fuck you over at any time."

There were debts that no one wanted to collect. But one of the parties expected it, longed for the opportunity to respond. The other, Emilio, just wanted to get past it, to move forward. He was surviving through a sort of truce in which it seemed like the other guy was always pointing a gun at him, waiting for him to cross the line, commit an imprudence, so that he could pull the trigger. That's how it felt: to live in the crosshairs of an automatic rifle.

Guasave is hell. Many hells. It's the bastion of one of the most warlike and violent cells organized by the Beltrán Leyva brothers. The group, not of dozens but of hundreds, maybe thousands, is led by a young man not yet thirty years old, Isidro Meza Flores, known as El Chapo Isidro. He's loved and idolized as much as he's feared.

In the style of older capos—fifty and up, like El Mayo and El Chapo, leaders of the Sinaloa Cartel, their enemies—these young bucks like to be accompanied by beautiful women, and not just one or two. They move around in Guasave and the municipalities of Sinaloa, Mocorito, and farther north. They also vie for control of the municipality of Salvador Alvarado and have a strong presence in Angostura and places as far south as Mazatlán and San Ignacio.

There, in Guasave, the veneration reaches such a level that at baseball games, for the local Algodoneros team in the Mexican Pacific League, the public address system at the stadium plays the ballad of El Chapo Isidro. Unofficial accounts indicate that when he arrives, people open a path to allow him and his thirty armed guards to pass. "Pure *morros* [kids], but those *batos* are killers just the same."

This group has made incursions in Culiacán, considered a sanctuary for the capos, to carry out executions and toss out decapitated victims, like the ones found on March 28, in an uninhabited place, in the 10 de Abril neighborhood, located north of the city.

On that occasion, there were five victims, all beheaded: Yahir Ernesto Noriega Loaiza, José Cruz González Castillo, Eduardo Flores Zazueta,

Marco Joshua, and Jaime Alejandro Higuera Larrañaga Cruz, who had been taken by armed commandos the previous Sunday night from a sports field located in the Infonavit Humaya development, according to the report of the State Ministerial Police. The murderers hung a blanket over the perimeter fence of the primary school Roberto Hernández Rodríguez with a handwritten message that read: "Look, you stinking fucking Chapo, you don't even control your own state where you are from, much less any other state, you *pendejo* traitor DEA informant who has turned in hundreds of the stinking scalps of your own people. Sincerely, El Z40."[4]

Arrogance

The area is its own Macondo, the legendary town that Gabriel García Márquez describes in *One Hundred Years of Solitude*: a place of dreams, yellow butterflies multiplying out of thin air, the magic of well-being without material progress, happiness just for belonging in the middle of the fiesta and the poverty, opulence in the bounty of its agricultural fields (some of the most productive in Sinaloa and the entire country), and lean wages for the workers. The whole area is also like Sasalpa. It is now, anyway. A hurried death in vehicles and houses torched during an assault perpetrated by a commando of at least forty men seeking to avenge the death of Rosario Angulo Soto, killed in an attack on the village of Comanitos. Both communities are located in the municipality of Mocorito. The attacks left Sasalpa stricken. Most of the inhabitants fled to the mountains and then to other villages, leaving dozens of cars and homes to burn. Now no one lives there.

That arrogance of determining, instantly, at the end of the dark barrel of an AK-47 automatic rifle, the lives, the homes, the fate, and the death of those who live in that region of Guasave and its surroundings. Of looks as sharp as knives, threats whose expiration date depends upon the capricious will of an armed group that acts like a gang, leaving devastation in its wake and ranking above all other authorities, because they are the government, the government that kidnaps, extorts, assaults, rapes, and kills.

"All those murderers, all of them, are still alive. And that's how they act, with arrogance. It takes one look to get any *pendejo* killed, they say, when someone annoys them by turning to face them a certain way. And it's not because they owe them money, for an affront, for the theft of drugs or merchandise worth millions of pesos, or to avenge the death of a relative. No. They kill for the simplest of looks," said a person who lived in Ruiz Cortines and went to live in Culiacán, where another hell awaits: the Sinaloa Cartel.

"That corridor," explained a journalist who asked to remain anonymous, "is one of death." Even people passing by, on the Mexico City–Nogales Highway, are assaulted and abused. They hold Batamote, Gabriel Leyva Solano, Ruiz Cortines, and the entirety of the municipalities of Sinaloa and Mocorito in the palm of their hand. All of it is theirs. "About 60 or 70 percent of homicides in the region are concentrated there; it's a trash dump full of dead people. Just look at where they killed those police officers . . . nearly twenty cops were killed in two attacks," he explained.

The reporter referred to the events of March 8 and July 16, 2011, on that same road in the same area. The first took a toll of seven policemen and one civilian killed—the latter had apparently been stopped by the officers before the shooting began. Another arrested civilian was released by the gunmen after the encounter. The July 16 attack was deadlier: it would appear that the triggermen thought that Francisco Córdova, the state secretary of public security, was traveling in the convoy of agents from the State Preventive Police after a meeting in the city of Los Mochis, the capital of the municipality of Ahome, about thirty miles northwest of Guasave. The assailants used AK-47 rifles and Barrett .50 caliber machine guns with armor-piercing capability. But the secretary of public security returned to Culiacán by helicopter and sent his agents and their escort on the ground. The convoy came under a fierce attack. Ten police were scattered on the asphalt of the federal highway afterward, and three were hospitalized with serious injuries.

El Chapo Isidro's people were under the control of the Beltrán Leyva brothers. Guasave and Los Mochis had been their territory when they operated as part of the Sinaloa Cartel. Once the unity of Beltrán Leyva, El Mayo, and El Chapo fell apart after the arrest—and alleged betrayal—of Alfredo Beltrán Leyva by the Mexican army in an operation in Culiacán in February 2008, they were left in control of the area and its market for cultivating, harvesting, and transporting drugs. When they made money before 2008, they bought luxury cars and homes. These homes later became safe houses. Half the town was already theirs. They took the rest by force.

And the children and young people who grew up with them, with those *pistoleros*, capos, and *caciques* of the local drug trade, followed in their footsteps. Seduced, stunned, resigned and wretched, they thought about the cash that came from that dirty business, the chance of escaping poverty and becoming the newly rich, the next masters and untouchables. But those bills were stained, even before they were printed and reached the banks. And so were those lost souls. Like poor Emilio, who slipped, and when he tried to recover from the quicksand and save himself and clean up his life, he fell again, this time defeated by those who had once recruited him with promises of paradise: the paradise of the goat horn.

Disappeared

No one disappears from this region without being seen and guarded, especially if they have pending accounts or have an unknown or "suspicious" character. He entered. He had no debts to repay, or so he felt. He went to see some relatives. They (not the relatives) followed him. He saw them in the rear-view mirror. They kept their distance and stayed there. At the third intersection, they rolled up on him. He was driving a car that was not new but in good condition. One of the gunmen, one of the guys with whom he'd grown up and who was part of the group that had engaged him for that transfer of drugs that cost him three years in a US prison blurted out: "You have no business here." Baffled, Emilio said that it was still his neighborhood, the place where he grew up, that he was a free citizen with nothing to fear, because he didn't owe anybody anything. The guy responded: "Don't come back," and he had nothing else to say.

Emilio had become a locksmith, and the Mexican army sought him out several times, before they went to execute a search warrant on someone's property. They had hired him, but he couldn't exactly have refused, he used to say. That's how he lived, from his business, a small one, in a strip mall south of the city of Culiacán.

Here and there, from the Sinaloan capital to that corridor of death. No one knows. They searched for him on trains, in the mountains, in the funeral homes, and among the wounded and hospitalized. And that's how it's been since September 10, 2009. One of the strongest versions of the story maintains that an armed group took him away, *lo levantó*. For this reason, the family filed complaint no. CLN/DAP/022/2009 with the state attorney general, who then assigned prosecutors in the town of Mocorito to handle the case.

Infiltrated

The director of the State Ministerial Police, the agency responsible for investigating this and other common crimes, always attended to Emilio's family members. When they arrived at his office, he would open the sitting room and give them the comfortable chairs and table with a fine finish on which to rest their elbows and forearms, those tired, hurt, and hopeful bodies. He gave them coffee and water, and more coffee and more water. He would say: "I'm with you, I support you. We're going to work on this. You will see. We will find him." Between coffee and coffee and other attentions, he called them several times by phone to tell them that they had found a body. That it could be him. The family sent one of its members to view photos and check the belongings. A few times they looked upon corpses on slabs in the morgue or at crime scenes. Again and again, he called them to report on new findings. And siblings and cousins and aunts and uncles finally gave up when the director, Silvio Isidro de Jesús Hernández Soto, with the rank of lieutenant colonel in the Mexican army, called again to tell them that the latest body had been identified by other family members, and it was not him.

Three or four days after Emilio's disappearance, ministerial officers found the body of a twentysomething young man near the community of Pericos, in the municipality of Mocorito. The town is located less than a hundred kilometers north of Culiacán. The victim had countless gunshot wounds and showed signs of having been tortured. Again the lieutenant colonel called. And soon backtracked: "No, it's not him. His relatives recognized him."

That lieutenant colonel was arrested by personnel of the Military Judicial Police and agents from the attorney general's office in mid-May 2012. A few days later, a federal judge granted an order of house arrest for forty days for his alleged complicity along with other senior military officers in organized crime, specifically with the Beltrán Leyva brothers in 2010.

A story by Gustavo Castillo, published in *La Jornada* on May 20, 2012, has the details:

> The attorney general's office (PGR) won court approval to keep General Ricardo Escorcia Vargas and Lieutenant Colonel Silvio Isidro de Jesús Hernández Soto under arrest for 40 days, pending investigation of their alleged ties to the Beltrán Leyva Cartel.
>
> From a court specializing in arrest and search warrants, the [Special] Prosecutor for Organized Crime (SIEDO) obtained an order that the two officers must remain in the custody of the attorney general in the so-called Federal Investigations Center, located in the Colonia Doctores in Mexico City.
>
> Escorcia Vargas and Silvio Isidro de Jesús Hernández added to the court orders that SIEDO had already obtained against General Tomás Ángeles Dauahare and Roberto Dawe González, who, according to the Federal Justice Department, allegedly protected the Beltrán Leyva Cartel operations, led by Héctor Beltrán since December 2010, when his brother Arturo, El Barbas, was shot dead in Cuernavaca, Morelos, by members of the navy.
>
> The PGR has the four military officers under house arrest presumably in order to obtain evidence of their responsibility for criminal acts, after two protected witnesses came forward. One was identified as Jennifer, whose real name is Roberto López Nájera. The other, identified as Mateo, is Sergio Villarreal Barragan, known in the Beltrán Leyva cartel as El Grande.
>
> According to SIEDO, the preliminary investigation PGR/OFDI/ EU IFDCS/112/2012 was opened in March of this year for drug crimes and organized crime, but General Ángeles Dauahare was arrested a week after taking part in a roundtable analysis of national security issues—convened by the Colosio Foundation, and attended by the PRI candidate for the presidency, Enrique Peña Nieto—which was held in San Luis Potosí.

Supposedly to prevent an attack, the PGR [has] reinforced perimeter security around the center since last Friday, placing dozens of soldiers to guard the building in effective coordination with the navy and elements of the Federal Ministerial Police.

Pleas

In a letter sent to the media in September 2009, the family of the deceased asked his captors for mercy, begged and pleaded with them in an open letter: "Hand him over, dead or alive." In another statement that some of Emilio's family members made to the media, they went further, imploring: "If you have or know of him, tell us, deliver him to us, alive or dead, so that we no longer have to suffer this ordeal of not knowing what happened to him and not having him with us." Emilio's wife demanded that the state government expedite the investigation and asked the public to report any knowledge of the case.

"As a family that has brothers and sisters, sons and daughters, mothers and fathers, we beg you to support us, to turn in those who have him, to know that we are good people and we know how to forgive, we don't harbor hatred or bitterness . . . let them turn him over however he is, alive or just his body . . . so that we can bury him."

The screams of a cadaver

There are many like him. Many thousands in this country. But none that yell at you, that speak to you, that wait for you. There are no dead like this. None like Emilio.

It all came down to a chance encounter with an expert from the Coordinated Criminal Investigation and Forensic Services (of which the medical examiner, SEMEFO, is a subunit), of the state attorney general's office. He saw a corpse. It was routine. Before placing it in a common grave in a cemetery in Culiacán, certain tests had to be made. Little was left of that person. But the final scientific ritual was well worth it, the morgue's official farewell.

The man looked and looked, and he looked again. He went through the belongings, the official staff reports from the prosecutor's office in

Mocorito, the bag with the few items that the murderers had left, along with what was left of the corpse: it was him, his friend's brother, the guy who had disappeared. It was December 1.

The cell phone rang—"I have your brother"—and the colors rose in the young woman's face. Red, purple, and blue. Her cheeks, chin, and eyelids trembled. Everything shook, off the Richter scale. Emilio's family members got in the car and headed to Culiacán. It took almost an hour and a half to get there, a long time. Life and death are always in a hurry. Each expects the other and is impatient. And the family's long wait converged on that date, in the morgue. One of the sisters lived closer, and she was told immediately. It was she who went first and then told the others by cell phone: "Yes, it is my brother Emilio."

Her friend showed them the few remaining bones of the deceased. There was very little, almost nothing to show. All there was to identify him was the fractured septum, some crooked teeth on the left side of his mouth, dust and more dust, and a brand of jeans that should be called To Die Just the Same, that had died like his frayed and transparent shirt: spread by the wind like the rest of him. A dusty blizzard standing and sitting in a bag, a funeral vessel, a dull ritual that for them was life and rest and peace and pain. But no tears: all of those had already been shed in a year and three months of waiting. Those 440 days had been one long nightmare for them.

"All that time he was mothballed, stacked, lost, as in an old filing cabinet, a drawer, exposed to the elements, the glare of the sun, the dust, and the wind, in a corner, in the courtyard of the funeral home in the community of Pericos, with other coffins and boxes of other corpses left by order of Rubén García Galván, an officer at the prosecutor's office, as an unknown," said one of Emilio's family members.

A document from the State Human Rights Commission, case number CEDH/III/327/10, notes that the prosecutor García Galván should have had the corpse and other evidence turned over to the Forensic Medical Service of the PGJE, that it could have been identified after being submitted for scientific testing. But the prosecutor did not do so. He kept it there mothballed, embraced by dust, at the faithful mercy of oblivion.

For this case, Garcia Galván was suspended. The CEDH ordered that the case be reviewed and serve as a precedent for the handling of similar records in the future, and it recommended a public apology to Emilio's family from the judicial authorities. In the end, the apology was private and intimate. Luis Cárdenas Fonseca, head of the prosecutor's office, visited the family at home to express his sorrow for the role prosecutors played in Emilio's disappearance and murder.

Find me, here I am

It was terrible. One of Emilio's closest relatives tells the story. They made the journey, and when the staff from the Ministerio Público and the funeral parlor in Pericos learned who they were, they bowed their heads and spoke softly. It was a pain without measure or remedy. They felt tears that wouldn't come, that dried up before escaping their eyes, because Emilio had been there all along. The corpse was the same one that the commander of the state police, Lt. Col. Silvio Isidro de Jesús Hernández, had told them that they had found and later hastened to conclude was not Emilio, that members of another family had come forward to identify. That hadn't been true, and they had no idea that this was the case or why. They didn't know any better. Now many things are clearer, many loose ends are tied up.

How can you refer to the irresponsibility of those investigating a disappearance and murder, if they never actually investigated it? How can you describe the grief, ridicule, incompetence, ineptitude, and irresponsibility of those who are supposedly looking for a body they already have in hand, a body that has slowly vanished and been consumed over 440 days, along with other "unknown" remains? It's the willful ignorance and vileness of a government that not only punishes the victims but extends their suffering as long as possible. "Imagine what we did not have to live through, to think about, for all that time. Disconcerted, not knowing the whereabouts of my brother, a human being. And the whole time he was in the hands of the attorney general's office, of those who are supposed to seek justice, who must seek justice. They had him all along."

In the bag of dust and bones, he was already gone, extinct and fragile. There was no sobbing now. The tears had been spent during the comings and goings. In the faces, the words, the bodies brown and bent by that awful tiredness, there was a mix of reunion and relief, of knowing about him without being able to reach out and embrace him. There was pain, but this was dulled by peace and harmony.

The men responsible are still at it, albeit cloaked in shadows. "There's no bitterness," they say, but there's no forgetting either. They are alive and well. The army knocks them down a peg, but they still kill policemen, they kidnap, they extort, they form new gangs, they escape, they crouch down low, and *Pum!* They attack once again. They are the masters. They own the place. They dole out destinies and lives. That's why looks and glances went extinct in these towns. They can get you killed.

"Did they find him? Is it him, my brother?" asked one of the older sisters in a dry voice, leaden and resigned. Come what may. The bad had come and gone, but it also remained. "No, we didn't find him, he found us." He had always been there, waiting, sitting, lying in the wind and the dust, screaming out for them, calling to them during those fifteen months of darkness.

Notes

INTRODUCTION

1. The first mentions of *levantones* in the news magazine *Proceso*, for example, are from 2003, and they appear in direct quotations. Neither the definition of the noun nor of the verb form of the term (*levantar*) was included in the 2010 edition of Luis Fernando Lara's canonical *Diccionario del español mexicano, Vol. II* (Mexico City: Colegio de México). On the evolving language of the drug war, see Guillermo Colín Sánchez, *Así se habla la delincuencia y otras más* (Mexico City: Porrúa, 1997); Fernando Escalante Gonzalbo, *El crimen como realidad y representación* (Mexico City: Colegio de México, 2012), 60.

2. According to Mexico's National Institute of Statistics and Geography (INEGI), the death toll from 2007–14 was 164,000. See also Jason Breslow, "The Staggering Death Toll of Mexico's Drug War," *Frontline*, July 27, 2015. The Mexican government's Registro Nacional de Personas Desaparecidas (https://rnped .segob.gob.mx) included 26,581 people as of October 1, 2015. On forced displacement, see *Desplazamiento Interno Forzado en México* (Mexico City: Comisión Mexicana de Defensa y Promoción de los Derechos Humanos A.C., 2014), http://cmdpdh.org/wp-content/uploads/2015/03/Desplazamiento-Interno -Forzado-en-Mex.pdf.

3. *Global Peace Index, 2015* (Institute for Economics & Peace), http:// economicsandpeace.org/wp-content/uploads/2015/06/Global-Peace-Index -Report-2015_0.pdf.

4. "México supera a España como la primera economía hispana," *El País*, April 14, 2015; GDP data for the World Bank (World Bank, http://data.world bank.org/country/mexico); social indicators from United Nations Development Programme (http://hdr.undp.org/en/countries/profiles/MEX).

5. "Se declara culpable detenido por asesinato de activista sinaloense," *Proceso*, May 23, 2014; "Niega la PGJE que sea poco creíble versión de homicidio

de Sandra Luz," *Ríodoce,* May 22, 2015; "Detienen en Sinaloa a presunto asesino de la activista Sandra Luz Hernández," *Aristegui Noticias,* May 21, 2014; "Pide la CNDH protección para familia de activista asesinada en Sinaloa," *Proceso,* May 21, 2014; "Cae en Sinaloa presunto homicida de la activista Sandra Luz Hernández," *Proceso,* May 20, 2014; "In Mexico, Activist Mother of Missing Man Is Slain," *Los Angeles Times,* May 20, 2014; "La procuraduría ignora pistas de Sandra Luz Hernández," *El Debate,* May, 18, 2014; "Video: Ella era Sandra Luz Hernández, activista asesinada en Sinaloa," *Aristegui Noticias,* May 15, 2014; "'Voy a ser una piedrita en el zapato'—Sandra Luz Hernández," *El Debate,* May 14, 2014; "La madre incómoda," *Noroeste,* May 14, 2014; "La Segob exige al gobierno de Sinaloa esclarecer asesinato de activista," *CNN México,* May 14, 2014; "Asesinan en Culiacán a madre activista; buscaba a su hijo," *Animal Político,* May 13, 2014; "México—Asesinato de la defensora de derechos humanos la Sra. Sandra Luz Hernandez," *Frontline Defenders,* May 6, 2014.

6. "Se plantan en Palacio Gobierno por justicia a Sandra Luz Hernández," *Noroeste,* April 15, 2015; "Con la mafia no se puede: La multiplicada tragedia de Sandra Luz Hernández," *Ríodoce,* March 29, 2015; "Inicia CEDH investigación de oficio por caso Sandra Luz Hernández," *Noroeste,* March 27, 2015; "Exhorta Malova a STJE a investigar tráfico de influencias en caso Sandra Luz," *Noroeste,* March 26, 2015; 'Influyentismo familiar' facilita liberar a homicida de Sandra," *El Debate,* March 24, 2015; "Absuelven a acusado de asesinar a activista," *Noroeste,* March 24, 2015; "Silencian a Sandra Luz," "Acusa Procurador tráfico de influencias para liberar a acusado de asesinato," *Noroeste,* December 29, 2014; "La sed de la justicia," *Noroeste,* December 8, 2014; "Los siete 'pecados' de la PGJE," *Noroeste,* November 15, 2014; "Mentira, la justicia por desapariciones forzadas," *Noroeste,* September 29, 2014.

7. "Las tres muertes de Sandra Luz," *Ríodoce,* May 25, 2014. Revised and updated with a full recounting of the case in Valdez Cárdenas, *Los huérfanos del narco* (Mexico City: Penguin Random House Grupo Editorial México, 2015).

8. The protest was timed to coincide with the commemoration of the massacre of unarmed student protestors in the Plaza de las Tres Culturas Tlatelolco, in Mexico City on October 2, 1968. For the initial story of the disappearance and the protests, see Carmen Bullosa and Mike Wallace, *A Narco History: How the United States and Mexico Jointly Created the Mexican Drug War* (New York: OR Books, 2015); "43 Missing Students, a Mass Grave, and a Suspect: Mexico's Police," *New York Times,* October 6, 2014; "Investigators in Mexico Detain Mayor and His Wife over Missing Students," *New York Times,* November 4, 2014; "Drug Gang Killed Students, Mexican Law Official Says," *New York Times,* November 7, 2014; "Mexico's Barbarous Tragedy," *New York Times,* November 10, 2014; "Ayotzinapa: A Timeline of the Mass Disappearance That Has Shaken Mexico," *Vice News,* December 9, 2014; "Iguala: Historia no oficial," *Proceso,* December 13, 2014.

9. *Informe Ayotzinapa: Investigación y primeras conclusiones de las desapariciones y homicidios de los normalistas de Ayotzinapa* (Mexico City: Grupo Interdisciplinario de Expertos Independientes, 2015), http://www.casede.org/BibliotecaCasede/Informe_AyotziGIEI.pdf.

10. While the phrase became ubiquitous, some of the first and clearest articulations of its meaning and import can be found on the website of Nuestra Aparente Rendición ("Our Apparent Surrender"), a volunteer organization formed by journalists, exiles, and victims' family members to defend freedom of expression in Mexico: http://nuestraaparenterendicion.com/.

11. See John P. Sullivan and Robert J. Bunker, eds., *Mexico's Criminal Insurgency: A Small Wars Journal—El Centro Anthology* (iUniverse, 2012); George Grayson, *Mexico: Narco-Violence and a Failed* State (New Brunswick: Transaction Publishers, 2011); Shannon O'Neil, "The Real War in Mexico: How Democracy Can Defeat the Drug Cartels," *Foreign Affairs* 88, no. 4 (July/August 2009), 63–77. Otherwise excellent pieces of journalism that misuse the "insurgency" label in their analysis include Ioan Grillo, *El Narco: Inside Mexico's Criminal Insurgency* (London: Bloomsbury, 2011); Sam Quiñones, "The Real War in Mexico," *Foreign Affairs*, no. 171 (March/April 2009), 76–80. For a careful analysis of the way in which the "failed state" discourse serves the interests of privatization, see Paul Kenny, Monica Serrano, and Arturo C. Sotomayor, *Mexico's Security Failure: Collapse into Criminal Violence* (London: Routledge, 2013).

12. Luis Astorga, *Drogas sin fronteras*, new ed. (Mexico City: Debolsillo, 2015).

13. Patricio Asfura-Heim and Ralph H. Espach, "The Rise of Mexico's Self-Defense Forces: Vigilante Justice South of the Border," *Foreign Affairs*, July/August, 2013.

14. *Sicario* is an archaic term for a hired assassin, derived from the Latin *sicarius* ("dagger"), recently revived as a generic term for drug cartel hit men. Ramón Joaquín Domínguez, *Diccionario nacional o gran diccionario clásico de la lengua española, quinta edición* (Madrid: Establecimiento de Mellado, 1853); *Diccionario de la lengua española, vigésima segunda edición* (Madrid: Real Academia Española, 1992, hereafter cited as *RAE* (1992). While the word was used to describe the perpetrators of certain high-profile assassinations and attempted assassinations throughout the twentieth century, its current usage is a phenomenon of the post-2006 drug war; it was not widely used to describe gunmen for organized crime in the 1990s or earlier. Some attribute its use to the Colombian Pablo Escobar, who was perhaps the first contemporary drug trafficker to use strategic assassination on a large scale and hire whole squads of assassins who were otherwise uninvolved in the drug trade.

15. After a shootout in Tamaulipas on May 19, 2010, which left four Zetas dead, one of them was identified as a member of the Kaibiles. National

Security Archives, http://www2.gwu.edu/~nsarchiv/NSAEBB/NSAEBB445/docs/20100528.PDF.

16. National Security Archive, http://nsarchive.gwu.edu/NSAEBB/NSAEBB445/docs/20100826.pdf

17. Howard Campbell, *Drug War Zone: Frontline Dispatches from the Streets of El Paso and Juárez* (Austin: University of Texas Press, 2009).

18. "¿Por qué el crimen organizado atenta contra la sociedad civil en México?" *El País*, October 12, 2014.

19. Benjamin Locks, "Extortion in Mexico: Why Mexico's Pain Won't End with the War on Drugs," *Yale Journal of International Affairs*, October 6, 2014, http://yalejournal.org/article_post/extortion-in-mexico-why-mexicos-pain-wont-end-with-the-war-on-drugs.

20. "Pemex Struggles to Stop Spike in Petroleum Theft," *Houston Chronicle*, August 16, 2014; "Mexican Crime Gangs Expand Fuel Thefts," *Wall Street Journal*, June 18, 2011; Ricardo Ravelo, *Zetas, franqicia criminal* (Mexico City: Ediciones, 2014); Diego Osorno, *La guerra de los zetas: viaje por la frontera de la necropolítica* (Mexico City: Vintage Español, 2013).

21. *Sin Embargo*, September 18, 2015. On homicide in Guerrero, see Semáforo Delictivo, guerrero.semaforo.com.mx/. On the ranking of the most violent municipalities, where Acapulco ranks behind San Pedro Sula, Honduras, and ahead of Caracas, Venezuela, see Consejo Ciudadano para la Seguridad Pública y la Justicia Penal, A.C.: http://www.seguridadjusticiaypaz.org.mx/biblioteca/prensa/send/6-prensa/199-the-50-most-violent-cities-in-the-world-2014. See also Jean Mendieta, *Acompañamiento integral a víctimas a las violencias en la Aquidióces de Acapulco: construcción de paz de cara a la crisis humanitaria en México* (Mexico City: Aquidióces de Acapulco, 2015).

22. Santiago Roel, "Narco-menudeo es la principal causa de la violencia en México," Semáforo Delictivo, 2014, http://www.semaforo.mx/content/narco-menudeo-es-la-principal-causa-de-la-violencia-en-mexico.

23. "Cinco adolescentes matan a un niño al 'jugar al secuestro' en Chihuahua," *La Jornada*, May 15, 2015.

24. "Niños de primaria 'juegan' a violar a compañera," *El Debate*, June 13, 2015.

25. "Buenos muchachos," *Proceso*, August 6, 2015.

26. "Asesinan y prenden fuego a una joven mujer," *El Debate*, April 27, 2015. On the broader pattern, see Julia Monárrez Fragoso, Luis Cervera Gómez, César Fuentes, and Rodolfo Rubio Salas, *Violencia contra las mujeres e inseguridad ciudadana en Ciudad Juárez* (Mexico City: Miguel Ángel de Porrúa/Colegio de la Frontera Norte, 2010), 374–86.

27. "Mujeres priistas piden indemnizar a víctima," *El Debate*, March 4, 2015; "'Se atenderá el caso de Ana Cecilia': Malova," *El Debate*, February 12, 2015; "En momentos sentí que me iba a matar," *El Debate*, February 10, 2015; "Habla

hermano de mujer que fue exhibida desnuda en Navolato," *El Debate,* January 31, 2015; "Exigen reclasificar el delito por caso de Navolato," *El Debate,* January 30, 2015; "Caso de mujer agredida en Navolato refleja machismo," *El Debate,* 28 enero 2015; "Jalaba con una cuerda a una mujer semidesnuda," *El Debate,* January 21, 2015.

28. Kimberly Heinle, Octavio Rodríguez Ferreira, and David A. Shirk, "Drug Violence in Mexico: Data and Analysis through 2013," Justice in Mexico Project, University of San Diego, April 2014, http://justiceinmexico.files.word press.com/2014/04/140415-dvm-2014-releasered1.pdf.

29. Pabo Piccato, "El significado político del homicidio en México en el siglo XX," *Cuicuilco* 15, no. 43: 56–78; Erik Aranda and Fernando Escalante Gonzalbo, *El homicidio en México entre 1990 y 2007* (Mexico City: Colegio de México, 2009); David Shirk and Alejandra Ríos Cázares, "Introduction: Reforming the Administration of Justice in Mexico," in *Reforming the Administration of Justice in Mexico,* ed. Wayne Cornelius and David Shirk (South Bend: University of Notre Dame Press/Center for U.S.-Mexican Studies, 2007), 1–49; Fernando Escalante Gonzalbo, "Homicidios 2008–2009: La muerte tiene permiso," *Nexos* 1 (January 2011), http://www.nexos.com.mx/?p=14089.

30. Heinle, Rodríguez, and Shirk, "Drug Violence in Mexico," 18–21.

31. According the *Global Study of Homicide 2013,* compiled by the United Nations Office on Drugs and Crime, the homicide rate in Mexico was 21.5 per 100,000 in 2012. In 2012, the average rate for South America and Central America was 25.7 per 100,000, and for Central America alone the rate was 34.3 per 100,000. For the period 2006–12, the period of the "drug war," the homicide rate averaged 59.9 per 100,000 in El Salvador, 43.1 per 100,000 in Guatemala, and 69.9 per 100,000 in Honduras. United Nations Office on Drugs and Crime, https://www.unodc.org/documents/data-and-analysis/statistics/GSH2013/2014_GLOBAL_HOMICIDE_BOOK_web.pdf.

32. In 2012, when the homicide rate per 100,000 inhabitants was 21.5 in Mexico, it was 25.2 in Brazil, 30.8 in Colombia, and 53.7 in Venezuela. Ibid.

33. Data from the FBI's Uniform Crime Report, aggregated in "New Orleans Murders Down in First Half of 2014, but Summer's Death Toll Climbing," *Times-Picayune,* August 21, 2014 (original data available "Crime in the United States, 2013," FBI, http://www.fbi.gov/about-us/cjis/ucr/crime-in-the-u.s/2013/crime-in-the-u.s.-2013/resource-pages/downloads/download-files); Heinle, Rodríguez, and Shirk, "Drug Violence in Mexico."

34. Murder has a very particular history in New Orleans, which includes racial biases familiar in other large American cities, along with contract enforcement in various black markets, due to its role as an international port, and entrenched police and political corruption.

35. "Despite Recent Shootings, Chicago Nowhere Near U.S. 'Murder Capital,'" Pew Research Center, July 14, 2014, http://www.pewresearch.org/fact

-tank/2014/07/14/despite-recent-shootings-chicago-nowhere-near-u-s-murder
-capital.

36. "Detroit Police Report 92.7 Percent Homicide Clearance Rate So Far in 2014," *MLive.com*, March 18, 2014; "New Orleans Murders Down in First Half of 2014, but Summer's Death Toll Climbing."

37. "Crime in the United States, 2012," FBI, http://www.fbi.gov/about -us/cjis/ucr/crime-in-the-u.s/2012/crime-in-the-u.s.-2012/offenses-known-to -law-enforcement/clearances.

38. Data from INEGI, compiled and analyzed in "98% de los homicidios cometidos en 2012 están impunes," *Animal Político*, July 17, 2013, http://www .animalpolitico.com/2013/07/98-de-los-homicidios-de-2012-en-la-impunidad. Survey data largely confirm the government figures for impunity. See *Encuesta Nacional de Victimización y Percepción sobre Seguridad Pública (ENVIPE) 2013*, Instituto Nacional de Estadística y Geografía (INEGI), http://www3.inegi.org.mx/ sistemas/tabuladosbasicos/tabgeneral.aspx?c=33623&s=est.

39. Semáforo Delictivo, http://www.semaforo.com.mx/.

40. The body of Daniel Parra Urías was found with two bullet holes in the head, sitting in his pickup truck on the shoulder of the Cuauhtémoc-Chihuahua highway late in the evening of March 20, 2009. "Ejecutado en carretera Chihuahua-Cuauhtémoc era padre de victima de masacre de Creel," XHEPL, http://xepl.com.mx/completa1.php?i=30097; "Creel: la masacre que el gobierno de Chihuahua olvidó," *Proceso*, August 17, 2014.

41. "Don Nepo y sus muertos vivientes," *Proceso*, December 1, 2011.

42. *El Debate*, October 16, 2014; *Proceso*, October 17, 2014; *Sin embargo*, October 27, 2014; "She Tweeted against the Mexican Cartels. They Tweeted Her Murder," *Daily Beast*, October 21, 2014.

43. The murder of Rubí Marisol Frayre Escobedo took place in Ciudad Juárez in 2008. "A dos años de la muerte de Marisela Escobedo, persiste exigencia de justicia," *Proceso*, December 8, 2012. The murder of Marisela Escobedo was captured on video: "Video del asesinato de Marisela Escobedo," *YouTube*, https://www.youtube.com/watch?v=7AM3G0D-hZA. The man likely responsible for both killings, Sergio Rafael Barraza, was killed in a shootout with police in 2012. "Cierran casos de asesinatos de Marisela Escobedo y su hija," *Animal Político*, November 23, 2012.

44. "Death of Susana Chavez, Female Activist in Ciudad Juarez, Not Tied to Organized Crime, State Says," *Los Angeles Times*, January 14, 2011; "Juarez Killings Activist Chavez Murdered in Mexico," *BBC*, January 12, 2011.

45. "Juicio Oral por feminicidio en Juárez implica a militares; las usaban para placer: testigo," *Sin Embargo*, June 28, 2015.

46. "Mexican Gangs Displaying Severed Heads," *Washington Post*, October 21, 2006; "Guatemalans Arrested in Case of Five Severed Heads," *Los Angeles Times*, September 13, 2006.

47. Sara Schatz, *Murder and Politics in Mexico: Political Killings in the Partido de la Revolución Democrática and its Consequences* (New York: Springer/Verlag, 2011), 90–91; Paul Eiss, "The Narco Media: A Reader's Guide," *Latin American Perspectives* 41, no. 2 (March 2014); Blog del Narco, *Dying for the Truth: Undercover inside the Mexican Drug War by the Fugitive Reporters of Blog del Narco* (Port Townsend, WA: Feral House, 2013); John Gibler, *To Die in Mexico* (San Francisco: City Lights Books, 2011), 7; Bunker, *Narcos over the Border*: Gangs Cartels, and Mercenaries. (Routledge).

48. "Hallan en Yucatán 12 decapitados; 11 de ellos muy cerca de Mérida," *La Jornada*, 29 agosto 2008.

49. Eiss, "The Narco Media: A Reader's Guide"; Gibler, *To Die in Mexico* (San Francisco: City Lights Books, 2011).

50. Blog del Narco, *Dying for the Truth*.

51. http://elnarcotube.com/4-mujeres-incluida-la-guera-loca-son-decapitadas-por-los-zetas.html.

52. "Interrogatorio a jovenes Zetas antes de ser colgados en Zacatecas capital," YouTube, https://www.youtube.com/watch?v=eRXbjRxuZPI.

53. Isabelle Rousseau, *Historia regional de Sinaloa: perfil socioeconómico* (Mexico City: Editorial Limusa: Colegio Nacional de Educación Profesional Técnica: Secretaria de Educación Pública, 2000).

54. Daniel Cosío Villegas, "¡Ya viene la bola!" *Historia Mexicana* 2, no. 2 (October–December 1952), 155–83.

55. Frolán Enciso, "Prólogo" in Diego Osorno, *El cártel de Sinaloa: Una historia del uso político del narco* (Mexico City: Grijalbo, 2012).

56. Helena Simonett, "Strike up the Tambora: A Social History of Sinaloan Band Music," *Latin American Music Review / Revista de Música Latinoamericana* 20, no. 1 (Spring/Summer 1999), 59–104; Everardo Mendoza Guerrero, *El léxico de Sinaloa* (Mexico City: Siglo Veintiuno Editores, 2002); Gabriela Polit Dueñas, *Narrating Narcos: Culiacán and Medellín* (Pittsburgh: University of Pittsburgh Press, 2013), 47–63; Luis Astoga, "Los corridos de traficantes de drogas en México y Colombia," *Revista Mexicana de Sociología* 59, no. 4 (October–December 1997), 245–61.

57. Rihan Yeh, "Two Publics in a Mexican Border City," *Cultural Anthropology* 27, no. 4 (2012): 713–35; Paul Vanderwood, *Juan Soldado: Rapist, Murderer, Martyr, Saint* (Durham: Duke University Press, 2004).

58. Froylán Enciso, *Nuestra historia narcótica* (2015); Astorga, *Drogas sin fronteras*; Julián Herbert, *La casa del color ajeno: crónica de un pequeño genocidio en La Laguna* (Mexico City: Lietratura Random House, 2015). See also Gabriela Recio, "US Prohibition and the Origins of the Drug Trade in Mexico, 1910–1930," *Journal of Latin American Studies* 34, no. 1 (February 2002), 21–42.

59. Osorno, *El cártel de Sinaloa.*

60. Juan Alberto Cedillo, *La Cosa Nostra en México (1938–1950)* (Mexico City: Grijalbo, 2011).

61. Osorno, *El cártel de Sinaloa*; Stephen R. Niblo, *Mexico in the 1940s: Modernity, Politics, and Corruption* (Rowman & Littlefield, 2000), 259–79.

62. Niblo, *Mexico in the 1940s*, 151; Astorga, *Drogas sin fronteras.*

63. Osorno, *El cártel de Sinaloa*; Enciso, *Nuestra historia narcótica.*

64. Osorno, *El cártel de Sinaloa.*

65. Matthew Lassiter and Kevin Kruse, "The Bulldozer Revolution: Suburbs and Southern History since World War II," *Journal of Southern History* 75, no. 30 (August 2009): 691–706; Christopher Sneddon, *Concrete Revolution: Large Dams, Cold War Geopolitics, and the US Bureau of Reclamation* (Chicago: University of Chicago Press, 2015).

66. The massive use of pesticides sends thousands of farm workers to the hospital every year. Angus Lindsay Wright, *The Death of Ramon Gonzalez: The Modern Agricultural Dilemma* (Austin: University of Texas Press, 1992), 54; David Runsten and Michael Kearney, *A Survey of Oaxacan Village Networks in California Agriculture* (Sacramento: California Institute for Rural Studies, 1994), A-16; Esther Schrader, "A Giant Spraying Sound," *Mother Jones* 20 (January/February 1995), http://www.motherjones.com/politics/1995/01/giant-spraying-sound.

67. Enciso, *Nuestra historia narcótica.*

68. "Lista de los mausoleos de lujo de los grandes capos del narco en México," *NarcoViolencia*, June 30, 2015, http://www.narcoviolencia.com.mx/2015/06/lista-de-los-mausoleos-de-lujo-de-los.html.

69. "Mexican Miracle" refers to the postwar boom in which GDP growth in Mexico topped 6 percent for twenty-five consecutive years. Osorno, *El cártel de Sinaloa.*

70. Luis Astorga, *Mitología del narcotraficante en México* (Mexico City: Plaza y Valdés, 1995), 99–103; Osorno, *El cártel de Sinaloa*; Malcolm Beith, *The Last Narco: Inside the Hunt for El Chapo* (New York: Grove Press, 2010), 29.

71. Astorga, *Drogas sin fronteras*; Enciso, *Nuestra historia narcótica*; José Luis García Cabrera, *1920–2000 ¡El Pastel! Parte Uno* (Mexico City: Palibrio, 2012), 53–55.

72. Operation Condor I targeted Sinaloa and the "Golden Triangle" areas bordering with Chihuahua and Durango; Condor II targeted Guerrero. CIA, "Latin America: Regional Political Analysis, October 1977 (accessed via Digital National Security Archive).

73. Richard Craig, "'Operation Condor': Mexico's Anti-drug Campaign Enters a New Era," *Journal of Interamerican Studies and World Affairs* 22, no. 3 (August 1980), 345–63.

74. Confidential cable to US Ambassador Vance, February 14, 1975 (accessed via Digital National Security Archive).

75. Memorandum to the President, May 19, 1977 (accessed via Digital National Security Archive). See also "The Sierra Madre's Amapola War," *Time*, February 21, 1977.

76. CIA, Latin America Regional Analysis, March 17, 1977 (accessed via Digital National Security Archive). Enciso, *Nuestra historia narcótica*.

77. *Informe Histórico a la Sociedad Mexicana—2006* (Mexico City: Procuraduría General de la República / Fiscalía Especial para Movimientos Sociales y Políticos del Pasado, 2006). Disappearances by state (of the 436 fully documented cases + "reasonable presumption" cases): Guerrero = 255 + 139; D.F. and Mexico City = 69 + 18; Sinaloa = 30 + 12; Jalisco = 24 + 9; other states = 58 +25. Research in newly declassified archives points to hundreds, if not thousands, of further disappearances in this period, but their pattern and geographic distribution generally hold. See Sergio Aguayo Quezada, *La Charola: Una historia de los servicios de inteligencia en México* (Mexico City: Editorial Ink, 2014); Alexander Aviña, *Specters of Revolution: Peasant Guerrillas in the Cold War Mexican Countryside* (Oxford: Oxford University Press, 2014); Jorge Luis Sierra Guzmán, *El enemigo interno* (Mexico City: Plaza y Valdés, 2003).

78. Jorge Luis Sierra Guzmán, *El enemigo interno* (Mexico City: Plaza y Valdés, 2003). Disappearances by state (of the 436 fully documented cases + "reasonable presumption" cases): Guerrero = 255 + 139; D.F. and Mexico City = 69 + 18; Sinaloa = 30 + 12; Jalisco = 24 + 9; other states = 58 +25.

79. *Informe de Actividades* (Chilpancingo: Comisión de la Verdad del Estado de Guerrero, 2014).

80. Ron Chepesiuk, *The Bullet or the Bribe: Taking Down Colombia's Cali Drug Cartel* (Westport: Greenwood Press, 2003), 27.

81. Osorno, *El cártel de Sinaloa*.

82. Peter Dale Scott and Jonathan Marshall, *Cocaine Politics: Drugs, Armies, and the CIA in Central America, Updated Edition* (Berkeley: University of California Press, 1998), 41–45.

83. Anabel Hernández, *Los señores del narco* (Mexico City: Delbolsillo, 2014); Grillo, *El Narco*; Beith, *The Last Narco*.

84. Carlos Moncada Ochoa, *Oficio de muerte: periodistas asesinados en el país de la impunidad* (Mexico City: Grijalbo, 2012).

85. James Kuykendall, *¿O plata, o plomo? Silver or Lead? The Abduction and Murder of DEA Agent Kiki Camarena* (Xlibris, 2005).

86. "'The CIA helped kill DEA agent Enrique "Kiki" Camarena,' say witnesses," *El País*, October 13, 2013.

87. Beith, *The Last Narco*.

88. CIA Narcotics Review, June 1986 (accessed via Digital National Security Archive).

89. "Fed Up, the Nation Launches a Crusade against Drugs," *Time*, September 15, 1986; "Drugs: So Hot, It's Killing People," *Time*, April 7, 1986.

90. Beith, *The Last Narco*; Grillo, *El Narco.*

91. "Confidential Report from US Embassy in Mexico to Secretary of State," June 1995 (accessed via Digital National Security Archive); Jesús Blancornelas, *El Cartel: Los Arrellano Félix, la mafia más poderosa en la historia de America Latina* (Mexico City: Del Bolsillo, 2010); "Mexico Arrests 4 in Killing of Human Rights Activist," *Los Angeles Times*, July 3, 1990; "Recuerdan a Norma Corona a 25 años de su muerte," *El Debate*, May 21, 2015; *Unceasing Abuses: Human Rights in Mexico One Year after the Introduction of Reform* (New York: Human Rights Watch, 1991).

92. Enciso, *Nuestra historia narcótica.*

93. Hernández, *Los Señores del narco.*

94. Osorno, *El cártel de Sinaloa*, 522; José Reveles, *El cártel incomodo: el fin de los Beltrán Leyva y la hegemonía del Chapo Guzmán* (Mexico City: Grijalbo, 2011).

95. The United States accused Sonora governor Manlio Fabio Beltrones (1991–97) of protecting Amado Carrillo Fuentes, the leader of the Juárez Cartel, and his name was included on a list of officials banned from receiving important appointments under President Ernesto Zedillo (1994–2000). DEA informants and personnel from the Centro de Investigación y Seguridad Nacional ("Center for Research and National Security"), CISEN, reported that he coordinated the handing out of millions of dollars in bribes, including the transfer of suitcases of cash from drug traffickers to Raúl Salinas de Gortari, brother of the now disgraced former president Carlos Salinas. "Another Mexican General Is Arrested and Charged with Links to Drug Cartel," *New York Times*, March 18, 1997; "Drug Ties Taint 2 Mexican Governors," *New York Times*, February 23, 1997; Jorge Chabat, "Mexico's War on Drugs: No Margin for Maneuver," *Annals of the American Academy of Political and Social Science* 582 (July 2002), 138–48.

96. "Policías matan policías," *Zeta*, August 4, 2014, http://zetatijuana .com/noticias/dobleplana/8260/policias-matan-policias; "Todos en Ciudad Obregón sabían de la presencia del güero Palma y de la protección que le daban las autoridades," *Proceso*, July 31, 1995; *Informe de la investigación del homicidio del licenciado Luis Donaldo Colosio Murriet: entorno político y nracotráfico, Tomo IV* (Mexico City: PGR/Subproduraduría Especial para el Caso Colosio, 2000) 414–15.

97. "De 1988 a la fecha han sido asesinados 696 militantes: PRD," *La Jornada*, November 2, 2007; Schatz, *Murder and Politics in Mexico.*

98. *Diccionario histórico y biográfico de la Revolución Mexicana, Tomo VI* (Mexico City: Instituto Nacional de Estudios Históricos de la Revolución Mexicana, Secretaría de Gobernación, 1990), 382.

99. Examples include the corridos of Benjamín Argumedo, Francisco Madero, Francisco Murguía, Emiliano Zapata, Pancho Villa, Felipe Ángeles, Heraclio Bernal, Macario Romero, Pascual Orozco, and many others. See Vicente T. Mendoza, *El corrido de la Revolución Mexicana* (Mexico City: Instituto Nacional de Estudios Históricos de la Revolución Mexicana, 1956); Armando de María y Campos, *La Revolución Mexicana a través de los corridos populares* (Mexico City: Instituto Nacional de Estudios Históricos de la Revolución Mexicana, 1962); Everard Meade, "Modern Warfare Meets 'Mexico's Evil Tradition': Death, Memory, and Media during the Mexican Revolution," *InterCulture* 5, no. 2 (June 2008), 119–49; John H. McDowell, "The Mexican Corrido: Formula and Theme in a Ballad Tradition," *Journal of American Folklore* 85, no. 337 (July–September 1972), 205–20; Américo Paredes and Ricard Bauman, eds., *Folklore and Culture on the Texas-Mexican Border* (Austin: CMAS/University of Texas Press, 1993).

100. George Yúdice, "Testimonio y concientización," *Revista de Crítica Literaria Latinoamericana* 18, no. 36 (1992), 211–32; Georg Gugelberger and Michael Kearney, "Voices for the Voiceless: Testimonial Literature in Latin America," *Latin American Perspectives* 18, no. 3 (Summer 1991), 3–14; Juan Ramón Duchesne, "Miguel Barnet y el testimonio como humanismo," *Revista de Crítica Literaria Latinoamericana* 13, no. 26 (1987), 155–60; Margaret Randall, "¿Que es, y como se hace un testimonio?," *Revista de Crítica Literaria Latinoamericana* 18, no. 36 (1992), 23–47.

101. Rigoberta Menchú, *I, Rigoberta Menchú: An Indian Woman from Guatemala*, 2nd ed., edited by Elizabeth Burgos, translated by Anne Wright (London: Verso: 2009); Beth E. Jörgensen, "Speaking from the Soapbox: Benita Galeana's 'Benita,'" *Latin American Literary Review* 28, no. 55 (January–June 2000), 46–66; Teresa Ortiz, *Never Again a World without Us: Voices of Mayan Women in Chiapas, Mexico* (Washington, D.C.: Epica Task Force, 2001). For a discussion of the politics of testimonial literature and its truth claims, see "If Truth Be Told: A Forum on David Stoll's 'Rigoberta Menchu and the Story of All Poor Guatemalans,'" special issue, *Latin American Perspectives* 26, no. 6 (November 1999).

102. Eduardo Galeano, *Century of the Wind*, Memory of Fire 3, translated by Cedrick Belfrage (New York: W. W. Norton, 1998).

103. *El País*, July 17, 2015.

104. "The Hunt for El Chapo," *New Yorker*, May 5, 2014.

105. Hernández, *Los Señores del narco*; Beith, *The Last Narco*.

106. José Reveles, *El cártel incomodo: el fin de los Beltrán Leyva y la hegemonía del Chapo Guzmán* (México: Grijalbo, 2011).

107. Arindrajit Dube, Oeindra Dube, and Omar García Ponce, "Cross-Border Spillover: U.S. Gun Laws and Violence in Mexico," *American Political Science Review* 107, no. 3, 397–417; Howard Campbell, "Drug Trafficking Stories: Everyday Forms of Narco-Folklore on the U.S. Mexico Border," *International Journal of Drug Policy* 16, no. 5, 326–33.

108. Daniel Sabet, "The Border Bottleneck: Drug Trafficking, Civil Society, and Incentives for Police Corruption," in *Deceiving (Dis)Appearances: Analyzing Current Developments in Europe and North America's Border Regions*, ed. Harlan Koff (Brussels: Peter Lang, 2007), 207–24.

109. Campbell, *Drug War Zone*; "Barrio Azteca" *Borderland Beat*, November 15, 2009, http://www.borderlandbeat.com/2009/11/barrio-azteca.html; *El Paso Times*, September 18, 2009; "Barrio Azteca" *InSight Crime*, February 1, 2014, http://www.insightcrime.org/mexico-organized-crime-news/barrio-azteca.

110. Alfredo Corchado, *Midnight in Mexico: A Reporter's Journey through a Country's Descent into Darkness* (New York: Penguin Books, 2013); Robert C. Bonner, "The New Cocaine Cowboys: How to Defeat Mexico's Drug Cartels," *Foreign Affairs* 89, no. 4 (July/August 2010), 35–47.

111. Beith, *The Last Narco*.

112. Ricardo Ravelo, *Zetas, franqicia criminal* (Mexico City: Ediciones, 2014); Diego Osorno, *La guerra de los zetas: viaje por la frontera de la necropolítica* (Mexico City: Vintage Español, 2013).

113. "Casino Royal: historias de una tragedia," *Proceso*, October 4, 2012; "Alacan con granadas casino en Monterrey; hay 53 muertos," August 25, 2011.

114. Eddie Muller, *Dark City: The Lost World of Film Noir* (New York: St. Martin's Griffin, 1998).

115. Robert Ricigliano, *Making Peace Last: A Toolbox for Sustainable* Peacebuilding (Boulder, Colo.: Paradigm, 2012); John Paul Lederach, *Reconcile: Conflict Transformation for Ordinary Christians* (New York: Herald Press, 2014); John Paul Lederach, "Compassionate Presence: Faith-Based Peacebuilding in the Face of Violence," Joan B. Kroc School of Peace Studies Distinguished Lecture Series, San Diego, 2012); Robert J. Scheiter, "A Practical Theology of Healing, Forgiveness, and Reconciliation," in *Peacebuilding: Catholic Theology, Ethics, and Praxis*, ed. Scott Appleby and Gerald Powers (New York: Orbis Books, 2010), 366–97.

CHAPTER 1

1. The Lacandones are a small group of indigenous ancestors of the ancient Maya who live along Mexico's far southern border with Guatemala. One of the oldest and most isolated indigenous groups in the state of Chiapas, the Lacandones now number fewer than a thousand. They have their own language, derived from Yucatec Maya, and they live in small communities dedicated to subsistence agriculture and foraging in the dense rainforest along the Usumacinta River and its tributaries.

2. The municipality of Choix sits in the far northeastern corner of Sinaloa, on the border with Sonora and Chihuahua. The wide, fertile Río Fuerte valley extends into the municipality from the southwest, linking it to the Pacific

coast at Topolobampo and Los Mochis, with the town of El Fuerte about half-way in between, cutting deep into the towering Sierra Madre Occidental. The municipal seat of Choix sits at about 350 meters above sea level, but the mountains immediately to the east and north climb thousands of meters from there, making it a gateway to the most remote parts of the Sierra, in Chihuahua to the north and east, and in Sinaloa to the south. Population density is very low, with about 32,000 residents dispersed in dozens of rural pueblos (about 9,300 live in the municipal seat).

3. *Tata* is a generic term for "patron" or "father."

4. Montes Azules sits in the center of a national park of the same name located in the far eastern part of the state of Chiapas, in a large and remote forest along the Guatemala border. The closest town of a reasonable size is Ocosingo, Chiapas, which is only 87 kilometers (54 miles) as the crow flies but 233 kilometers (145 miles)—or a minimum of about three and a half hours driving—by any passable road. The trip to Choix, Sinaloa, from Ocosingo, Chiapas, is about 2,600 kilometers (over 1,600 miles), depending on the route taken.

5. See note 2 for this chapter.

6. While it used to apply strictly to assassins or contract killers, *sicario* has evolved into a generic term for all gunmen and enforcers of the drug trade.

7. Ramiro is not a native Spanish speaker, as noted in the text, but he was interviewed in Spanish and thus his phrasing is a bit awkward at times.

8. The DIF is part of the Heath Ministry (Secretaría de Salud), and it combines the functions of child protection and custody familiar to departments of children and family services, welfare and assistance programs for impoverished women and children, disaster relief, and general public health.

9. La Santa Muerte ("Saint Death"), is a female figure of death, or the Grim Reaper, around whom a popular cult has arisen celebrating her as the patron saint of outcasts, criminals, and those wronged by the authorities. The use of a generic female figure of death in cultural metaphors and rituals is centuries old, but as a symbol of Mexican cultural nationalism often used as a rhetorical device for political satire, the symbol dates to the late nineteenth century. Juan Miguel Lope Blanch's 2,500-entry dictionary of death-related terms in Mexico includes sixty different names just for the figure of death, all of them female. Claudio Lomnitz labels the figure of death "Mexico's national totem" in his *Death and the Idea of Mexico* (Brooklyn: Zone Books, 2005), 11–58. Drug traffickers and contrabandists along the US-Mexico border have used Santa Muerte icons and images for good luck since the 1960s, but the symbol has taken on darker connotations (e.g., a celebration of killing, rather than death itself) during post-2006 escalation of violence. See Campbell, *Drug War Zone*. The specific religious cult of La Santa Muerte, however, has little to do with drug trafficking or the border. Headquartered in Tepito, a neighborhood in Mexico City infamous for

its markets and its thieves since colonial times, the cult has served as a rebellious symbol of local identity and independence since the early twentieth century. Over the last decade, however, the cult has become wildly popular, both as a fleeting fetish and as a devotional node that has attracted tens of thousands of pilgrims to Tepito. "Inside Santa Muerte, Mexico's Cult of Death—in Pictures," *Guardian*, September 12, 2015.

10. Machaca is a type of shredded beef popular in northern Mexico.

11. Infonavit (Instituto del Fondo Nacional de la Vivienda para los Trabajadores) is a federal agency charged with providing affordable housing to working-class Mexicans. Its name refers to planned and government subsidized housing developments, without carrying the same social connotations—urban racial segregation and neglect—as public housing in the United States.

12. *Compa* is shortened form of *compañero*, used to convey "buddy" or "pal."

13. *Pendejo* literally means a pubic hair (going back to Antonio de Nebrija's 1495 Castilian-Latin dictionary), but it is more commonly used to refer to a foolish or stupid person. While it still counts as an expletive, it is somewhat disassociated from its literal meaning (in a way that most sexual expletives are not), and thus it is less explicit and severe. Indeed, the most recent version of the *Diccionario de la Real Academia Española* includes the verb form *pendejar*—to do or say stupid things—without any reference to the original noun.

14. Surutato is a town of about nine hundred inhabitants that sits on a narrow, high plateau at an elevation of 1,460 meters (4,790 feet). It is located forty kilometers (twenty-five miles) due north from the municipal seat of Badiraguato, up a steep green valley cut by two tributaries of the Huamaya River and far off the main highway. Surutato looks down upon two major waterfalls and is home to numerous scenic overlooks popular with eco-tourists. The town is poor—only about half of its households are connected to the municipal water supply—but it has been the focal point of several pioneering rural development and education projects, including the establishment in 1978 of the Centro de Estudios Justo Sierra, which has provided post-secondary education to residents of the surrounding highlands since its founding.

15. The reference is to the Centro de Estudios Justo Sierra (see preceding note).

16. *Bato* (sometimes *vato*), meaning a person, a guy, a buddy, et cetera, is used in a very similar manner to "dude" in contemporary American English, although its origins follow an inverse trajectory. The *Real Academia Española* (1992) defines *bato* as "hombre tonto o rústico y de pocos alcances" ("a stupid or rustic man, dim-witted") or as vulgar form of *padre* ("father" or "daddy"). Dictionaries going back to the sixteenth century underscore the usage of the word to define rusticity, and some even include a man whose stammering or stuttering

indicates that he is an ignorant rustic. Over the course of the twentieth century, this pejorative term for a rustic was transformed by criminal and *pachuco* (urban working-class or borderlands) slang into a term of rebellious endearment, meaning "one of us" (as rural Mexicans and migrants were incorporated into the broader body politic after the Mexican Revolution but subject to pervasive discrimination and ridicule). It also figures in Guillermo Colín Sánchez's comprehensive dictionary of criminal slang (*Así se habla la delincuencia y otras más*) as a generic term for "amigo, sujeto, individuo, hombre, compañero, persona" (friend, subject, man, colleague/partner, person). "Dude," by contrast, began as a pejorative term for an urban, upper-class dandy or swell, over-concerned with dress and decorum, who did not fit into more organic rural settings (and couldn't handle them), and it was later applied to dandified city folk who visited ranches in the American West. In the twentieth century, "dude" was appropriated by urban Afro-American culture as a term of rebellious endearment and belonging, meaning "one of us" (as black Americans asserted their freedom to dress and style themselves how they wanted, despite segregation and racism). From there it was disseminated into mass culture as a generic term for a person, a friend, et cetera, much like *bato.*

CHAPTER 2

1. The original Steel City and home to Altos Hornos de México (Mexico's first steel company, founded in 1942), Monclova is about a three-hour drive southwest of the US-Mexico border at Piedras Negras, Texas, and five hours southwest of San Antonio, Texas.

2. The origin of the term "the coast is clear," *no hay moros en la costa* ("there are no Moors on the coast"), is a Spanish phrase that referred to smugglers and raiders on the Iberian coast. Shakespeare used it in *Henry VI,* and it was popularized thereafter.

3. The Policía Ministerial del Estado de Sinaloa (PME), or State Ministerial Police, serve the state attorney general and the governor directly and have jurisdiction over all of Sinaloa. The Ministerial Police replaced the former Judicial Police in 2000 in a process that unfolded in all of Mexico's thirty-one states as part of major police reform aimed at cleaning up overlapping or conflicting jurisdictions and eliminating corruption (for which the Judicial Police were notorious in many states, Sinaloa in particular). Known as *los café con leche* ("café au lait") for their light brown uniforms, the Judicial Police in many states acted as personal police for various governors and regional crime bosses.

4. *Empatrullados* refers to those who ride around in *patrullas* ("patrol cars").

5. *Trolo* is a variation on the word *cholo,* or "homeboy," from Mexican and borderlands slang for a gangster or someone streetwise (not to be confused with

trolo from Argentine slang, which is derogatory term for a homosexual male, akin to "fag" or "faggot" in English).

6. The State Ministerial Police play an investigative role in law enforcement, directed by a series of special prosecutors who handle particular kinds of crime, often in collaboration with the Federal Ministerial Police, which replaced the Federal Investigations Agency (AFI) in 2009, which in turn replaced the Federal Judicial Police in 2000). The broader range of ordinary police functions in Sinaloa is carried out by municipal police departments with the help of the State Preventive Police (PEP). The development of ministerial police forces across the country has been part of a wave of efforts over the last decade to curb police corruption and improve law enforcement by way of specialization and the streamlining of chains of command. These efforts have produced an alphabet soup of special task forces and police agencies, but there is little evidence that they have thwarted official collusion with organized crime or improved the effectiveness of law enforcement.

7. The term *camarada* ("comrade") has become ubiquitous in Mexican slang, particularly in Culiacán, as a general informal reference to a friend, fellow traveler, et cetera.

8. Apodaca is a municipality just outside of Monterrey, Nuevo León, in northeastern Mexico, not far from the Texas border.

CHAPTER 3

1. Cofradía is a small rural community in the highlands, up the Río Tamazula due east of Culiacán and next to the Sanaloa Dam and reservoir.

2. José Luis Ibarra Velázquez was murdered, along with his brother José Blas, on February 23, 2012, in downtown Culiacán. His widow, Martha Olivia López López, was shot to death and her car riddled with bullets outside of her Culiacán home on November 18, 2012.

3. *Sardito* is a diminutive form of *sardo*, which is a colloquial derivation from *sardina* ("sardine"), a mocking term for soldiers, based on their matching uniforms and the fact that they are often packed into transports. In contemporary colloquial Mexican Spanish, *pinche*, derived from *pinchar* ("to poke or stab") and *pinche* ("lowliest of household servants"), is used as an expletive equivalent in meaning to the English verb "to fuck" and its derivatives, but less severe—something akin to "screwed" in contemporary American usage. Its relative mildness compared to other terms with the same usage—such as *chingado*—is important to note. Indeed, dictionaries of classic Mexican criminal slang do not include a sexual connotation but rather use *pinche* to denote something ugly, miserable, or distasteful. *RAE* (1992), 1762; Colín Sánchez, *Así se habla la delincuencia*, 221.

4. *La maña* is used to mean the drug trade, or organized crime more specifically. *Maña* literally means "dexterity," "skill," or "shrewdness," especially

in business dealings, and over the modern period, thanks to descriptions of pick-pockets, burglars, and con men, it came to be associated with vice and bad habits as well. Sebastián de Covarrubias, *Tesoro de la lengua castellana o española* (Madrid: Luis Sánchez,1611), 1072; *RAE* (1992), 1466.

5. The Nahuatl word *tlacuache* ("opossum") is used colloquially in Mexico to refer to a moron or a beggar.

6. *Morro* and *morra* are used to mean "boy" and "girl," equivalent to *muchacho* ("young person"), either literally or as an ironic term of endearment or affection. The term is medieval in origin, and it appears in the earliest Spanish dictionaries as a pastoral word for the muzzle of an animal (or anything sharing its shape). In descriptions of people, it also carried the connotation of a simpleton or ignoramus (similar in origin to the English "moron"), copied from a Greek word *moríon* for the head of the penis, or, in feminine form, testicles, a word that was later used to describe small rocks. Girolamo Vittori, *Tesoro de las tres lenguas francesa, italiana y española. Thresor des trois langues françoise, italienne et espagnolle* (Geneva: Philippe Albert & Alexandre Pernet, 1609), 430; Francisco del Rosal, *Origen y etimología de todos los vocablos originales de la Lengua Castellana. Obra inédita de el Dr. Francisco de el Rosal, médico natual de Córdova, copiada y puesta en claro puntualmente del mismo manuscrito original, que está casi ilegible, e ilustrada con alguna[s] notas y varias adiciones por el P. Fr. Miguel Zorita de Jesús María, religioso augustino recoleto* (Madrid, 1611). Its contemporary usage has its origins in criminal and borderlands slang. Colín Sánchez, *Así se habla la delincuencia*, 184–85.

7. *Gacho* means literally "ugly," "bad," or "disagreeable," but it is used ironically to mean bold, difficult, or daring as well. *RAE* (1992); Colín Sánchez, *Así se habla la delincuencia*, 129.

8. *Tacuache* is an alternate form of the Nahuatl word *tlacuache* ("opossum"), used in Mexico. Colloquially it refers to a moron or a beggar.

9. *Plebes*, as in the Latin term for "commoners," or people without privileges, is used colloquially in Sinaloa to mean "kids" or as a term of affection for one's particular friends and associates as fellow commoners, as in the American English terms "peeps" as a short form of "people" or "my people." Elsewhere, the term refers to the lowest social class. *RAE* (1992), 1785. In Mexican criminal slang, *plebe*—more commonly *ser bien plebe* ("to be a good plebe")—refers to being crude, common, or discourteous. Colín Sánchez, *Así se habla la delincuencia*, 224.

10. *Al chile*, literally "hot pepper–style" or "like a pepper," is used to mean "by force." *La neta*, from the adjective *neto/a*, meaning "pure" or "clean," is a colloquial declarative used to mean "the truth," similar to "for real" or "true that" in colloquial American English. *RAE* (1992), 1577; Colín Sánchez, *Así se habla la delincuencia*, 85.

11. *Bronca*, the noun, is used to describe a dispute, fight, quarrel, or problem in colloquial Mexican usage. The phrase *de la bronca* means "in on the joke" or "in on the action." *RAE* (1992), 358; Colín Sánchez, *Así se habla la delincuencia*, 48.

CHAPTER 4

1. In the original, Valdez quotes: "'tas pendejo, pero bien pendejo." The state-of-being use of *pendejo* translates well into "stupid" and makes greater sense than leaving it in the original nominal form.

2. *Impunidad* ("impunity") and the adjective *impune* refer, literally, to a lack of punishment, and they can be traced back to the Latin *impūnitās*, meaning exemption from punishment. But in contemporary usage they have as much to do with acknowledging a criminal act as such, publicly identifying those responsible, and pursuing and prosecuting them as they do with actual punishment.

CHAPTER 5

1. *Chilo*, a working-class variant of *chido*, is preferred in Culiacán over the latter term, which is widely used in Mexican youth slang for "beautiful" or "cool."

2. Founded in 1997, Oportunidades (now known as Progresa) is a social welfare program based on conditional cash transfers whereby mothers receive direct payments for enrolling their families in educational and health care programs.

3. The same phenomenon is called *pizzo* in Sicily.

4. Z40 was the code name of Miguel Ángel Treviño Morales, a notorious Zetas commander, arrested in July 2013.

Index

Cities in Mexico are identified by state.

314INDEX